W9-ABC-167

The "Spray." From a photograph taken in Australian waters.

SAILING ALONE

AROUND THE WORLD

Captain Joshua Slocum

ILLUSTRATED BY

THOMAS FOGARTY AND GEORGE VARIAN

DOVER PUBLICATIONS, INC. NEW YORK

Copyright © 1956 by Dover Publications, Inc.
All rights reserved under Pan American and
International Copyright Conventions.

Published in Canada by General Publishing Com-
pany, Ltd., 30 Lesmill Road, Don Mills, Toronto,
Ontario.
Published in the United Kingdom by Constable
and Company, Ltd., 10 Orange Street, London
WC 2.

This Dover edition, first published in 1956, is
an unabridged republication of the work originally
published by the Century Company in 1900, with
a new Introduction by Geoffrey Mott-Smith.

Standard Book Number: 486-20326-3
Library of Congress Catalog Card Number: 59-7670

Manufactured in the United States of America
Dover Publications, Inc.
180 Varick Street
New York, N.Y. 10014

TO THE ONE WHO SAID:
"THE 'SPRAY' WILL COME BACK."

INTRODUCTION

In the early morning of June 27, 1898, a 37-foot yawl edged gingerly into the harbor of Newport, R. I., which was mined against Spanish raiders. From the guard-ship in the harbor came no warning shot, but rather a welcoming hail, *"Spray,* ahoy!" For the fame of the little craft had preceded her. She had sailed clear round the world, a voyage of 46,000 miles.

Other small vessels before the *Spray* had sailed around the world. The ships of Magellan were puny by modern standards. But the *Spray* established an epic "first" in history—never before had any craft circumnavigated the globe with a one-man crew.

"I was aware that no other vessel had sailed in this manner around the globe, but would have been loath to say another could not do it . . . I was greatly amused, therefore, by the flat assertions of an expert that it could not be done."

So wrote Joshua Slocum, the builder, owner, captain, and one-man crew of the *Spray.* That is as near to an explanation as he ever gave why he "resolved on a voyage around the world, and as the wind in the morning of April 24, 1895, was fair, at noon . . . weighed anchor, set sail, and filled away from Boston . . ." Someone had said it could not be done; therefore, Joshua Slocum had to do it.

This book is Slocum's own story of the voyage. It was written soon after his return, and was first published serially in *The Century Illustrated Monthly Magazine*, 1899-1900. The Century Company put it in book form on March 3, 1900. The book rapidly became a best-seller and was reprinted many times. Some persons living today may remember when it was required reading in the public schools. For it is more than the record of an epic voyage: it is a masterpiece of vivid story-telling. The pace is as swift as was the *Spray* herself. From native reticence (as much as from literary cunning) Slocum does not elaborate upon the hazards of the voyage nor on his preparations to cope with them. The voyage is invested with a deceptive air of casualness that often becomes downright comical. One reads with a chuckle how the captain "lamented the day I had allowed on board the goat that ate my chart"; how the captain, swamped while going ashore in his life-boat, "suddenly remembered I could not swim"; how the initial plan of sailing eastward through the Mediterranean ran afoul of a pirate at Gibraltar, so that the *Spray* went westward around the world instead!

Few words are expended, also in the matter of the chronometer. Rather than expend fifteen dollars in the repair of his chronometer, Slocum set off without a timepiece. Later he repaired the omission by purchase of the "famous tin clock" for one dollar. Here, perhaps, the captain had tongue in cheek; as his son and biographer Victor Slocum takes pains to explain, the captain had long relied on the lunar method for his longitude.

Joshua Slocum was born on a farm at Wilmot, Annapolis County, Nova Scotia, on February 20th,

1844. His father was John Slocombe (sic), a man of 6 feet in height, 200 pounds weight, a Methodist deacon and stern disciplinarian. His mother was Sarah Jane Southern, the daughter of a lighthouse keeper. On both sides the ancestors were seafaring folk. Joshua was the fifth child of John and Sarah.

In 1852, John exchanged his farm for a shoemaking shop at Westport, a town on Brier Island, which lies at the entrance to the bay of Fundy. At the age of ten, Joshua was put to work pegging boots. He hated the arduous labor, and two years later ran away from home to work aboard the fishing schooners in nearby St. Mary's Bay. In 1860 his mother died; he then left the Bay for deepsea sailing. Together with a chum, Cheney, he shipped out of St. John on a droger bound for Dublin. (Says Victor Slocum, droger was an opprobrious epithet for "an ill-found, ill-fed, and leaky vessel.")

From Dublin, Slocum went to Liverpool, and shipped as an ordinary seaman on the British *Tanjore* bound for China. During the next several years he sailed far and wide on British ships carrying chiefly coal and grain. He rounded Cape Horn twice, touched at Batavia, the Moluccas, Manila, Hong Kong, Saigon, Singapore, San Francisco. At sea, he prepared himself for the Board of Trade examination and at the age of 18 received his certificate as second mate.

He was attracted to San Francisco, the center of a booming coastal trade, and became an American citizen there. He went salmon fishing in the Columbia River, fur hunting in British Columbia; he designed an improved boat for gill fishing, and the design was purchased at sight by a Columbia fishery.

After these shoreside activities, Slocum in 1869 returned to the sea, piloting a coastal schooner carrying grain from Frisco to Seattle. His first command as captain was the bark *Washington,* built in Puget Sound. He was sent on a voyage to Sydney, Australia, whence he was to go to Alaska on a pioneer salmon-fishing expedition. (Alaska was purchased from Russia in 1867.)

At Sydney, Slocum met Virginia Albert Walker, the daughter of an American couple. He married her on January 31st, 1871. She accompanied him in the *Washington* on the voyage to Alaska, and on most of his voyages thereafter. None of their four children was born on the soil of the United States. Victor was born aboard the *Constitution,* Garfield at Hong Kong, Benjamin at Sydney, and Jessie at Olongapo, P. I.

The *Washington* was the first American vessels to enter Cooke Inlet, Alaska, after the Russians withdrew. The salmon fishing expedition was a great success, but ship dragged her anchor in a gale, went ashore near the Kasilof River, and was a total loss. But Slocum contrived to get the valuable catch of salmon back to San Francisco. The owners of the *Washington* then gave him command of the barkentine *Constitution,* in which he sailed to Honolulu, and later to Mexican ports.

During 1874-6, Slocum commanded the *Benjamin Aymar,* plying in th South Seas. When her owner sold her, the Slocum menage was stranded in the Philippine Islands. Nothing daunted, the captain took on the task of organizing native workmen to build a 150-ton steamship for a young naval architect, Edward Johnson. The ways were set up on Subig Bay, and the hull was later towed 60 miles to Pasig, near Manila, for finishing. In part payment for the work, Johnson gave Slocum a 90-ton schooner, the *Pato*. Slocum retrieved his fortunes with inter-island trips on the *Pato*, carrying lumber. Then he was fired by the idea of resuming the hunt for salmon. Refitted at Hong Kong, the *Pato* set out for the Okhotsk Sea, but made so large a catch that she continued clear across the North Pacific to Victoria, B. C., a voyage of 8,200 miles, to sell her cargo in the profitable West Coast market.

Victor Slocum says "The few months that *Pato* was in East Portland was the writer's first experience, really, in living on land." During this period Joshua traveled alone by rail to Nova Scotia to visit his relations. On this trip he acted as correspondent for the San Francisco *Bee*; all his life he was interested in writing and came to hope for a successful literary career.

The *Pato* was sailed to Hawaii and there sold. In 1878, Slocum bought the *Amethyst*, fitted her for the timber trade, and began to carry timber and coal between Honolulu, Manila, Nagasaki, Shanghai, Vladivostok. In 1880, he sold the *Amethyst* at Hong Kong and bought an interest in the *Northern Light*, a full-rigged ship (skysails on every mast!) Slocum says the *Northern Light* was his "best command" and "the finest American sailing-vessel afloat." But two years later he sold out his interest and bought the bark *Aquidneck*, in which he sailed to Pernambuco and Buenos Aires. His wife Virginia died on July 25, 1885, and was buried at Buenos Aires. In the following year he married Henrietta Elliott, a first cousin.

The *Aquidneck* commenced to ply between Baltimore and South American ports, where Slocum met a variety of misadventures. In a mutiny, he was forced to shoot two men. He stood trial in a Brazilian court and was duly acquitted. A few months later (1887) his vessel ran aground on a sandbar in the harbor of Anontina, near Rio. Despite all efforts, the ship broke up and was a total loss. The Slocum family was marooned on a foreign shore, with scarce the funds for passage home.

Joshua's experience in shipbuilding now stood him in good stead. Enlisting native help, he designed and built a 35-foot craft combining the hull of "a Cape Ann dory with the rig of a Chinese sampan." Ready for christening on May 13, 1888, the festival day commemorating the liberation of the Brazilian slaves, this uncouth vessel was christened *Liberdade* (Liberty). On June 24th the Slocum family embarked in her and set sail for the United States.

Had it not been for the overshadowing feat of the *Spray*, Joshua Slocum would probably be remembered as the intrepid mariner who guided an open boat 5,510 miles, from Paranagua, Brazil, to Cape Roman, S. C., encumbered as much as helped by a wife and two small children (Victor and Garfield). Slocum wrote the story of this epic in *Voyage of the Liberdade*, which he published at his own expense in 1890. The book is little known, even among enthusiastic readers of *Sailing Alone Around the World*. The feat did not pass, however, wholly without recognition. Slocum was taken to meet President Theodore Roosevelt, and the *Liberdade* was placed on view at the Smithsonian Institution.

These events brought no rehabilitation of Slocum's sunken fortunes. He speaks of "One midwinter day in 1892, in Boston, where I had been cast up from the old ocean, so to speak, a year or two before, I was cogitating whether I should apply for a command, or go to work in a shipyard . . ." Instead, he built (or rather, rebuilt) the *Spray*.

With the embarkation on the fantastic project of a solo voyage around the world, Slocum's fortunes changed. As ship after ship reported passage of the *Spray*, as enthralled audiences in port after port listened to tales of her adventures, as news stories went humming in the newly-laid cables from strange lands to the metropolitan newspapers, worldwide interest was evoked in the adventure. The world spoke in that hail of welcome when the captain returned safely, "*Spray*, ahoy!"

Royalties from the book enabled Slocum to buy his first home, a house at West Tisbury on Martha's Vineyard. But he could not wholly abandon the sea. In the autumn of 1905, 1907, and 1908 he made solo cruises in the *Spray* to the West Indies. On November 14th, he set out once more on his "winter vacation."

Now, the captain had always considered himself a lucky man. In the North Pacific the *Pato* ran short of salt and was on the point of jettisoning the greater part of her fine catch, when along came the *Constitution*, about to jettison an excess supply of salt! Again, when the pirate chased him at Gibraltar, the captain had been nearly swamped by a heavy sea, but the same sea disabled the pursuing felucca. The *Spray* herself was a colossally lucky find; she weathered many gales in which larger vessels foundered; she kept a straight course for thousands of miles with a lashed steering wheel; exhaustive analysis of her lines and construction by a naval architect brought the verdict that her design was the most perfect, for her purposes, ever conceived.

But after the *Spray* set sail in 1909, she was never heard from again. Somewhere on the high seas the captain's luck ran out.

Geoffrey Mott-Smith
1956

CONTENTS

CHAPTER I

CHAPTER II

CHAPTER III

CHAPTER IV

CHAPTER V

CHAPTER VI

CHAPTER VII

CHAPTER VIII

CHAPTER IX

CHAPTER X

CHAPTER XI

CHAPTER XII

CHAPTER XIII

CHAPTER XIV

CHAPTER XV

CHAPTER XVI

CHAPTER XVII

CHAPTER XVIII

CHAPTER XIX

CHAPTER XX

CHAPTER XXI

APPENDIX

LINES AND SAIL-PLAN OF THE " SPRAY "

LIST OF ILLUSTRATIONS

SAILING ALONE AROUND
THE WORLD

CHAPTER I

A blue-nose ancestry with Yankee proclivities — Youthful fondness
for the sea — Master of the ship *Northern Light* — Loss of the
Aquidneck — Return home from Brazil in the canoe *Liberdade* —
The gift of a "ship" — The rebuilding of the *Spray* — Conundrums
in regard to finance and calking — The launching of the *Spray*.

IN the fair land of Nova Scotia, a maritime prov-
ince, there is a ridge called North Mountain,
overlooking the Bay of Fundy on one side and
the fertile Annapolis valley on the other. On the
northern slope of the range grows the hardy spruce-
tree, well adapted for ship-timbers, of which many
vessels of all classes have been built. The people
of this coast, hardy, robust, and strong, are disposed
to compete in the world's commerce, and it is
nothing against the master mariner if the birthplace mentioned on his certificate be Nova Scotia.
I was born in a cold spot, on coldest North Moun-

tain, on a cold February 20, though I am a citizen
of the United States — a naturalized Yankee, if it
may be said that Nova Scotians are not Yankees
in the truest sense of the word. On both sides my
family were sailors; and if any Slocum should be
found not seafaring, he will show at least an inclination to whittle models of boats and contemplate
voyages. My father was the sort of man who, if
wrecked on a desolate island, would find his way
home, if he had a jack-knife and could find a tree.
He was a good judge of a boat, but the old clay
farm which some calamity made his was an anchor
to him.   He was not afraid of a capful of wind, and
he never took a back seat at a camp-meeting or a
good, old-fashioned revival.

As for myself, the wonderful sea charmed me
from the first. At the age of eight I had already
been afloat along with other boys on the bay,
with chances greatly in favor of being drowned.
When a lad I filled the important post of cook on
a fishing-schooner; but I was not long in the galley, for the crew mutinied at the appearance of my
first duff, and "chucked me out" before I had a
chance to shine as a culinary artist. The next step
toward the goal of happiness found me before the
mast in a full-rigged ship bound on a foreign voyage. Thus I came "over the bows," and not in
through the cabin windows, to the command of a
ship.

My best command was that of the magnificent
ship *Northern Light*, of which I was part-owner. I
had a right to be proud of her, for at that time —
in the eighties — she was the finest American sail-

ing-vessel afloat. Afterward I owned and sailed
the *Aquidneck*, a little bark which of all man's
handiwork seemed to me the nearest to perfection
of beauty, and which in speed, when the wind
blew, asked no favors of steamers. I had been
nearly twenty years a shipmaster when I quit her

Drawn by W. Taber.

The *Northern Light*, Captain Joshua Slocum,
bound for Liverpool, 1885.

deck on the coast of Brazil, where she was wrecked.
My home voyage to New York with my family was
made in the canoe *Liberdade*, without accident.

My voyages were all foreign. I sailed as freighter
and trader principally to China, Australia, and
Japan, and among the Spice Islands. Mine was
not the sort of life to make one long to coil up
one's ropes on land, the customs and ways of which
I had finally almost forgotten. And so when times

for freighters got bad, as at last they did, and I
tried to quit the sea, what was there for an old sailor
to do ? I was born in the breezes, and I had studied
the sea as perhaps few men have studied it, neglecting all else. Next in attractiveness, after seafaring, came ship-building. I longed to be master in
both professions, and in a small way, in time, I accomplished my desire. From the decks of stout
ships in the worst gales I had made calculations as
to the size and sort of ship safest for all weather
and all seas. Thus the voyage which I am now to
narrate was a natural outcome not only of my love
of adventure, but of my lifelong experience.

One midwinter day of 1892, in Boston, where I
had been cast up from old ocean, so to speak, a year
or two before, I was cogitating whether I should
apply for a command, and again eat my bread and
butter on the sea, or go to work at the shipyard,
when I met an old acquaintance, a whaling-captain,
who said: "Come to Fairhaven and I'll give you a
ship. But," he added, "she wants some repairs."
The captain's terms, when fully explained, were
more than satisfactory to me. They included all
the assistance I would require to fit the craft for
sea. I was only too glad to accept, for I had already found that I could not obtain work in the
shipyard without first paying fifty dollars to a society, and as for a ship to command — there were
not enough ships to go round. Nearly all our tall
vessels had been cut down for coal-barges, and were
being ignominiously towed by the nose from port
to port, while many worthy captains addressed
themselves to Sailors' Snug Harbor.

The next day I landed at Fairhaven, opposite New Bedford, and found that my friend had something of a joke on me. For seven years the joke had been on him. The "ship" proved to be a very antiquated sloop called the *Spray*, which the neighbors declared had been built in the year 1. She was affectionately propped up in a field, some distance from salt water, and was covered with canvas. The people of Fairhaven, I hardly need say, are thrifty and observant. For seven years they had asked, "I wonder what Captain Eben Pierce is going to do with the old *Spray*?" The day I appeared there was a buzz at the gossip exchange: at last some one had come and was actually at work on the old *Spray*. "Breaking her up, I s'pose?" "No; going to rebuild her." Great was the amazement. "Will it pay?" was the question which for a year or more I answered by declaring that I would make it pay.

My ax felled a stout oak-tree near by for a keel, and Farmer Howard, for a small sum of money, hauled in this and enough timbers for the frame of the new vessel. I rigged a steam-box and a pot for a boiler. The timbers for ribs, being straight saplings, were dressed and steamed till supple, and then bent over a log, where they were secured till set. Something tangible appeared every day to show for my labor, and the neighbors made the work sociable. It was a great day in the *Spray* shipyard when her new stem was set up and fastened to the new keel. Whaling-captains came from far to survey it. With one voice they pronounced it "A 1," and in their opinion "fit

to smash ice." The oldest captain shook my hand
warmly when the breast-hooks were put in, declaring that he could see no reason why the *Spray*
should not "cut in bow-head" yet off the coast of
Greenland. The much-esteemed stem-piece was
from the butt of the smartest kind of a pasture
oak. It afterward split a coral patch in two at the
Keeling Islands, and did not receive a blemish.
Better timber for a ship than pasture white oak
never grew. The breast-hooks, as well as all the
ribs, were of this wood, and were steamed and bent
into shape as required. It was hard upon March
when I began work in earnest; the weather was
cold; still, there were plenty of inspectors to back
me with advice. When a whaling-captain hove
in sight I just rested on my adz awhile and
"gammed" with him.

New Bedford, the home of whaling-captains, is
connected with Fairhaven by a bridge, and the
walking is good. They never "worked along up"
to the shipyard too often for me. It was the
charming tales about arctic whaling that inspired
me to put a double set of breast-hooks in the *Spray*,
that she might shunt ice.

The seasons came quickly while I worked.
Hardly were the ribs of the sloop up before apple-
trees were in bloom. Then the daisies and the
cherries came soon after. Close by the place where
the old *Spray* had now dissolved rested the ashes
of John Cook, a revered Pilgrim father. So the
new *Spray* rose from hallowed ground. From the
deck of the new craft I could put out my hand and
pick cherries that grew over the little grave. The

planks for the new vessel, which I soon came to put
on, were of Georgia pine an inch and a half thick.
The operation of putting them on was tedious, but,
when on, the calking was easy. The outward edges
stood slightly open to receive the calking, but the
inner edges were so close that I could not see daylight between them. All the butts were fastened by
through bolts, with screw-
nuts tightening them to
the timbers, so that there
would be no complaint
from them. Many bolts
with screw-nuts were used
in other parts of the construction, in all about a
thousand. It was my pur-
pose to make my vessel
stout and strong.

Cross-section of the *Spray*.

Now, it is a law in Lloyd's
that the *Jane* repaired all
out of the old until she is
entirely new is still the *Jane*. The *Spray* changed
her being so gradually that it was hard to say at
what point the old died or the new took birth,
and it was no matter. The bulwarks I built up
of white-oak stanchions fourteen inches high,
and covered with seven-eighth-inch white pine.
These stanchions, mortised through a two-inch
covering-board, I calked with thin cedar wedges.
They have remained perfectly tight ever since.
The deck I made of one-and-a-half-inch by three-
inch white pine spiked to beams, six by six inches,
of yellow or Georgia pine, placed three feet apart.

The deck-inclosures were one over the aperture of the main hatch, six feet by six, for a cooking-galley, and a trunk farther aft, about ten feet by twelve, for a cabin. Both of these rose about three feet above the deck, and were sunk sufficiently into the hold to afford head-room. In the spaces along the sides of the cabin, under the deck, I arranged a berth to sleep in, and shelves for small storage, not forgetting a place for the medicine-chest. In the midship hold, that is, the space between cabin and galley, under the deck, was room for provision of water, salt beef, etc., ample for many months.

The hull of my vessel being now put together as strongly as wood and iron could make her, and the various rooms partitioned off, I set about " calking ship." Grave fears were entertained by some that at this point I should fail. I myself gave some thought to the advisability of a "professional calker." The very first blow I struck on the cotton with the calking-iron, which I thought was right, many others thought wrong. " It 'll crawl!" cried a man from Marion, passing with a basket of clams on his back. "It 'll crawl!" cried another from West Island, when he saw me driving cotton into the seams. Bruno simply wagged his tail. Even Mr. Ben J——, a noted authority on whaling-ships, whose mind, however, was said to totter, asked rather confidently if I did not think " it would crawl." " How fast will it crawl ? " cried my old captain friend, who had been towed by many a lively sperm-whale. "Tell us how fast," cried he, "that we may get into port in time." How-

"It'll crawl!"

Thomas Fogarty.

ever, I drove a thread of oakum on top of the cotton, as from the first I had intended to do. And Bruno again wagged his tail. The cotton never "crawled." When the calking was finished, two coats of copper paint were slapped on the bottom, two of white lead on the topsides and bulwarks. The rudder was then shipped and painted, and on the following day the *Spray* was launched. As she rode at her ancient, rust-eaten anchor, she sat on the water like a swan.

The *Spray's* dimensions were, when finished, thirty-six feet nine inches long, over all, fourteen feet two inches wide, and four feet two inches deep in the hold, her tonnage being nine tons net and twelve and seventy-one hundredths tons gross.

Then the mast, a smart New Hampshire spruce, was fitted, and likewise all the small appurtenances necessary for a short cruise. Sails were bent, and away she flew with my friend Captain Pierce and me, across Buzzard's Bay on a trial-trip—all right. The only thing that now worried my friends along the beach was, "Will she pay?" The cost of my new vessel was $553.62 for materials, and thirteen months of my own labor. I was several months more than that at Fairhaven, for I got work now and then on an occasional whale-ship fitting farther down the harbor, and that kept me the overtime.

CHAPTER II

Failure as a fisherman — A voyage around the world projected —
From Boston to Gloucester — Fitting out for the ocean voyage —
Half of a dory for a ship's boat — The run from Gloucester to
Nova Scotia — A shaking up in home waters — Among old friends.

I SPENT a season in my new craft fishing on
the coast, only to find that I had not the cunning properly to bait a hook. But at last the time
arrived to weigh anchor and get to sea in earnest.
I had resolved on a voyage around the world, and
as the wind on the morning of April 24, 1895, was
fair, at noon I weighed anchor, set sail, and filled
away from Boston, where the *Spray* had been
moored snugly all winter. The twelve-o'clock whis-
tles were blowing just as the sloop shot ahead under
full sail. A short board was made up the harbor
on the port tack, then coming about she stood seaward, with her boom well off to port, and swung
past the ferries with lively heels. A photographer
on the outer pier at East Boston got a picture of her
as she swept by, her flag at the peak throwing its
folds clear. A thrilling pulse beat high in me. My
step was light on deck in the crisp air. I felt that
there could be no turning back, and that I was engaging in an adventure the meaning of which I
thoroughly understood. I had taken little advice

from any one, for I had a right to my own opinions
in matters pertaining to the sea.   That the best of
sailors might do worse than even I alone was borne
in upon me not a league from Boston docks, where
a great steamship, fully manned, officered, and piloted, lay stranded and broken.   This was the *Ve-
netian.*   She was broken completely in two over a
ledge.   So in the first hour of my lone voyage I had
proof that the *Spray* could at least do better than
this full-handed steamship, for I was already farther
on my voyage than she.   "Take warning, *Spray,*
and have a care," I uttered aloud to my bark, passing fairylike silently down the bay.

The wind freshened, and the *Spray* rounded Deer
Island light, going at the rate of seven knots.
Passing it, she squared away direct for Gloucester,
where she was to procure some fishermen's stores.
Waves dancing joyously across Massachusetts Bay
met the sloop coming out, to dash themselves instantly into myriads of sparkling gems that hung
about her breast at every surge.   The day was perfect, the sunlight clear and strong.   Every particle
of water thrown into the air became a gem, and the
Spray, making good her name as she dashed ahead,
snatched necklace after necklace from the sea, and
as often threw them away.   We have all seen miniature rainbows about a ship's prow, but the *Spray*
flung out a bow of her own that day, such as I
had never seen before.   Her good angel had embarked on the voyage; I so read it in the sea.

Bold Nahant was soon abeam, then Marblehead
was put astern.   Other vessels were outward bound,
but none of them passed the *Spray* flying along on

her course. I heard the clanking of the dismal bell on Norman's Woe as we went by; and the reef where the schooner *Hesperus* struck I passed close aboard. The "bones" of a wreck tossed up lay bleaching on the shore abreast. The wind still freshening, I settled the throat of the mainsail to ease the sloop's helm, for I could hardly hold her before it with the whole mainsail set. A schooner ahead of me lowered all sail and ran into port under bare poles, the wind being fair. As the *Spray* brushed by the stranger, I saw that some of his sails were gone, and much broken canvas hung in his rigging, from the effects of a squall.

I made for the cove, a lovely branch of Gloucester's fine harbor, again to look the *Spray* over and again to weigh the voyage, and my feelings, and all that. The bay was feather-white as my little vessel tore in, smothered in foam. It was my first experience of coming into port alone, with a craft of any size, and in among shipping. Old fishermen ran down to the wharf for which the *Spray* was heading, apparently intent upon braining herself there. I hardly know how a calamity was averted, but with my heart in my mouth, almost, I let go the wheel, stepped quickly forward, and downed the jib. The sloop naturally rounded in the wind, and just ranging ahead, laid her cheek against a mooring-pile at the windward corner of the wharf, so quietly, after all, that she would not have broken an egg. Very leisurely I passed a rope around the post, and she was moored. Then a cheer went up from the little crowd on the wharf. "You could n't 'a' done it better," cried an old

skipper, " if you weighed a ton ! "   Now, my weight
was rather less than the fifteenth part of a ton,
but I said nothing, only putting on a look of careless indifference to say for me, " Oh, that 's nothing "; for some of the ablest sailors in the world
were looking at me, and my wish was not to appear
green, for I had a mind to stay in Gloucester several days.   Had I uttered a word it surely would
have betrayed me, for I was still quite nervous and
short of breath.

I remained in Gloucester about two weeks, fitting out with the various articles for the voyage
most readily obtained there.   The owners of the
wharf where I lay, and of many fishing-vessels, put
on board dry cod galore, also a barrel of oil to calm
the waves.   They were old skippers themselves,
and took a great interest in the voyage.   They also
made the *Spray* a present of a " fisherman's own "
lantern, which I found would throw a light a great
distance round.   Indeed, a ship that would run
another down having such a good light aboard
would be capable of running into a light-ship.   A
gaff, a pugh, and a dip-net, all of which an old
fisherman declared I could not sail without, were
also put aboard.   Then, too, from across the cove
came a case of copper paint, a famous antifouling
article, which stood me in good stead long after.
I slapped two coats of this paint on the bottom of
the *Spray* while she lay a tide or so on the hard
beach.

For a boat to take along, I made shift to cut a
castaway dory in two athwartships, boarding up
the end where it was cut.   This half-dory I could

hoist in and out by the nose easily enough, by hooking the throat-halyards into a strop fitted for the purpose. A whole dory would be heavy and awkward to handle alone. Manifestly there was not room on deck for more than the half of a boat, which, after all, was better than no boat at all, and was large enough for one man. I perceived, moreover, that the newly arranged craft would answer for a washing-machine when placed athwartships, and also for a bath-tub. Indeed, for the former office my razeed dory gained such a reputation on the voyage that my washerwoman at Samoa would not take no for an answer. She could see with one eye that it was a new invention which beat any Yankee notion ever brought by missionaries to the islands, and she had to have it.

The want of a chronometer for the voyage was all that now worried me. In our newfangled notions of navigation it is supposed that a mariner cannot find his way without one; and I had myself drifted into this way of thinking. My old chronometer, a good one, had been long in disuse. It would cost fifteen dollars to clean and rate it. Fifteen dollars! For sufficient reasons I left that timepiece at home, where the Dutchman left his anchor. I had the great lantern, and a lady in Boston sent me the price of a large two-burner cabin lamp, which lighted the cabin at night, and by some small contriving served for a stove through the day.

Being thus refitted I was once more ready for sea, and on May 7 again made sail. With little room in which to turn, the *Spray*, in gathering headway, scratched the paint off an old, fine-weather craft in the fairway, being puttied and painted for a summer voyage. " Who 'll pay for that ? " growled the painters. " I will," said I. " With the main-sheet," echoed the captain of the *Bluebird*, close by, which was his way of saying that I was off. There was nothing to pay for above five cents' worth of paint, maybe, but such a din was raised between the old " hooker " and the *Bluebird*, which now took up my case, that the first cause of it was forgotten altogether. Anyhow, no bill was sent after me.

The weather was mild on the day of my departure from Gloucester. On the point ahead, as the *Spray* stood out of the cove, was a lively picture, for the front of a tall factory was a flutter of handkerchiefs and caps. Pretty faces peered out of the windows from the top to the bottom of the building, all smiling *bon voyage*. Some hailed me to know where away and why alone. Why ? When I made as if to stand in, a hundred pairs of arms reached out, and said come, but the shore was dangerous ! The sloop worked out of the bay against a light southwest wind, and about noon squared away off Eastern Point, receiving at the same time a hearty salute — the last of many kindnesses to her at Gloucester. The wind freshened off the point, and skipping along smoothly, the *Spray* was soon off Thatcher's Island lights. Thence shaping her course east, by compass, to go north of Cashes Ledge and the Amen Rocks, I sat and considered the matter all over again, and asked myself once more whether it were best to sail beyond the ledge and rocks at all. I had only said that I would sail round the world in the *Spray*, "dangers of the sea excepted," but I must have said it very much in earnest. The "charter-party" with myself seemed to bind me, and so I sailed on. Toward night I hauled the sloop to the wind, and baiting a hook, sounded for bottom-fish, in thirty fathoms of water, on the edge of Cashes Ledge. With fair success I hauled till dark, landing on deck three cod and two haddocks, one hake, and, best of all, a small halibut, all plump and spry. This, I thought, would be the place to take in a good stock of provisions above what I already had; so I put out a sea-anchor that would hold her head to windward. The current being southwest, against the wind, I felt quite sure I would find the *Spray* still on the bank or near it in the morning. Then "stradding" the cable and putting my great lantern in the rigging, I lay down, for the first time at sea alone, not to sleep, but to doze and to dream.

I had read somewhere of a fishing-schooner hooking her anchor into a whale, and being towed a long way and at great speed. This was exactly what happened to the *Spray* — in my dream! I could not shake it off entirely when I awoke and found that it was the wind blowing and the heavy sea now running that had disturbed my short rest. A scud was flying across the moon. A storm was brewing; indeed, it was already stormy. I reefed the sails, then hauled in my sea-anchor, and setting what canvas the sloop could carry, headed her away for Monhegan light, which she made before daylight on the morning of the 8th. The wind being free, I ran on into Round Pond harbor, which

2

is a little port east from Pemaquid.   Here I rested
a day, while the wind rattled among the pine-trees
on shore.   But the following day was fine enough,

" 'No dorg nor no cat.' "

and I put to sea, first writing up my log from Cape
Ann, not omitting a full account of my adventure
with the whale.

The *Spray*, heading east, stretched along the coast among many islands and over a tranquil sea. At evening of this day, May 10, she came up with a considerable island, which I shall always think of as the Island of Frogs, for the *Spray* was charmed by a million voices. From the Island of Frogs we made for the Island of Birds, called Gannet Island, and sometimes Gannet Rock, whereon is a bright, intermittent light, which flashed fitfully across the *Spray's* deck as she coasted along under its light and shade. Thence shaping a course for Briar's Island, I came among vessels the following afternoon on the western fishing-grounds, and after speaking a fisherman at anchor, who gave me a wrong course, the *Spray* sailed directly over the southwest ledge through the worst tide-race in the Bay of Fundy, and got into Westport harbor in Nova Scotia, where I had spent eight years of my life as a lad.

The fisherman may have said "east-southeast," the course I was steering when I hailed him; but I thought he said "east-northeast," and I accordingly changed it to that. Before he made up his mind to answer me at all, he improved the occasion of his own curiosity to know where I was from, and if I was alone, and if I did n't have "no dorg nor no cat." It was the first time in all my life at sea that I had heard a hail for information answered by a question. I think the chap belonged to the Foreign Islands. There was one thing I was sure of, and that was that he did not belong to Briar's Island, because he dodged a sea that slopped over the rail, and stopping to brush the water from his

face, lost a fine cod which he was about to ship.
My islander would not have done that. It is known
that a Briar Islander, fish or no fish on his hook,
never flinches from a sea. He just tends to his
lines and hauls or "saws." Nay, have I not seen
my old friend Deacon W. D——, a good man of the

The deacon's dream.

island, while listening to a sermon in the little
church on the hill, reach out his hand over the
door of his pew and "jig" imaginary squid in the
aisle, to the intense delight of the young people,
who did not realize that to catch good fish one
must have good bait, the thing most on the deacon's mind.

I was delighted to reach Westport. Any port at
all would have been delightful after the terrible
thrashing I got in the fierce sou'west rip, and to

find myself among old schoolmates now was charming. It was the 13th of the month, and 13 is my
lucky number — a fact registered long before Dr.
Nansen sailed in search of the north pole with his
crew of thirteen. Perhaps he had heard of my
success in taking a most extraordinary ship successfully to Brazil with that number of crew. The very
stones on Briar's Island I was glad to see again,
and I knew them all. The little shop round the
corner, which for thirty-five years I had not seen,
was the same, except that it looked a deal smaller.
It wore the same shingles — I was sure of it; for
did not I know the roof where we boys, night after
night, hunted for the skin of a black cat, to be
taken on a dark night, to make a plaster for a poor
lame man? Lowry the tailor lived there when
boys were boys. In his day he was fond of the
gun. He always carried his powder loose in the
tail pocket of his coat. He usually had in his
mouth a short dudeen; but in an evil moment he
put the dudeen, lighted, in the pocket among the
powder. Mr. Lowry was an eccentric man.

At Briar's Island I overhauled the *Spray* once
more and tried her seams, but found that even the
test of the sou'west rip had started nothing. Bad
weather and much head wind prevailing outside, I
was in no hurry to round Cape Sable. I made a
short excursion with some friends to St. Mary's
Bay, an old cruising-ground, and back to the
island. Then I sailed, putting into Yarmouth the
following day on account of fog and head wind. I
spent some days pleasantly enough in Yarmouth,
took in some butter for the voyage, also a barrel of

potatoes, filled six barrels of water, and stowed all
under deck.   At Yarmouth, too, I got my famous
tin clock, the only timepiece I carried on the whole
voyage.   The price of it was a dollar and a half,
but on account of the face being smashed the merchant let me have it for a dollar.

Captain Slocum's chronometer.

CHAPTER III

I NOW stowed all my goods securely, for the boisterous Atlantic was before me, and I sent the topmast down, knowing that the *Spray* would be the wholesomer with it on deck. Then I gave the lanyards a pull and hitched them afresh, and saw that the gammon was secure, also that the boat was lashed, for even in summer one may meet with bad weather in the crossing.

In fact, many weeks of bad weather had prevailed. On July 1, however, after a rude gale, the wind came out nor'west and clear, propitious for a good run. On the following day, the head sea having gone down, I sailed from Yarmouth, and let go my last hold on America. The log of my first day on the Atlantic in the *Spray* reads briefly: "9:30 A. M. sailed from Yarmouth. 4:30 P. M. passed Cape Sable; distance, three cables from the land. The sloop making eight knots. Fresh breeze N. W." Before the sun went down I was taking my supper

of strawberries and tea in smooth water under the
lee of the east-coast land, along which the *Spray*
was now leisurely skirting.

At noon on July 3 Ironbound Island was abeam.
The *Spray* was again at her best. A large schooner
came out of Liverpool, Nova Scotia, this morning,
steering eastward. The *Spray* put her hull down
astern in five hours. At 6:45 P. M. I was in close
under Chebucto Head light, near Halifax harbor. I
set my flag and squared away, taking my departure
from George's Island before dark to sail east of
Sable Island. There are many beacon lights along
the coast. Sambro, the Rock of Lamentations,
carries a noble light, which, however, the liner
Atlantic, on the night of her terrible disaster, did
not see. I watched light after light sink astern as
I sailed into the unbounded sea, till Sambro, the
last of them all, was below the horizon. The *Spray*
was then alone, and sailing on, she held her course.
July 4, at 6 A. M., I put in double reefs, and at 8:30
A. M. turned out all reefs. At 9:40 P. M. I raised the
sheen only of the light on the west end of Sable
Island, which may also be called the Island of
Tragedies. The fog, which till this moment had
held off, now lowered over the sea like a pall. I
was in a world of fog, shut off from the universe.
I did not see any more of the light. By the lead,
which I cast often, I found that a little after midnight I was passing the east point of the island,
and should soon be clear of dangers of land and
shoals. The wind was holding free, though it was
from the foggy point, south-southwest. It is said
that within a few years Sable Island has been

reduced from forty miles in length to twenty, and that of three lighthouses built on it since 1880, two have been washed away and the third will soon be engulfed.

"'Good evening, sir.'"

On the evening of July 5 the *Spray*, after having steered all day over a lumpy sea, took it into her head to go without the helmsman's aid. I had been steering southeast by south, but the wind hauling forward a bit, she dropped into a smooth lane, heading southeast, and making about eight knots, her very best work. I crowded on sail to cross the track of the liners without loss of time, and to reach as soon as possible the friendly Gulf Stream. The fog lifting before night, I was afforded a look at the sun just as it was touching the sea. I watched it go down and out of sight. Then I turned my face eastward, and there, apparently at the very end of the bowsprit, was the smiling full moon rising out of the sea. Neptune himself coming over the bows could not have startled me more. "Good evening, sir," I cried; "I 'm glad to see you." Many a long talk since then I have had with the man in the moon; he had my confidence on the voyage.

About midnight the fog shut down again denser than ever before. One could almost "stand on it." It continued so for a number of days, the wind increasing to a gale. The waves rose high, but I had a good ship. Still, in the dismal fog I felt myself drifting into loneliness, an insect on a straw in the midst of the elements. I lashed the helm, and my vessel held her course, and while she sailed I slept.

During these days a feeling of awe crept over me. My memory worked with startling power. The ominous, the insignificant, the great, the small, the wonderful, the commonplace—all appeared before my mental vision in magical succession. Pages of my history were recalled which had been so long forgotten that they seemed to belong to a previous existence. I heard all the voices of the past laughing, crying, telling what I had heard them tell in many corners of the earth.

The loneliness of my state wore off when the gale was high and I found much work to do. When fine weather returned, then came the sense of solitude, which I could not shake off. I used my voice often, at first giving some order about the affairs of a ship, for I had been told that from disuse I should lose my speech. At the meridian altitude of the sun I called aloud, "Eight bells," after the custom on a ship at sea. Again from my cabin I cried to an imaginary man at the helm, "How does she head, there?" and again, "Is she on her course?" But getting no reply, I was reminded the more palpably of my condition. My voice sounded hollow on the empty air, and I dropped the practice. However, it was not long before the thought came to me that when I was a lad I used to sing; why not try that now, where it would disturb no one? My musical talent had never bred envy in others, but out on the Atlantic, to realize what it meant, you should have heard me sing. You should have seen the porpoises leap when I pitched my voice for the waves and the sea and all that was in it. Old turtles, with large eyes, poked their heads up out of the sea as I sang "Johnny Boker," and "We 'll Pay Darby Doyl for his Boots," and the like. But the porpoises were, on the whole, vastly more appreciative than the turtles; they jumped a deal higher. One day when I was humming a favorite chant, I think it was "Babylon 's a-Fallin'," a porpoise jumped higher than the bowsprit. Had the *Spray* been going a little faster she would have scooped him in. The sea-birds sailed around rather shy.

July 10, eight days at sea, the *Spray* was twelve
hundred miles east of Cape Sable. One hundred
and fifty miles a day for so small a vessel must be
considered good sailing. It was the greatest run
the *Spray* ever made before or since in so few days.
On the evening of July 14, in better humor than
ever before, all hands cried, "Sail ho!" The sail
was a barkantine, three points on the weather bow,
hull down. Then came the night. My ship was
sailing along now without attention to the helm.
The wind was south; she was heading east. Her
sails were trimmed like the sails of the nautilus.
They drew steadily all night. I went frequently
on deck, but found all well. A merry breeze kept
on from the
south. Early
in the morn-
ing of the
15th the
Spray was
close aboard
the stranger, which proved to
be *La Vaguisa* of Vigo, twenty-
three days from Philadelphia,
bound for Vigo. A lookout
from his masthead had spied
the *Spray* the evening before.
The captain, when I came near
enough, threw a line to me and
sent a bottle of wine across
slung by the neck, and very good wine it was. He
also sent his card, which bore the name of Juan
Gantes. I think he was a good man, as Spaniards

"He also sent his card."

go. But when I asked him to report me "all well" (the *Spray* passing him in a lively manner), he hauled his shoulders much above his head; and when his mate, who knew of my expedition, told him that I was alone, he crossed himself and made for his cabin. I did not see him again. By sundown he was as far astern as he had been ahead the evening before.

There was now less and less monotony. On July 16 the wind was northwest and clear, the sea smooth, and a large bark, hull down, came in sight on the lee bow, and at 2:30 P. M. I spoke the stranger. She was the bark *Java* of Glasgow, from Peru for Queenstown for orders. Her old captain was bearish, but I met a bear once in Alaska that looked pleasanter. At least, the bear seemed pleased to meet me, but this grizzly old man! Well, I suppose my hail disturbed his siesta, and my little sloop passing his great ship had somewhat the effect on him that a red rag has upon a bull. I had the advantage over heavy ships, by long odds, in the light winds of this and the two previous days. The wind was light; his ship was heavy and foul, making poor headway, while the *Spray*, with a great mainsail bellying even to light winds, was just skipping along as nimbly as one could wish. "How long has it been calm about here?" roared the captain of the *Java*, as I came within hail of him. "Dunno, cap'n," I shouted back as loud as I could bawl. "I have n't been here long." At this the mate on the forecastle wore a broad grin. "I left Cape Sable fourteen days ago," I added. (I was now well across toward

Chart of the *Spray's* course around the world — April 24, 1895, to July 3, 1898.

the Azores.) "Mate," he roared to his chief officer
— "mate, come here and listen to the Yankee's
yarn. Haul down the flag, mate, haul down the
flag!" In the best of humor, after all, the *Java*
surrendered to the *Spray*.

The acute pain of solitude experienced at first
never returned. I had penetrated a mystery, and,
by the way, I had sailed through a fog. I had met
Neptune in his wrath, but he found that I had not
treated him with contempt, and so he suffered me
to go on and explore.

In the log for July 18 there is this entry: "Fine
weather, wind south-southwest. Porpoises gamboling all about. The S. S. *Olympia* passed at
11:30 A. M., long. W. 34° 50'."

"It lacks now three minutes of the half-hour,"
shouted the captain, as he gave me the longitude
and the time. I admired the businesslike air of the
Olympia; but I have the feeling still that the captain was just a little too precise in his reckoning.
That may be all well enough, however, where there
is plenty of sea-room. But over-confidence, I believe, was the cause of the disaster to the liner *Atlantic*, and many more like her. The captain knew
too well where he was. There were no porpoises
at all skipping along with the *Olympia!* Porpoises
always prefer sailing-ships. The captain was a
young man, I observed, and had before him, I
hope, a good record.

Land ho! On the morning of July 19 a mystic
dome like a mountain of silver stood alone in the
sea ahead. Although the land was completely
hidden by the white, glistening haze that shone in

the sun like polished silver, I felt quite sure that it
was Flores Island. At half-past four P. M. it was
abeam. The haze in the meantime had disappeared.
Flores is one hundred and seventy-four miles from
Fayal, and although it is a high island, it remained
many years undiscovered after the principal group
of the islands had been colonized.

Early on the morning of July 20 I saw Pico
looming above the clouds on the starboard bow.
Lower lands burst forth as the sun burned away

The island of Pico.

the morning fog, and island after island came into
view. As I approached nearer, cultivated fields
appeared, "and oh, how green the corn!" Only
those who have seen the Azores from the deck of a
vessel realize the beauty of the mid-ocean picture.

At 4:30 P. M. I cast anchor at Fayal, exactly
eighteen days from Cape Sable. The American
consul, in a smart boat, came alongside before
the *Spray* reached the breakwater, and a young
naval officer, who feared for the safety of my vessel, boarded, and offered his services as pilot. The
youngster, I have no good reason to doubt, could
have handled a man-of-war, but the *Spray* was too
small for the amount of uniform he wore. However, after fouling all the craft in port and sinking
a lighter, she was moored without much damage to

herself. This wonderful pilot expected a "gratifica-
tion," I understood, but whether for the reason that
his government, and not I, would have to pay the
cost of raising the lighter, or because he did not
sink the *Spray*, I could never make out. But I
forgive him.

It was the season for fruit when I arrived at the
Azores, and there was soon more of all kinds of it
put on board than I knew what to do with. Islanders are always the kindest people in the world,
and I met none anywhere kinder than the good
hearts of this place. The people of the Azores are
not a very rich community. The burden of taxes
is heavy, with scant privileges in return, the air
they breathe being about the only thing that is not
taxed. The mother-country does not even allow
them a port of entry for a foreign mail service. A
packet passing never so close with mails for Horta
must deliver them first in Lisbon, ostensibly to be
fumigated, but really for the tariff from the packet.
My own letters posted at Horta reached the United
States six days behind my letter from Gibraltar,
mailed thirteen days later.

The day after my arrival at Horta was the feast
of a great saint. Boats loaded with people came
from other islands to celebrate at Horta, the capital, or Jerusalem, of the Azores. The deck of the
Spray was crowded from morning till night with
men, women, and children. On the day after the
feast a kind-hearted native harnessed a team and
drove me a day over the beautiful roads all about
Fayal, "because," said he, in broken English,
"when I was in America and could n't speak a

3

word of English, I found it hard till I met some one
who seemed to have time to listen to my story, and
I promised my good saint then that if ever a
stranger came to my country I would try to make
him happy." Unfortunately, this gentleman brought
along an interpreter, that I might "learn more of
the country." The fellow was nearly the death of
me, talking of ships and voyages, and of the boats
he had steered, the last thing in the world I wished
to hear. He had sailed out of New Bedford, so he
said, for "that Joe Wing they call 'John.'" My
friend and host found hardly a chance to edge in a
word. Before we parted my host dined me with
a cheer that would have gladdened the heart of a
prince, but he was quite alone in his house. "My
wife and children all rest there," said he, pointing
to the churchyard across the way. "I moved to
this house from far off," he added, "to be near the
spot, where I pray every morning."

I remained four days at Fayal, and that was two
days more than I had intended to stay. It was the
kindness of the islanders and their touching simplicity which detained me. A damsel, as innocent
as an angel, came alongside one day, and said she
would embark on the *Spray* if I would land her at
Lisbon. She could cook flying-fish, she thought,
but her forte was dressing *bacalhao*. Her brother
Antonio, who served as interpreter, hinted that,
anyhow, he would like to make the trip. Antonio's
heart went out to one John Wilson, and he was
ready to sail for America by way of the two capes
to meet his friend. "Do you know John Wilson
of Boston?" he cried. "I knew a John Wilson," I

Chart of the *Spray's* Atlantic voyages from Boston to Gibraltar, thence to the Strait of Magellan, in 1895, and finally homeward bound from the Cape of Good Hope in 1898.

said, "but not of Boston." "He had one daughter and one son," said Antonio, by way of identifying his friend. If this reaches the right John Wilson, I am told to say that "Antonio of Pico remembers him."

CHAPTER IV

Squally weather in the Azores — High living — Delirious from cheese
and plums — The pilot of the *Pinta* — At Gibraltar — Compliments
exchanged with the British navy — A picnic on the Morocco
shore.

I SET sail from Horta early on July 24. The southwest wind at the time was light, but squalls came
up with the sun, and I was glad enough to get reefs
in my sails before I had gone a mile. I had hardly
set the mainsail, double-reefed, when a squall of wind
down the mountains struck the sloop with such
violence that I thought her mast would go. However, a quick helm brought her to the wind. As it
was, one of the weather lanyards was carried away
and the other was stranded. My tin basin, caught
up by the wind, went flying across a French school-
ship to leeward. It was more or less squally all
day, sailing along under high land; but rounding
close under a bluff, I found an opportunity to mend
the lanyards broken in the squall. No sooner had
I lowered my sails when a four-oared boat shot out
from some gully in the rocks, with a customs officer
on board, who thought he had come upon a smug-
gler. I had some difficulty in making him compre-
hend the true case. However, one of his crew, a
sailorly chap, who understood how matters were,
while we palavered jumped on board and rove off

the new lanyards I had already prepared, and with
a friendly hand helped me "set up the rigging."
This incident gave the turn in my favor. My story
was then clear to all. I have found this the way
of the world. Let one be without a friend, and see
what will happen!

Passing the island of Pico, after the rigging was
mended, the *Spray* stretched across to leeward of
the island of St. Michael's, which she was up with
early on the morning of July 26, the wind blowing
hard. Later in the day she passed the Prince of
Monaco's fine steam-yacht bound to Fayal, where,
on a previous voyage, the prince had slipped his
cables to "escape a reception" which the padres of
the island wished to give him. Why he so dreaded
the "ovation" I could not make out. At Horta
they did not know. Since reaching the islands I
had lived most luxuriously on fresh bread, butter,
vegetables, and fruits of all kinds. Plums seemed
the most plentiful on the *Spray*, and these I ate
without stint. I had also a Pico white cheese that
General Manning, the American consul-general,
had given me, which I supposed was to be eaten,
and of this I partook with the plums. Alas! by
night-time I was doubled up with cramps. The
wind, which was already a smart breeze, was increasing somewhat, with a heavy sky to the sou'-
west. Reefs had been turned out, and I must turn
them in again somehow. Between cramps I got
the mainsail down, hauled out the earings as best I
could, and tied away point by point, in the double
reef. There being sea-room, I should, in strict pru-
dence, have made all snug and gone down at once

to my cabin.   I am a careful man at sea, but this
night, in the coming storm, I swayed up my sails,
which, reefed though they were, were still too much
in such heavy weather; and I saw to it that the
sheets were securely belayed.   In a word, I should
have laid to, but did not.   I gave her the double-
reefed mainsail and whole jib instead, and set her
on her course.   Then I went below, and threw myself upon the cabin floor in great pain.   How long
I lay there I could not tell, for I became delirious.
When I came to, as I thought, from my swoon, I
realized that the sloop was plunging into a heavy
sea, and looking out of the companionway, to my
amazement I saw a tall man at the helm.   His
rigid hand, grasping the spokes of the wheel, held
them as in a vise.   One may imagine my astonishment.   His rig was that of a foreign sailor, and the
large red cap he wore was cockbilled over his left
ear, and all was set off with shaggy black whiskers.
He would have been taken for a pirate in any part
of the world.   While I gazed upon his threatening
aspect I forgot the storm, and wondered if he had
come to cut my throat.   This he seemed to divine.
" Señor," said he, doffing his cap, " I have come to
do you no harm."   And a smile, the faintest in the
world, but still a smile, played on his face, which
seemed not unkind when he spoke.   " I have come
to do you no harm.   I have sailed free," he said,
"but was never worse than a *contrabandista*.   I am
one of Columbus's crew," he continued.   " I am the
pilot of the *Pinta* come to aid you.   Lie quiet,
señor captain," he added, " and I will guide your
ship to-night.   You have a *calentura*, but you will

be all right to-morrow." I thought what a very
devil he was to carry sail. Again, as if he read my
mind, he exclaimed: "Yonder is the *Pinta* ahead;

The apparition at the wheel.

we must overtake her. Give her sail; give her
sail! *Vale, vale, muy vale!*" Biting off a large quid
of black twist, he said: "You did wrong, captain,
to mix cheese with plums. White cheese is never

safe unless you know whence it comes. *Quien sabe*, it may have been from *leche de Capra* and becoming capricious —— "

"Avast, there!" I cried. "I have no mind for moralizing."

I made shift to spread a mattress and lie on that instead of the hard floor, my eyes all the while fastened on my strange guest, who, remarking again that I would have "only pains and calentura," chuckled as he chanted a wild song:

> High are the waves, fierce, gleaming,
> High is the tempest roar!
> High the sea-bird screaming!
> High the Azore!

I suppose I was now on the mend, for I was peevish, and complained: "I detest your jingle. Your Azore should be at roost, and would have been were it a respectable bird!" I begged he would tie a rope-yarn on the rest of the song, if there was any more of it. I was still in agony. Great seas were boarding the *Spray*, but in my fevered brain I thought they were boats falling on deck, that careless draymen were throwing from wagons on the pier to which I imagined the *Spray* was now moored, and without fenders to breast her off. "You'll smash your boats!" I called out again and again, as the seas crashed on the cabin over my head. "You'll smash your boats, but you can't hurt the *Spray*. She is strong!" I cried.

I found, when my pains and calentura had gone, that the deck, now as white as a shark's tooth from seas washing over it, had been swept of every-

thing movable. To my astonishment, I saw now
at broad day that the *Spray* was still heading as I
had left her, and was going like a race-horse.
Columbus himself could not have held her more
exactly on her course. The sloop had made ninety
miles in the night through a rough sea. I felt
grateful to the old pilot, but I marveled some that
he had not taken in the jib. The gale was moder-
ating, and by noon the sun was shining. A meridian altitude and the distance on the patent log,
which I always kept towing, told me that she had
made a true course throughout the twenty-four
hours. I was getting much better now, but was
very weak, and did not turn out reefs that day or
the night following, although the wind fell light;
but I just put my wet clothes out in the sun when
it was shining, and lying down there myself, fell
asleep. Then who should visit me again but my
old friend of the night before, this time, of course,
in a dream. " You did well last night to take my
advice," said he, " and if you would, I should like
to be with you often on the voyage, for the love
of adventure alone." Finishing what he had to
say, he again doffed his cap and disappeared as
mysteriously as he came, returning, I suppose, to
the phantom *Pinta*. I awoke much refreshed, and
with the feeling that I had been in the presence of
a friend and a seaman of vast experience. I gathered up my clothes, which by this time were dry,
then, by inspiration, I threw overboard all the
plums in the vessel.

July 28 was exceptionally fine. The wind from
the northwest was light and the air balmy. I over-

hauled my wardrobe, and bent on a white shirt against nearing some coasting-packet with genteel folk on board. I also did some washing to get the salt out of my clothes. After it all I was hungry, so I made a fire and very cautiously stewed a dish of pears and set them carefully aside till I had made a pot of delicious coffee, for both of which I could afford sugar and cream. But the crowning dish of all was a fish-hash, and there was enough of it for two. I was in good health again, and my appetite was simply ravenous. While I was dining I had a large onion over the double lamp stewing for a luncheon later in the day. High living to-day!

In the afternoon the *Spray* came upon a large turtle asleep on the sea. He awoke with my harpoon through his neck, if he awoke at all. I had much difficulty in landing him on deck, which I finally accomplished by hooking the throat-halyards to one of his flippers, for he was about as heavy as my boat. I saw more turtles, and I rigged a burton ready with which to hoist them in; for I was obliged to lower the mainsail whenever the halyards were used for such purposes, and it was no small matter to hoist the large sail again. But the turtle-steak was good. I found no fault with the cook, and it was the rule of the voyage that the cook found no fault with me. There was never a ship's crew so well agreed. The bill of fare that evening was turtle-steak, tea and toast, fried potatoes, stewed onions; with dessert of stewed pears and cream.

Sometime in the afternoon I passed a barrel-buoy adrift, floating light on the water. It was painted red, and rigged with a signal-staff about

six feet high. A sudden change in the weather
coming on, I got no more turtle or fish of any sort
before reaching port. July 31 a gale sprang up
suddenly from the north, with heavy seas, and I
shortened sail. The *Spray* made only fifty-one
miles on her course that day. August 1 the gale
continued, with heavy seas. Through the night
the sloop was reaching, under close-reefed mainsail and bobbed jib. At 3 P. M. the jib was washed
off the bowsprit and blown to rags and ribbons.
I bent the "jumbo" on a stay at the night-heads.
As for the jib, let it go; I saved pieces of it, and,
after all, I was in want of pot-rags.

On August 3 the gale broke, and I saw many
signs of land. Bad weather having made itself
felt in the galley, I was minded to try my hand at
a loaf of bread, and so rigging a pot of fire on deck
by which to bake it, a loaf soon became an accomplished fact. One great feature about ship's cooking is that one's appetite on the sea is always good
— a fact that I realized when I cooked for the
crew of fishermen in the before-mentioned boyhood
days. Dinner being over, I sat for hours reading
the life of Columbus, and as the day wore on I
watched the birds all flying in one direction, and
said, "Land lies there."

Early the next morning, August 4, I discovered
Spain. I saw fires on shore, and knew that the
country was inhabited. The *Spray* continued on
her course till well in with the land, which was
that about Trafalgar. Then keeping away a point,
she passed through the Strait of Gibraltar, where
she cast anchor at 3 P. M. of the same day, less

than twenty-nine days from Cape Sable. At the finish of this preliminary trip I found myself in excellent health, not overworked or cramped, but as well as ever in my life, though I was as thin as a reef-point.

Two Italian barks, which had been close along-

Coming to anchor at Gibraltar.

side at daylight, I saw long after I had anchored, passing up the African side of the strait. The *Spray* had sailed them both hull down before she reached Tarifa. So far as I know, the *Spray* beat everything going across the Atlantic except the steamers.

All was well, but I had forgotten to bring a bill

of health from Horta, and so when the fierce old
port doctor came to inspect there was a row.   That,
however, was the very thing needed.   If you want
to get on well with a true Britisher you must first
have a deuce of a row with him.   I knew that well
enough, and so I fired away, shot for shot, as best
I could.   " Well, yes," the doctor admitted at last,
" your crew are healthy enough, no doubt, but who
knows the diseases of your last port ? " — a reasonable enough remark.   " We ought to put you in
the fort, sir!" he blustered; "but never mind.
Free pratique, sir!   Shove off, cockswain!"   And
that was the last I saw of the port doctor.

But on the following morning a steam-launch,
much longer than the *Spray*, came alongside,— or
as much of her as could get alongside,— with compliments from the senior naval officer, Admiral
Bruce, saying there was a berth for the *Spray* at
the arsenal.   This was around at the new mole.
I had anchored at the old mole, among the native
craft, where it was rough and uncomfortable.   Of
course I was glad to shift, and did so as soon as
possible, thinking of the great company the *Spray*
would be in among battle-ships such as the *Collingwood*, *Balfleur*, and *Cormorant*, which were at that
time stationed there, and on board all of which I
was entertained, later, most royally.

" ' Put it thar!' as the Americans say," was the
salute I got from Admiral Bruce, when I called at
the admiralty to thank him for his courtesy of
the berth, and for the use of the steam-launch
which towed me into dock.   " About the berth,
it is all right if it suits, and we 'll tow you out

when you are ready to go. But, say, what repairs
do you want? Ahoy the *Hebe*, can you spare your
sailmaker? The *Spray* wants a new jib. Construction and repair, there! will you see to the
Spray? Say, old man, you must have knocked
the devil out of her coming over alone in twenty-

The *Spray* at anchor off Gibraltar.

nine days! But we 'll make it smooth for you
here!" Not even her Majesty's ship the *Collingwood* was better looked after than the *Spray* at
Gibraltar.

Later in the day came the hail: "*Spray* ahoy!
Mrs. Bruce would like to come on board and
shake hands with the *Spray*. Will it be con-
venient to-day?" "Very!" I joyfully shouted.

On the following day Sir F. Carrington, at the time governor of Gibraltar, with other high officers of the garrison, and all the commanders of the battle-ships, came on board and signed their names in the *Spray's* log-book. Again there was a hail, "*Spray* ahoy!" "Hello!" "Commander Reynolds's compliments. You are invited on board H. M. S. *Collingwood*, 'at home' at 4:30 P. M. Not later than 5:30 P. M." I had already hinted at the limited amount of my wardrobe, and that I could never succeed as a dude. "You are expected, sir, in a stovepipe hat and a claw-hammer coat!" "Then I can't come." "Dash it! come in what you have on; that is what we mean." "Aye, aye, sir!" The *Collingwood's* cheer was good, and had I worn a silk hat as high as the moon I could not have had a better time or been made more at home. An Englishman, even on his great battle-ship, unbends when the stranger passes his gangway, and when he says "at home" he means it.

That one should like Gibraltar would go without saying. How could one help loving so hospitable a place? Vegetables twice a week and milk every morning came from the palatial grounds of the admiralty. "*Spray* ahoy!" would hail the admiral. "*Spray* ahoy!" "Hello!" "To-morrow is your vegetable day, sir." "Aye, aye, sir!"

I rambled much about the old city, and a gunner piloted me through the galleries of the rock as far as a stranger is permitted to go. There is no excavation in the world, for military purposes, at all approaching these of Gibraltar in conception or execution. Viewing the stupendous works, it became hard to realize that one was within the Gibraltar of his little old Morse geography.

Before sailing I was invited on a picnic with the governor, the officers of the garrison, and the commanders of the war-ships at the station; and a royal affair it was. Torpedo-boat No. 91, going twenty-two knots, carried our party to the Morocco shore and back. The day was perfect — too fine, in fact, for comfort on shore, and so no one landed at Morocco. No. 91 trembled like an aspen-leaf as she raced through the sea at top speed. Sublieutenant Boucher, apparently a mere lad, was in command, and handled his ship with the skill of an older sailor. On the following day I lunched with General Carrington, the governor, at Line Wall House, which was once the Franciscan convent. In this interesting edifice are preserved relics of the fourteen sieges which Gibraltar has seen. On the next day I supped with the admiral at his residence, the palace, which was once the convent of the Mercenaries. At each place, and all about, I felt the friendly grasp of a manly hand, that lent me vital strength to pass the coming long days at sea. I must confess that the perfect discipline, order, and cheerfulness at Gibraltar were only a second wonder in the great stronghold. The vast amount of business going forward caused no more excitement than the quiet sailing of a well-appointed ship in a smooth sea. No one spoke above his natural voice, save a boatswain's mate now and then. The Hon. Horatio J. Sprague, the venerable United States consul at Gibraltar, honored the *Spray* with a visit on Sunday, August 24, and was much pleased to find that our British cousins had been so kind to her.

CHAPTER V

MONDAY, August 25, the *Spray* sailed from Gibraltar, well repaid for whatever deviation she
had made from a direct course to reach the place.
A tug belonging to her Majesty towed the sloop into
the steady breeze clear of the mount, where her sails
caught a volant wind, which carried her once more
to the Atlantic, where it rose rapidly to a furious
gale. My plan was, in going down this coast, to
haul offshore, well clear of the land, which here-
abouts is the home of pirates; but I had hardly
accomplished this when I perceived a felucca
making out of the nearest port, and finally following in the wake of the *Spray*. Now, my course
to Gibraltar had been taken with a view to proceed
up the Mediterranean Sea, through the Suez Canal,
down the Red Sea, and east about, instead of a
western route, which I finally adopted. By officers
of vast experience in navigating these seas, I was
influenced to make the change. Longshore pirates
on both coasts being numerous, I could not afford

to make light of the advice. But here I was, after all, evidently in the midst of pirates and thieves! I changed my course; the felucca did the same, both vessels sailing very fast, but the distance growing less and less between us. The *Spray* was doing nobly; she was even more than at her best; but, in spite of all I could do, she would broach now and then. She was carrying too much sail for safety. I must reef or be dismasted and lose all, pirate or no pirate. I must reef, even if I had to grapple with him for my life.

I was not long in reefing the mainsail and sweating it up — probably not more than fifteen minutes; but the felucca had in the meantime so shortened the distance between us that I now saw the tuft of hair on the heads of the crew,— by which, it is said, Mohammed will pull the villains up into heaven,— and they were coming on like the wind. From what I could clearly make out now, I felt them to be the sons of generations of pirates, and I saw by their movements that they were now preparing to strike a blow. The exultation on their faces, however, was changed in an instant to a look of fear and rage. Their craft, with too much sail on, broached to on the crest of a great wave. This one great sea changed the aspect of affairs suddenly as the flash of a gun. Three minutes later the same wave overtook the *Spray* and shook her in every timber. At the same moment the sheet-strop parted, and away went the main-boom, broken short at the rigging. Impulsively I sprang to the jib-halyards and down-haul, and instantly downed the jib. The head-sail being off, and the helm put hard down, the sloop came in the wind with a bound. While shivering there, but a moment though it was, I got the mainsail down and secured inboard, broken boom and all. How I got the boom in before the sail was torn I hardly know; but not a stitch of it was broken. The mainsail being secured, I hoisted away the jib, and, without looking round, stepped quickly to the cabin and snatched down my loaded rifle and cartridges at hand; for I made mental calculations that the pirate would by this time have recovered his course and be close aboard, and that when I saw him it would be better for me to be looking at him along the barrel of a gun. The piece was at my shoulder when I peered into the mist, but there was no pirate within a mile. The wave and squall that carried away my boom dismasted the felucca outright. I perceived his thieving crew, some dozen or more of them, struggling to recover their rigging from the sea. Allah blacken their faces!

I sailed comfortably on under the jib and forestaysail, which I now set. I fished the boom and furled the sail snug for the night; then hauled the sloop's head two points offshore to allow for the set of current and heavy rollers toward the land. This gave me the wind three points on the starboard quarter and a steady pull in the headsails. By the time I had things in this order it was dark, and a flying-fish had already fallen on deck. I took him below for my supper, but found myself too tired to cook, or even to eat a thing already prepared. I do not remember to have been more tired before or since in all my life than I was at the finish of that day. Too fatigued to sleep, I rolled about with the motion of the vessel till near midnight, when I made shift to dress my fish and prepare a dish of tea. I fully realized now, if I had not before, that the voyage ahead would call for exertions ardent and lasting. On August 27 nothing could be seen of the Moor, or his country either, except

Chased by pirates.

two peaks, away in the east through the clear atmosphere of morning. Soon after the sun rose even these were obscured by haze, much to my satisfaction.

The wind, for a few days following my escape from the pirates, blew a steady but moderate gale, and the sea, though agitated into long rollers, was not uncomfortably rough or dangerous, and while sitting in my cabin I could hardly realize that any

sea was running at all, so easy was the long, swing-
ing motion of the sloop over the waves. All dis-
tracting uneasiness and excitement being now over,
I was once more alone with myself in the realiza-
tion that I was on the mighty sea and in the hands
of the elements. But I was happy, and was becoming more and more interested in the voyage.

Columbus, in the *Santa Maria*, sailing these seas
more than four hundred years before, was not so
happy as I, nor so sure of success in what he had
undertaken. His first troubles at sea had already
begun. His crew had managed, by foul play or
otherwise, to break the ship's rudder while running
before probably just such a gale as the *Spray* had
passed through; and there was dissension on the
Santa Maria, something that was unknown on the
Spray.

After three days of squalls and shifting winds I
threw myself down to rest and sleep, while, with
helm lashed, the sloop sailed steadily on her course.

September 1, in the early morning, land-clouds
rising ahead told of the Canary Islands not far
away. A change in the weather came next day:
storm-clouds stretched their arms across the sky;
from the east, to all appearances, might come a
fierce harmattan, or from the south might come the
fierce hurricane. Every point of the compass
threatened a wild storm. My attention was turned
to reefing sails, and no time was to be lost over it,
either, for the sea in a moment was confusion
itself, and I was glad to head the sloop three points
or more away from her true course that she might
ride safely over the waves. I was now scudding

her for the channel between Africa and the island of Fuerteventura, the easternmost of the Canary Islands, for which I was on the lookout. At 2 P. M., the weather becoming suddenly fine, the island stood in view, already abeam to starboard, and not more than seven miles off. Fuerteventura is twenty-seven hundred feet high, and in fine weather is visible many leagues away.

The wind freshened in the night, and the *Spray* had a fine run through the channel. By daylight, September 3, she was twenty-five miles clear of all the islands, when a calm ensued, which was the precursor of another gale of wind that soon came on, bringing with it dust from the African shore. It howled dismally while it lasted, and though it was not the season of the harmattan, the sea in the course of an hour was discolored with a reddish-brown dust. The air remained thick with flying dust all the afternoon, but the wind, veering north-west at night, swept it back to land, and afforded the *Spray* once more a clear sky. Her mast now bent under a strong, steady pressure, and her belly-ing sail swept the sea as she rolled scuppers under, courtesying to the waves. These rolling waves thrilled me as they tossed my ship, passing quickly under her keel. This was grand sailing.

September 4, the wind, still fresh, blew from the north-northeast, and the sea surged along with the sloop. About noon a steamship, a bullock-droger, from the river Plate hove in sight, steering north-east, and making bad weather of it. I signaled her, but got no answer. She was plunging into the head sea and rolling in a most astonishing manner, and from the way she yawed one might have said that a wild steer was at the helm.

On the morning of September 6 I found three flying-fish on deck, and a fourth one down the fore-scuttle as close as possible to the frying-pan. It was the best haul yet, and afforded me a sumptuous breakfast and dinner.

The *Spray* had now settled down to the trade-winds and to the business of her voyage. Later in the day another droger hove in sight, rolling as badly as her predecessor. I threw out no flag to this one, but got the worst of it for passing under her lee. She was, indeed, a stale one! And the poor cattle, how they bellowed! The time was when ships passing one another at sea backed their topsails and had a " gam," and on parting fired guns; but those good old days have gone. People have hardly time nowadays to speak even on the broad ocean, where news is news, and as for a salute of guns, they cannot afford the powder. There are no poetry-enshrined freighters on the sea now; it is a prosy life when we have no time to bid one another good morning.

My ship, running now in the full swing of the trades, left me days to myself for rest and recuperation. I employed the time in reading and writing, or in whatever I found to do about the rigging and the sails to keep them all in order. The cooking was always done quickly, and was a small matter, as the bill of fare consisted mostly of flying-fish, hot biscuits and butter, potatoes, coffee and cream — dishes readily prepared.

On September 10 the *Spray* passed the island of

St. Antonio, the northwesternmost of the Cape
Verdes, close aboard. The landfall was wonder-
fully true, considering that no observations for
longitude had been made. The wind, northeast,
as the sloop drew by the island, was very squally,
but I reefed her sails snug, and steered broad from
the highland of blustering St. Antonio. Then
leaving the Cape Verde Islands out of sight astern,
I found myself once more sailing a lonely sea and
in a solitude supreme all around. When I slept
I dreamed that I was alone. This feeling never
left me; but, sleeping or waking, I seemed always
to know the position of the sloop, and I saw my
vessel moving across the chart, which became a
picture before me.

One night while I sat in the cabin under this
spell, the profound stillness all about was broken
by human voices alongside! I sprang instantly
to the deck, startled beyond my power to tell.
Passing close under lee, like an apparition, was
a white bark under full sail. The sailors on board
of her were hauling on ropes to brace the yards,
which just cleared the sloop's mast as she swept
by. No one hailed from the white-winged flier,
but I heard some one on board say that he saw
lights on the sloop, and that he made her out
to be a fisherman. I sat long on the starlit deck
that night, thinking of ships, and watching the
constellations on their voyage.

On the following day, September 13, a large four-
masted ship passed some distance to windward,
heading north.

The sloop was now rapidly drawing toward the

region of doldrums, and the force of the trade-winds was lessening. I could see by the ripples that a counter-current had set in. This I estimated to be about sixteen miles a day. In the heart of the counter-stream the rate was more than that setting eastward.

September 14 a lofty three-masted ship, heading north, was seen from the masthead. Neither this ship nor the one seen yesterday was within signal distance, yet it was good even to see them. On the following day heavy rain-clouds rose in the south, obscuring the sun; this was ominous of doldrums. On the 16th the *Spray* entered this gloomy region, to battle with squalls and to be harassed by fitful calms; for this is the state of the elements between the northeast and the southeast trades, where each wind, struggling in turn for mastery, expends its force whirling about in all directions. Making this still more trying to one's nerve and patience, the sea was tossed into confused cross-lumps and fretted by eddying currents. As if something more were needed to complete a sailor's discomfort in this state, the rain poured down in torrents day and night. The *Spray* struggled and tossed for ten days, making only three hundred miles on her course in all that time. I did n't say anything!

On September 23 the fine schooner *Nantasket* of Boston, from Bear River, for the river Plate, lumber-laden, and just through the doldrums, came up with the *Spray*, and her captain passing a few words, she sailed on. Being much fouled on the bottom by shell-fish, she drew along with her fishes

which had been following the *Spray*, which was
less provided with that sort of food. Fishes will
always follow a foul ship. A barnacle-grown log
adrift has the same attraction for deep-sea fishes.
One of this little school of deserters was a dolphin
that had followed the *Spray* about a thousand
miles, and had been content to eat scraps of food
thrown overboard from my table; for, having been
wounded, it could not dart through the sea to prey
on other fishes. I had become accustomed to seeing the dolphin, which I knew by its scars, and
missed it whenever it took occasional excursions
away from the sloop. One day, after it had been
off some hours, it returned in company with three
yellowtails, a sort of cousin to the dolphin. This
little school kept together, except when in danger
and when foraging about the sea. Their lives
were often threatened by hungry sharks that came
round the vessel, and more than once they had
narrow escapes. Their mode of escape interested
me greatly, and I passed hours watching them.
They would dart away, each in a different direction, so that the wolf of the sea, the shark, pursuing one, would be led away from the others; then
after a while they would all return and rendezvous
under one side or the other of the sloop. Twice
their pursuers were diverted by a tin pan, which I
towed astern of the sloop, and which was mistaken
for a bright fish; and while turning, in the peculiar
way that sharks have when about to devour their
prey, I shot them through the head.

Their precarious life seemed to concern the
yellowtails very little, if at all. All living beings,

without doubt, are afraid of death. Nevertheless, some of the species I saw huddle together as
though they knew they were created for the larger
fishes, and wished to give the least possible trouble
to their captors. I have seen, on the other hand,
whales swimming in a circle around a school of
herrings, and with mighty exertion "bunching"
them together in a whirlpool set in motion by their
flukes, and when the small fry were all whirled
nicely together, one or the other of the leviathans,
lunging through the center with open jaws, take in
a boat-load or so at a single mouthful. Off the
Cape of Good Hope I saw schools of sardines or
other small fish being treated in this way by great
numbers of cavally-fish. There was not the slightest
chance of escape for the sardines, while the cavally
circled round and round, feeding from the edge of
the mass. It was interesting to note how rapidly
the small fry disappeared; and though it was repeated before my eyes over and over, I could hardly
perceive the capture of a single sardine, so dexterously was it done.

Along the equatorial limit of the southeast trade-
winds the air was heavily charged with electricity,
and there was much thunder and lightning. It was
hereabout I remembered that, a few years before,
the American ship *Alert* was destroyed by lightning.
Her people, by wonderful good fortune, were rescued on the same day and brought to Pernambuco,
where I then met them.

On September 25, in the latitude of 5° N., longitude 26° 30′ W., I spoke the ship *North Star* of
London. The great ship was out forty-eight days

from Norfolk, Virginia, and was bound for Rio, where we met again about two months later. The *Spray* was now thirty days from Gibraltar.

The *Spray's* next companion of the voyage was a swordfish, that swam alongside, showing its tall fin out of the water, till I made a stir for my harpoon, when it hauled its black flag down and disappeared. September 30, at half-past eleven in the morning, the *Spray* crossed the equator in longitude 29° 30′ W. At noon she was two miles south of the line. The southeast trade-winds, met, rather light, in about 4° N., gave her sails now a stiff full sending her handsomely over the sea toward the coast of Brazil, where on October 5, just north of Olinda Point, without further incident, she made the land, casting anchor in Pernambuco harbor about noon: forty days from Gibraltar, and all well on board. Did I tire of the voyage in all that time? Not a bit of it! I was never in better trim in all my life, and was eager for the more perilous experience of rounding the Horn.

It was not at all strange in a life common to sailors that, having already crossed the Atlantic twice and being now half-way from Boston to the Horn, I should find myself still among friends. My determination to sail westward from Gibraltar not only enabled me to escape the pirates of the Red Sea, but, in bringing me to Pernambuco, landed me on familiar shores. I had made many voyages to this and other ports in Brazil. In 1893 I was employed as master to take the famous Ericsson ship *Destroyer* from New York to Brazil to go against the rebel Mello and his party. The *De-*

stroyer, by the way, carried a submarine cannon of enormous length.

In the same expedition went the *Nictheroy*, the ship purchased by the United States government during the Spanish war and renamed the *Buffalo*. The *Destroyer* was in many ways the better ship of the two, but the Brazilians in their curious war sank her themselves at Bahia. With her sank my hope of recovering wages due me; still, I could but try to recover, for to me it meant a great deal. But now within two years the whirligig of time had brought the Mello party into power, and although it was the legal government which had employed me, the so-called "rebels" felt under less obligation to me than I could have wished.

During these visits to Brazil I had made the acquaintance of Dr. Perera, owner and editor of "El Commercio Jornal," and soon after the *Spray* was safely moored in Upper Topsail Reach, the doctor, who is a very enthusiastic yachtsman, came to pay me a visit and to carry me up the waterway of the lagoon to his country residence. The approach to his mansion by the waterside was guarded by his armada, a fleet of boats including a Chinese sampan, a Norwegian pram, and a Cape Ann dory, the last of which he obtained from the *Destroyer*. The doctor dined me often on good Brazilian fare, that I might, as he said, "salle gordo" for the voyage; but he found that even on the best I fattened slowly.

Fruits and vegetables and all other provisions necessary for the voyage having been taken in, on the 23d of October I unmoored and made ready

for sea. Here I encountered one of the unforgiving
Mello faction in the person of the collector of customs, who charged the *Spray* tonnage dues when
she cleared, notwithstanding that she sailed with a
yacht license and should have been exempt from
port charges. Our consul reminded the collector
of this and of the fact—without much diplomacy, I
thought—that it was I who brought the *Destroyer*
to Brazil.   "Oh, yes," said the bland collector;
" we remember it very well," for it was now in a
small way his turn.

Mr. Lungrin, a merchant, to help me out of the
trifling difficulty, offered to freight the *Spray* with
a cargo of gunpowder for Bahia, which would have
put me in funds; and when the insurance com-
panies refused to take the risk on cargo shipped on
a vessel manned by a crew of only one, he offered
to ship it without insurance, taking all the risk
himself. This was perhaps paying me a greater
compliment than I deserved. The reason why I
did not accept the business was that in so doing I
found that I should vitiate my yacht license and
run into more expense for harbor dues around the
world than the freight would amount to.   Instead
of all this, another old merchant friend came to my
assistance, advancing the cash direct.

While at Pernambuco I shortened the boom,
which had been broken when off the coast of Morocco, by removing the broken piece, which took
about four feet off the inboard end; I also refitted
the jaws. On October 24, 1895, a fine day even as
days go in Brazil, the *Spray* sailed, having had
abundant good cheer. Making about one hundred

miles a day along the coast, I arrived at Rio de
Janeiro November 5, without any event worth
mentioning, and about noon cast anchor near
Villaganon, to await the official port visit. On the
following day I bestirred myself to meet the highest
lord of the admiralty and the ministers, to inquire
concerning the matter of wages due me from the
beloved *Destroyer*. The high official I met said :
" Captain, so far as we are concerned, you may
have the ship, and if you care to accept her we
will send an officer to show you where she is." I
knew well enough where she was at that moment.
The top of her smoke-stack being awash in Bahia,
it was more than likely that she rested on the
bottom there. I thanked the kind officer, but declined his offer.

The *Spray*, with a number of old shipmasters on
board, sailed about the harbor of Rio the day before she put to sea. As I had decided to give the
Spray a yawl rig for the tempestuous waters of
Patagonia, I here placed on the stern a semicircular
brace to support a jigger mast. These old captains
inspected the *Spray's* rigging, and each one con-
tributed something to her outfit. Captain Jones,
who had acted as my interpreter at Rio, gave her
an anchor, and one of the steamers gave her a
cable to match it. She never dragged Jones's
anchor once on the voyage, and the cable not only
stood the strain on a lee shore, but when towed off
Cape Horn helped break combing seas astern that
threatened to board her.

CHAPTER VI

ON November 28 the *Spray* sailed from Rio de Janeiro, and first of all ran into a gale of wind, which tore up things generally along the coast, doing considerable damage to shipping. It was well for her, perhaps, that she was clear of the land. Coasting along on this part of the voyage, I observed that while some of the small vessels I fell in with were able to outsail the *Spray* by day, they fell astern of her by night. To the *Spray* day and night were the same; to the others clearly there was a difference. On one of the very fine days experienced after leaving Rio, the steamship *South Wales* spoke the *Spray* and unsolicited gave the longitude by chronometer as 48° W., "as near as I can make it," the captain said. The *Spray*, with her tin clock, had exactly the same reckoning. I was feeling at ease in my primitive method of navigation, but it startled me not a little to find my position by account verified by the ship's chronometer.

On December 5 a barkantine hove in sight, and

for several days the two vessels sailed along the
coast together. Right here a current was experienced setting north, making it necessary to hug
the shore, with which the *Spray* became rather familiar. Here I confess a weakness: I hugged the
shore entirely too close. In a word, at daybreak
on the morning of December 11 the *Spray* ran hard
and fast on the beach. This was annoying; but I
soon found that the sloop was in no great danger.
The false appearance of the sand-hills under a
bright moon had deceived me, and I lamented now
that I had trusted to appearances at all. The sea,
though moderately smooth, still carried a swell
which broke with some force on the shore. I managed to launch my small dory from the deck, and
ran out a kedge-anchor and warp; but it was too
late to kedge the sloop off, for the tide was falling
and she had already sewed a foot. Then I went
about "laying out" the larger anchor, which was
no easy matter, for my only life-boat, the frail
dory, when the anchor and cable were in it, was
swamped at once in the surf, the load being too
great for her. Then I cut the cable and made two
loads of it instead of one. The anchor, with forty
fathoms bent and already buoyed, I now took and
succeeded in getting through the surf; but my
dory was leaking fast, and by the time I had rowed
far enough to drop the anchor she was full to the
gunwale and sinking. There was not a moment to
spare, and I saw clearly that if I failed now all
might be lost. I sprang from the oars to my feet,
and lifting the anchor above my head, threw it
clear just as she was turning over. I grasped her

gunwale and held on as she turned bottom up, for
I suddenly remembered that I could not swim.
Then I tried to right her, but with too much eager-
ness, for she rolled clean over, and left me as before,
clinging to her gunwale, while my body was still in
the water.   Giving a moment to cool reflection, I
found that although the wind was blowing moderately toward the land, the current was carrying
me to sea, and that something would have to be
done.   Three
times   I   had
been under wa-
ter, in trying to
right the dory,
and I was just
saying, "Now I
lay me," when
I   was   seized
by a determina-
tion to try yet

"I suddenly remembered that I could not swim."

once more, so that no one of the prophets of
evil I had left behind me could say, "I told you
so."   Whatever the danger may have been, much
or little, I can truly say that the moment was the
most serene of my life.

After righting the dory for the fourth time, I
finally succeeded by the utmost care in keeping her
upright while I hauled myself into her and with
one of the oars, which I had recovered, paddled to
the shore, somewhat the worse for wear and pretty
full of salt water.   The position of my vessel, now
high and dry, gave me anxiety.   To get her afloat
again was all I thought of or cared for.   I had little

difficulty in carrying the second part of my cable
out and securing it to the first, which I had taken
the precaution to buoy before I put it into the boat.
To bring the end back to the sloop was a smaller
matter still, and I believe I chuckled above my
sorrows when I found that in all the haphazard
my judgment or my good genius had faithfully
stood by me. The cable reached from the anchor
in deep water to the sloop's windlass by just enough
to secure a turn and no more. The anchor had
been dropped at the right distance from the vessel.
To heave all taut now and wait for the coming tide
was all I could do.

I had already done enough work to tire a stouter
man, and was only too glad to throw myself on the
sand above the tide and rest; for the sun was
already up, and pouring a generous warmth over
the land. While my state could have been worse,
I was on the wild coast of a foreign country, and
not entirely secure in my property, as I soon found
out. I had not been long on the shore when I heard
the patter, patter of a horse's feet approaching along
the hard beach, which ceased as it came abreast of
the sand-ridge· where I lay sheltered from the
wind. Looking up cautiously, I saw mounted on a
nag probably the most astonished boy on the whole
coast. He had found a sloop! "It must be mine,"
he thought, "for am I not the first to see it on the
beach?" Sure enough, there it was all high and
dry and painted white. He trotted his horse
around it, and finding no owner, hitched the nag
to the sloop's bobstay and hauled as though he
would take her home; but of course she was too

heavy for one horse to move. With my skiff, however, it was different; this he hauled some distance, and concealed behind a dune in a bunch of tall grass. He had made up his mind, I dare say, to bring more horses and drag his bigger prize away, anyhow, and was starting off for the settlement a mile or so away for the reinforcement when I discovered myself to him, at which he seemed displeased and disappointed. "Buenos dias, muchacho," I said. He grunted a reply, and eyed me keenly from head to foot. Then bursting into a volley of questions,— more than six Yankees could ask, —he wanted to know, first, where my ship was from, and how many days she had been coming. Then he asked what I was doing here ashore so early in the morning. "Your questions are easily answered," I replied; "my ship is from the moon, it has taken her a month to come, and she is here for a cargo of boys." But the intimation of this enterprise, had I not been on the alert, might have cost me dearly; for while I spoke this child of the campo coiled his lariat ready to throw, and instead of being himself carried to the moon, he was apparently thinking of towing me home by the neck, astern of his wild cayuse, over the fields of Uruguay.

The exact spot where I was stranded was at the Castillo Chicos, about seven miles south of the dividing-line of Uruguay and Brazil, and of course the natives there speak Spanish. To reconcile my early visitor, I told him that I had on my ship biscuits, and that I wished to trade them for butter and milk. On hearing this a broad grin lighted up his face, and showed that he was greatly interested,

A double surprise.

and that even in Uruguay a ship's biscuit will cheer
the heart of a boy and make him your bosom friend.
The lad almost flew home, and returned quickly
with butter, milk, and eggs. I was, after all, in a
land of plenty. With the boy came others, old and
young, from neighboring ranches, among them a
German settler, who was of great assistance to me
in many ways.

A coast-guard from Fort Teresa, a few miles
away, also came, "to protect your property from
the natives of the plains," he said. I took occasion
to tell him, however, that if he would look after
the people of his own village, I would take care of
those from the plains, pointing, as I spoke, to the
nondescript "merchant" who had already stolen
my revolver and several small articles from my
cabin, which by a bold front I had recovered. The
chap was not a native Uruguayan. Here, as in
many other places that I visited, the natives
themselves were not the ones discreditable to the
country.

Early in the day a despatch came from the port
captain of Montevideo, commanding the coast-
guards to render the *Spray* every assistance. This,
however, was not necessary, for a guard was already
on the alert, and making all the ado that would become the wreck of a steamer with a thousand emi-
grants aboard. The same messenger brought word
from the port captain that he would despatch a
steam-tug to tow the *Spray* to Montevideo. The officer was as good as his word; a powerful tug arrived
on the following day; but, to make a long story
short, with the help of the German and one soldier

and one Italian, called "Angel of Milan," I had already floated the sloop and was sailing for port with the boom off before a fair wind. The adventure cost the *Spray* no small amount of pounding on the hard sand; she lost her shoe and part of her false keel, and received other damage, which, however, was readily mended afterward in dock.

On the following day I anchored at Maldonado. The British consul, his daughter, and another young lady came on board, bringing with them a basket of fresh eggs, strawberries, bottles of milk, and a great loaf of sweet bread. This was a good landfall, and better cheer than I had found at Maldonado once upon a time when I entered the port with a stricken crew in my bark, the *Aquidneck.*

In the waters of Maldonado Bay a variety of fishes abound, and fur-seals in their season haul out on the island abreast the bay to breed. Currents on this coast are greatly affected by the prevailing winds, and a tidal wave higher than that ordinarily produced by the moon is sent up the whole shore of Uruguay before a southwest gale, or lowered by a northeaster, as may happen. One of these waves having just receded before the northeast wind which brought the *Spray* in left the tide now at low ebb, with oyster-rocks laid bare for some distance along the shore. Other shellfish of good flavor were also plentiful, though small in size. I gathered a mess of oysters and mussels here, while a native with hook and line, and with mussels for bait, fished from a point of detached rocks for bream, landing several good-sized ones.

The fisherman's nephew, a lad about seven years old, deserves mention as the tallest blasphemer, for a short boy, that I met on the voyage. He called his old uncle all the vile names under the sun for not helping him across the gully. While he swore roundly in all the moods and tenses of the Spanish language, his uncle fished on, now and then congratulating his hopeful nephew on his accomplishment. At the end of his rich vocabulary the urchin sauntered off into the fields, and shortly returned with a bunch of flowers, and with all smiles handed them to me with the innocence of an angel. I remembered having seen the same flower on the banks of the river farther up, some years before. I asked the young pirate why he had brought them to me. Said he, "I don't know; I only wished to do so." Whatever the influence was that put so amiable a wish in this wild pampa boy, it must be far-reaching, thought I, and potent, seas over.

Shortly after, the *Spray* sailed for Montevideo, where she arrived on the following day and was greeted by steam-whistles till I felt embarrassed and wished that I had arrived unobserved. The voyage so far alone may have seemed to the Uruguayans a feat worthy of some recognition; but there was so much of it yet ahead, and of such an arduous nature, that any demonstration at this point seemed, somehow, like boasting prematurely.

The *Spray* had barely come to anchor at Montevideo when the agents of the Royal Mail Steamship Company, Messrs. Humphreys & Co., sent word that they would dock and repair her free of expense and give me twenty pounds sterling, which they did to the letter, and more besides. The calkers at Montevideo paid very careful attention to the work of making the sloop tight. Carpenters mended the keel and also the life-boat (the dory), painting it till 1 hardly knew it from a butterfly.

Christmas of 1895 found the *Spray* refitted even to a wonderful makeshift stove which was contrived from a large iron drum of some sort punched full of holes to give it a draft; the pipe reached straight up through the top of the forecastle. Now, this was not a stove by mere courtesy. It was always hungry, even for green wood; and in cold, wet days off the coast of Tierra del Fuego it stood me in good stead. Its one door swung on copper hinges, which one of the yard apprentices, with laudable pride, polished till the whole thing blushed like the brass binnacle of a P. & O. steamer.

The *Spray* was now ready for sea. Instead of proceeding at once on her voyage, however, she made an excursion up the river, sailing December 29. An old friend of mine, Captain Howard of Cape Cod and of River Plate fame, took the trip in her to Buenos Aires, where she arrived early on the following day, with a gale of wind and a current so much in her favor that she outdid herself. I was glad to have a sailor of Howard's experience on board to witness her performance of sailing with no living being at the helm. Howard sat near the binnacle and watched the compass while the sloop held her course so steadily that one would have declared that the card was nailed fast.

Not a quarter of a point did she deviate from her course. My old friend had owned and sailed a pilot-sloop on the river for many years, but this feat took the wind out of his sails at last, and he cried, "I 'll be stranded on Chico Bank if ever I saw the like of it!" Perhaps he had never given his sloop a chance to show what she could do. The point I make for the *Spray* here, above all other points, is that she sailed in shoal water and in a strong current, with other difficult and unusual conditions. Captain Howard took all this into account.

In all the years away from his native home Howard had not forgotten the art of making fish chowders; and to prove this he brought along some fine rockfish and prepared a mess fit for kings. When the savory chowder was done, chocking the pot securely between two boxes on the cabin floor, so that it could not roll over, we helped ourselves and swapped yarns over it while the *Spray* made her own way through the darkness on the river. Howard told me stories about the Fuegian cannibals as she reeled along, and I told him about the pilot of the *Pinta* steering my vessel through the storm off the coast of the Azores, and that I looked for him at the helm in a gale such as this. I do not charge Howard with superstition,— we are none of us superstitious,— but when I spoke about his returning to Montevideo on the *Spray* he shook his head and took a steam-packet instead.

I had not been in Buenos Aires for a number of years. The place where I had once landed from packets, in a cart, was now built up with magnifi-

cent docks. Vast fortunes had been spent in re-
modeling the harbor; London bankers could tell you
that. The port captain, after assigning the *Spray*
a safe berth, with his compliments, sent me word
to call on him for anything I might want while in
port, and I felt quite sure that his friendship was
sincere. The sloop was well cared for at Buenos
Aires; her dockage and tonnage dues were all free,
and the yachting fraternity of the city welcomed
her with a good will. In town I found things not
so greatly changed as about the docks, and I soon
felt myself more at home.

From Montevideo I had forwarded a letter from
Sir Edward Hairby to the owner of the " Standard,"
Mr. Mulhall, and in reply to it was assured of a
warm welcome to the warmest heart, I think, outside of Ireland. Mr. Mulhall, with a prancing
team, came down to the docks as soon as the
Spray was berthed, and would have me go to his
house at once, where a room was waiting. And
it was New Year's day, 1896. The course of the
Spray had been followed in the columns of the
" Standard."

Mr. Mulhall kindly drove me to see many im-
provements about the city, and we went in search
of some of the old landmarks. The man who sold
" lemonade " on the plaza when first I visited this
wonderful city I found selling lemonade still at
two cents a glass; he had made a fortune by it.
His stock in trade was a wash-tub and a neighboring hydrant, a moderate supply of brown sugar,
and about six lemons that floated on the sweetened
water. The water from time to time was renewed

from the friendly pump, but the lemon "went on forever," and all at two cents a glass.

But we looked in vain for the man who once sold whisky and coffins in Buenos Aires; the march of civilization had crushed him — memory only clung to his name. Enterprising man that he was, I fain

At the sign of the comet.

would have looked him up. I remember the tiers of whisky-barrels, ranged on end, on one side of the store, while on the other side, and divided by a thin partition, were the coffins in the same order, of all sizes and in great numbers. The unique arrangement seemed in order, for as a cask was emptied a coffin might be filled. Besides cheap whisky and many other liquors, he sold "cider," which he manufactured from damaged Malaga

raisins. Within the scope of his enterprise was
also the sale of mineral waters, not entirely blame-
less of the germs of disease. This man surely ca-
tered to all the tastes, wants, and conditions of
his customers.

Farther along in the city, however, survived the
good man who wrote on the side of his store, where
thoughtful men might read and learn: "This
wicked world will be destroyed by a comet! The
owner of this store is therefore bound to sell out
at any price and avoid the catastrophe." My friend
Mr. Mulhall drove me round to view the fearful
comet with streaming tail pictured large on the
trembling merchant's walls.

I unshipped the sloop's mast at Buenos Aires
and shortened it by seven feet. I reduced the
length of the bowsprit by about five feet, and even
then I found it reaching far enough from home;
and more than once, when on the end of it reefing
the jib, I regretted that I had not shortened it
another foot.

CHAPTER VII

Weighing anchor at Buenos Aires — An outburst of emotion at the mouth of the Plate — Submerged by a great wave — A stormy entrance to the strait — Captain Samblich's happy gift of a bag of carpet-tacks — Off Cape Froward — Chased by Indians from Fortescue Bay — A miss-shot for "Black Pedro" — Taking in supplies of wood and water at Three Island Cove — Animal life.

ON January 26, 1896, the *Spray*, being refitted and well provisioned in every way, sailed from Buenos Aires. There was little wind at the start; the surface of the great river was like a silver disk, and I was glad of a tow from a harbor tug to clear the port entrance. But a gale came up soon after, and caused an ugly sea, and instead of being all silver, as before, the river was now all mud. The Plate is a treacherous place for storms. One sailing there should always be on the alert for squalls. I cast anchor before dark in the best lee I could find near the land, but was tossed miserably all night, heartsore of choppy seas. On the following morning I got the sloop under way, and with reefed sails worked her down the river against a head wind. Standing in that night to the place where pilot Howard joined me for the up-river sail, I took a departure, shaping my course to clear Point Indio on the one hand, and the English Bank on the other.

A great wave off the Patagonian coast.

I had not for many years been south of these regions. I will not say that I expected all fine sailing on the course for Cape Horn direct, but while I worked at the sails and rigging I thought only of onward and forward. It was when I anchored in the lonely places that a feeling of awe crept over me. At the last anchorage on the monotonous and muddy river, weak as it may seem, I gave way to my feelings. I resolved then that I would anchor no more north of the Strait of Magellan.

On the 28th of January the *Spray* was clear of Point Indio, English Bank, and all the other dangers of the River Plate. With a fair wind she then bore away for the Strait of Magellan, under all sail, pressing farther and farther toward the wonderland of the South, till I forgot the blessings of our milder North.

My ship passed in safety Bahia Blanca, also the Gulf of St. Matias and the mighty Gulf of St. George. Hoping that she might go clear of the destructive tide-races, the dread of big craft or little along this coast, I gave all the capes a berth of about fifty miles, for these dangers extend many miles from the land. But where the sloop avoided one danger she encountered another. For, one day, well off the Patagonian coast, while the sloop was reaching under short sail, a tremendous wave, the culmination, it seemed, of many waves, rolled down upon her in a storm, roaring as it came. I had only a moment to get all sail down and myself up on the peak halliards, out of danger, when I saw the mighty crest towering masthead-high above me. The mountain of water submerged my vessel. She shook in every timber and reeled under the weight of the sea, but rose quickly out of it, and rode grandly over the rollers that followed. It may have been a minute that from my hold in the rigging I could see no part of the *Spray's* hull. Perhaps it was even less time than that, but it seemed a long while, for under great excitement one lives fast, and in a few seconds one may think a great deal of one's past life. Not only did the past, with electric speed, flash before me, but I had time while in my hazardous position for resolutions for the future that would take a long time to fulfil. The first one was, I remember, that if the *Spray* came through this danger I would dedicate my best energies to building a larger ship on her lines, which I hope yet to do. Other promises, less easily kept, I should have made under protest. However, the incident, which filled me with fear, was only one more test of the *Spray's* seaworthiness. It reassured me against rude Cape Horn.

From the time the great wave swept over the *Spray* until she reached Cape Virgins nothing occurred to move a pulse and set blood in motion. On the contrary, the weather became fine and the sea smooth and life tranquil. The phenomenon of mirage frequently occurred. An albatross sitting on the water one day loomed up like a large ship; two fur-seals asleep on the surface of the sea appeared like great whales, and a bank of haze I could have sworn was high land. The kaleidoscope then changed, and on the following day I sailed in a world peopled by dwarfs.

On February 11 the *Spray* rounded Cape Virgins
and entered the Strait of Magellan. The scene
was again real and gloomy; the wind, northeast,
and blowing a gale, sent feather-white spume along
the coast; such a sea ran as would swamp an ill-
appointed ship. As the sloop neared the entrance

Entrance to the Strait of Magellan.

to the strait I observed that two great tide-races
made ahead, one very close to the point of the land
and one farther offshore. Between the two, in a
sort of channel, through combers, went the *Spray*
with close-reefed sails. But a rolling sea followed
her a long way in, and a fierce current swept
around the cape against her; but this she stemmed,
and was soon chirruping under the lee of Cape
Virgins and running every minute into smoother
water. However, long trailing kelp from sunken
rocks waved forebodingly under her keel, and the
wreck of a great steamship smashed on the beach
abreast gave a gloomy aspect to the scene.

I was not to be let off easy. The Virgins would
collect tribute even from the *Spray* passing their
promontory. Fitful rain-squalls from the northwest followed the northeast gale. I reefed the

sloop's sails, and sitting in the cabin to rest my
eyes, I was so strongly impressed with what in all
nature I might expect that as I dozed the very air
I breathed seemed to warn me of danger. My
senses heard "*Spray* ahoy!" shouted in warning.
I sprang to the deck, wondering who could be
there that knew the *Spray* so well as to call out her
name passing in the dark; for it was now the
blackest of nights all around, except away in
the southwest, where the old familiar white arch,
the terror of Cape Horn, rapidly pushed up by
a southwest gale. I had only a moment to douse
sail and lash all solid when it struck like a shot
from a cannon, and for the first half-hour it was
something to be remembered by way of a gale.
For thirty hours it kept on blowing hard. The
sloop could carry no more than a three-reefed mainsail and forestaysail; with these she held on stoutly
and was not blown out of the strait. In the height
of the squalls in this gale she doused all sail, and
this occurred often enough.

After this gale followed only a smart breeze, and
the *Spray*, passing through the narrows without
mishap, cast anchor at Sandy Point on February
14, 1896.

Sandy Point (Punta Arenas) is a Chilean coal-
ing-station, and boasts about two thousand inhabitants, of mixed nationality, but mostly Chileans.
What with sheep-farming, gold-mining, and hunting, the settlers in this dreary land seemed not the
worst off in the world. But the natives, Patagonian
and Fuegian, on the other hand, were as squalid
as contact with unscrupulous traders could make

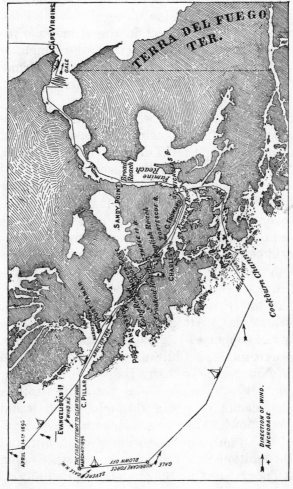

The course of the *Spray* through the Strait of Magellan.

them. A large percentage of the business there
was traffic in "fire-water." If there was a law
against selling the poisonous stuff to the natives,
it was not enforced. Fine specimens of the Patagonian race, looking smart in the morning when
they came into town, had repented before night of
ever having seen a white man, so beastly drunk
were they, to say nothing about the peltry of which
they had been robbed.

The port at that time was free, but a custom-
house was in course of construction, and when it
is finished, port and tariff dues are to be collected.
A soldier police guarded the place, and a sort of
vigilante force besides took down its guns now
and then; but as a general thing, to my mind,
whenever an execution was made they killed the
wrong man. Just previous to my arrival the governor, himself of a jovial turn of mind, had sent a
party of young bloods to foray a Fuegian settlement and wipe out what they could of it on account of the recent massacre of a schooner's crew
somewhere else. Altogether the place was quite
newsy and supported two papers — dailies, I think.
The port captain, a Chilean naval officer, advised
me to ship hands to fight Indians in the strait
farther west, and spoke of my stopping until a
gunboat should be going through, which would
give me a tow. After canvassing the place, however, I found only one man willing to embark, and
he on condition that I should ship another "mon
and a doog." But as no one else was willing to
come along, and as I drew the line at dogs, I said
no more about the matter, but simply loaded my

guns. At this point in my dilemma Captain Pedro Samblich, a good Austrian of large experience, coming along, gave me a bag of carpet-tacks, worth more than all the fighting men and dogs of Tierra del Fuego. I protested that I had no use for carpet-tacks on board. Samblich smiled at my want of experience, and maintained stoutly that I would have use for them. "You must use them with discretion," he said; "that is to say, don't step on them yourself." With this remote hint about the use of the tacks I got on all right, and saw the way to maintain clear decks at night without the care of watching.

Samblich was greatly interested in my voyage, and after giving me the tacks he put on board bags of biscuits and a large quantity of smoked venison. He declared that my bread, which was ordinary sea-biscuits and easily broken,

The man who would n't ship without another "mon and a doog."

was not nutritious as his, which was so hard that I could break it only with a stout blow from a maul. Then he gave me, from his own sloop, a compass which was certainly better than mine, and offered to unbend her mainsail for me if I would accept it. Last of all, this large-hearted man brought out a bottle of Fuegian gold-dust from a place where it had been *cached* and begged me to help myself from it, for use farther along on the voyage. But

A Fuegian Girl.

I felt sure of success without this draft on a friend, and I was right. Samblich's tacks, as it turned out, were of more value than gold.

The port captain finding that I was resolved to go, even alone, since there was no help for it, set up no further objections, but advised me, in case the savages tried to surround me with their canoes, to shoot straight, and begin to do it in time, but to avoid killing them if possible, which I heartily agreed to do. With these simple injunctions the officer gave me my port clearance free of charge, and I sailed on the same day, February 19, 1896. It was not without thoughts of strange and stirring adventure beyond all I had yet encountered that I now sailed into the country and very core of the savage Fuegians.

A fair wind from Sandy Point brought me on the first day to St. Nicholas Bay, where, so I was told, I might expect to meet savages; but seeing no signs of life, I came to anchor in eight fathoms of water, where I lay all night under a high mountain. Here I had my first experience with the terrific squalls, called williwaws, which extended from this point on through the strait to the Pacific. They were compressed gales of wind that Boreas handed down over the hills in chunks. A full-blown williwaw will throw a ship, even without sail on, over on her beam ends; but, like other gales, they cease now and then, if only for a short time.

February 20 was my birthday, and I found myself alone, with hardly so much as a bird in sight, off Cape Froward, the southernmost point of the continent of America. By daylight in the morning I was getting my ship under way for the bout ahead.

The sloop held the wind fair while she ran thirty miles farther on her course, which brought her to Fortescue Bay, and at once among the natives' signal-fires, which blazed up now on all sides. Clouds flew over the mountain from the west all day; at night my good east wind failed, and in its stead a gale from the west soon came on. I gained anchorage at twelve o'clock that night, under the lee of a little island, and then prepared myself a cup of coffee, of which I was sorely in need; for, to tell the truth, hard beating in the heavy squalls and against the current had told on my strength. Finding that the anchor held, I drank my beverage, and named the place Coffee Island. It lies to the south of Charles Island, with only a narrow channel between.

By daylight the next morning the *Spray* was again under way, beating hard; but she came to

Looking west from Fortescue Bay, where the *Spray* was chased by Indians.
(From a photograph.)

in a cove in Charles Island, two and a half miles
along on her course. Here she remained undis-
turbed two days, with both anchors down in a bed
of kelp. Indeed, she might have remained undis-
turbed indefinitely had not the wind moderated;
for during these two days it blew so hard that no
boat could venture out on the strait, and the natives being away to other hunting-grounds, the isl-
and anchorage was safe. But at the end of the
fierce wind-storm fair weather came; then I got
my anchors, and again sailed out upon the strait.

Canoes manned by savages from Fortescue now
came in pursuit. The wind falling light, they
gained on me rapidly till coming within hail, when
they ceased paddling, and a bow-legged savage
stood up and called to me, "Yammerschooner!
yammerschooner!" which is their begging term.
I said, "No!" Now, I was not for letting on
that I was alone, and so I stepped into the
cabin, and, passing through the hold, came out at
the fore-scuttle, changing my clothes as I went
along. That made two men. Then the piece of
bowsprit which I had sawed off at Buenos Aires,
and which I had still on board, I arranged forward
on the lookout, dressed as a seaman, attaching a
line by which I could pull it into motion. That
made three of us, and we did n't want to "yammerschooner"; but for all that the savages came
on faster than before. I saw that besides four at
the paddles in the canoe nearest to me, there were
others in the bottom, and that they were shifting
hands often. At eighty yards I fired a shot across
the bows of the nearest canoe, at which they all

stopped, but only for a moment. Seeing that they persisted in coming nearer, I fired the second shot so close to the chap who wanted to "yammer-schooner" that he changed his mind quickly enough and bellowed with fear, "Bueno jo via Isla," and sitting down in his canoe, he rubbed his starboard cat-head for some time. I was thinking of the good port captain's advice when I pulled the trigger, and must have aimed pretty straight; however, a miss was as good as a mile for Mr. "Black Pedro," as he it was, and no other, a leader in several bloody massacres. He made for the island now, and the others followed him. I knew by his Spanish lingo and by his full beard that he was the villain I have named, a renegade mongrel, and the worst murderer in Tierra del Fuego. The authorities had been in search of him for two years. The Fuegians are not bearded.

So much for the first day among the savages. I came to anchor at midnight in Three Island Cove, about twenty miles along from Fortescue Bay. I saw on the opposite side of the strait signal-fires, and heard the barking of dogs, but where I lay it was quite deserted by natives. I have always taken it as a sign that where I found birds sitting about, or seals on the rocks, I should not find savage Indians. Seals are never plentiful in these waters, but in Three Island Cove I saw one on the rocks, and other signs of the absence of savage men.

On the next day the wind was again blowing a gale, and although she was in the lee of the land, the sloop dragged her anchors, so that I had to get her under way and beat farther into the cove, where

A brush with Fuegians.

I came to in a landlocked pool. At another time or place this would have been a rash thing to do, and it was safe now only from the fact that the gale which drove me to shelter would keep the Indians from crossing the strait. Seeing this was the case, I went ashore with gun and ax on an island, where I could not in any event be surprised, and there felled trees and split about a cord of fire-wood, which loaded my small boat several times.

While I carried the wood, though I was morally sure there were no savages near, I never once went to or from the skiff without my gun. While I had that and a clear field of over eighty yards about me I felt safe.

The trees on the island, very scattering, were a sort of beech and a stunted cedar, both of which made good fuel. Even the green limbs of the beech, which seemed to possess a resinous quality, burned readily in my great drum-stove. I have described my method of wooding up in detail, that the reader who has kindly borne with me so far may see that in this, as in all other particulars of my voyage, I took great care against all kinds of surprises, whether by animals or by the elements. In the Strait of Magellan the greatest vigilance was necessary. In this instance I reasoned that I had all about me the greatest danger of the whole voyage — the treachery of cunning savages, for which I must be particularly on the alert.

The *Spray* sailed from Three Island Cove in the morning after the gale went down, but was glad to return for shelter from another sudden gale. Sailing again on the following day, she fetched Borgia

Bay, a few miles on her course, where vessels had anchored from time to time and had nailed boards on the trees ashore with name and date of harboring carved or painted. Nothing else could I see to indicate that civilized man had ever been there. I had taken a survey of the gloomy place with my spy-glass, and was getting my boat out to land and

A bit of friendly assistance.
(After a sketch by Midshipman Miguel Arenas.)

take notes, when the Chilean gunboat *Huemel* came in, and officers, coming on board, advised me to leave the place at once, a thing that required little eloquence to persuade me to do. I accepted the captain's kind offer of a tow to the next anchorage, at the place called Notch Cove, eight miles farther along, where I should be clear of the worst of the Fuegians.

We made anchorage at the cove about dark that night, while the wind came down in fierce williwaws from the mountains. An instance of Magellan weather was afforded when the *Huemel*, a well-appointed gunboat of great power, after attempting on the following day to proceed on her voyage, was obliged by sheer force of the wind to return and take up anchorage again and remain till the gale abated; and lucky she was to get back!

Meeting this vessel was a little godsend. She was commanded and officered by high-class sailors and educated gentlemen. An entertainment that was gotten up on her, impromptu, at the Notch would be hard to beat anywhere. One of her midshipmen sang popular songs in French, German, and Spanish, and one (so he said) in Russian. If the audience did not know the lingo of one song from another, it was no drawback to the merriment.

I was left alone the next day, for then the *Huemel* put out on her voyage the gale having abated. I spent a day taking in wood and water; by the end of that time the weather was fine. Then I sailed from the desolate place.

There is little more to be said concerning the *Spray's* first passage through the strait that would differ from what I have already recorded. She anchored and weighed many times, and beat many days against the current, with now and then a "slant" for a few miles, till finally she gained anchorage and shelter for the night at Port Tamar, with Cape Pillar in sight to the west. Here I felt the throb of the great ocean that lay before me. I knew now that I had put a world behind me, and that I was opening out another world ahead. I had passed the haunts of savages. Great piles of granite mountains of bleak and lifeless aspect were now astern; on some of them not even a speck of moss had ever grown. There was an unfinished newness all about the land. On the hill back of Port Tamar a small beacon had been thrown up, showing that some man had been there. But how could one tell but that he had died of loneliness and grief? In a bleak land is not the place to enjoy solitude.

Throughout the whole of the strait west of Cape Froward I saw no animals except dogs owned by savages. These I saw often enough, and heard them yelping night and day. Birds were not plentiful. The scream of a wild fowl, which I took for a loon, sometimes startled me with its piercing cry. The steamboat duck, so called because it propels itself over the sea with its wings, and resembles a miniature side-wheel steamer in its motion, was sometimes seen scurrying on out of danger. It never flies, but, hitting the water instead of the air with its wings, it moves faster than a rowboat or a canoe. The few fur-seals I saw were very shy; and of fishes I saw next to none at all. I did not catch one; indeed, I seldom or never put a hook over during the whole voyage. Here in the strait I found great abundance of mussels of an excellent quality. I fared sumptuously on them. There was a sort of swan, smaller than a Muscovy duck, which might have been brought down with the gun, but in the loneliness of life about the dreary country I found myself in no mood to make one life less, except in self-defense.

CHAPTER VIII

From Cape Pillar into the Pacific — Driven by a tempest toward Cape Horn — Captain Slocum's greatest sea adventure — Reaching the strait again by way of Cockburn Channel — Some savages find the carpet-tacks — Danger from firebrands — A series of fierce williwaws — Again sailing westward.

IT was the 3d of March when the *Spray* sailed from Port Tamar direct for Cape Pillar, with the wind from the northeast, which I fervently hoped might hold till she cleared the land; but there was no such good luck in store. It soon began to rain and thicken in the northwest, boding no good. The *Spray* neared Cape Pillar rapidly, and, nothing loath, plunged into the Pacific Ocean at once, taking her first bath of it in the gathering storm. There was no turning back even had I wished to do so, for the land was now shut out by the darkness of night. The wind freshened, and I took in a third reef. The sea was confused and treacherous. In such a time as this the old fisherman prayed, "Remember, Lord, my ship is small and thy sea is so wide!" I saw now only the gleaming crests of the waves. They showed white teeth while the sloop balanced over them. "Everything for an offing," I cried, and to this end I carried on all the sail she would bear. She ran all night with a free sheet, but on the morning of March 4 the

98

wind shifted to southwest, then back suddenly to northwest, and blew with terrific force. The *Spray*, stripped of her sails, then bore off under bare poles. No ship in the world could have stood up against so violent a gale. Knowing that this storm might continue for many days, and that it would be impossible to work back to the westward along the coast outside of Tierra del Fuego, there seemed nothing to do but to keep on and go east about,

Cape Pillar.

after all. Anyhow, for my present safety the only course lay in keeping her before the wind. And so she drove southeast, as though about to round the Horn, while the waves rose and fell and bellowed their never-ending story of the sea; but the Hand that held these held also the *Spray*. She was running now with a reefed forestaysail, the sheets flat amidship. I paid out two long ropes to steady her course and to break combing seas astern, and I lashed the helm amidship. In this trim she ran before it, shipping never a sea. Even while the storm raged at its worst, my ship was wholesome and noble. My mind as to her seaworthiness was put at ease for aye.

When all had been done that I could do for the safety of the vessel, I got to the fore-scuttle, between seas, and prepared a pot of coffee over a wood fire, and made a good Irish stew. Then, as before and afterward on the *Spray*, I insisted on warm meals. In the tide-race off Cape Pillar, however, where the sea was marvelously high, uneven, and crooked, my appetite was slim, and for a time I postponed cooking. (Confidentially, I was seasick!)

The first day of the storm gave the *Spray* her actual test in the worst sea that Cape Horn or its wild regions could afford, and in no part of the world could a rougher sea be found than at this particular point, namely, off Cape Pillar, the grim sentinel of the Horn.

Farther offshore, while the sea was majestic, there was less apprehension of danger. There the *Spray* rode, now like a bird on the crest of a wave, and now like a waif deep down in the hollow between seas; and so she drove on. Whole days passed, counted as other days, but with always a thrill — yes, of delight.

On the fourth day of the gale, rapidly nearing the pitch of Cape Horn, I inspected my chart and pricked off the course and distance to Port Stanley, in the Falkland Islands, where I might find my way and refit, when I saw through a rift in the clouds a high mountain, about seven leagues away on the port beam. The fierce edge of the gale by this time had blown off, and I had already bent a square-sail on the boom in place of the mainsail, which was torn to rags. I hauled in the trailing ropes, hoisted this awkward sail reefed, the forestaysail being already set, and under this sail brought her at once on the wind heading for the land, which appeared as an island in the sea. So it turned out to be, though not the one I had supposed.

I was exultant over the prospect of once more entering the Strait of Magellan and beating through again into the Pacific, for it was more than rough on the outside coast of Tierra del Fuego. It was indeed a mountainous sea. When the sloop was in the fiercest squalls, with only the reefed forestaysail set, even that small sail shook her from keelson to truck when it shivered by the leech. Had I harbored the shadow of a doubt for her safety, it would have been that she might spring a leak in the garboard at the heel of the mast; but she never called me once to the pump. Under pressure of the smallest sail I could set she made for the land like a race-horse, and steering her over the crests of the waves so that she might not trip was nice work. I stood at the helm now and made the most of it.

Night closed in before the sloop reached the land, leaving her feeling the way in pitchy darkness. I saw breakers ahead before long. At this I wore ship and stood offshore, but was immediately startled by the tremendous roaring of breakers again ahead and on the lee bow. This puzzled me, for there should have been no broken water where I supposed myself to be. I kept off a good bit, then wore round, but finding broken water also there, threw her head again offshore. In this way, among dangers, I spent the rest of the night. Hail

and sleet in the fierce squalls cut my flesh till the
blood trickled over my face; but what of that? It
was daylight, and the sloop was in the midst of the
Milky Way of the sea, which is northwest of Cape
Horn, and it was the white breakers of a huge sea
over sunken rocks which had threatened to engulf
her through the night. It was Fury Island I had
sighted and steered for, and what a panorama was
before me now and all around! It was not the
time to complain of a broken skin. What could I
do but fill away among the breakers and find a
channel between them, now that it was day? Since
she had escaped the rocks through the night, surely
she would find her way by daylight. This was the
greatest sea adventure of my life. God knows how
my vessel escaped.

The sloop at last reached inside of small islands
that sheltered her in smooth water. Then I climbed
the mast to survey the wild scene astern. The
great naturalist Darwin looked over this seascape
from the deck of the *Beagle*, and wrote in his journal,
"Any landsman seeing the Milky Way would have
nightmare for a week." He might have added, "or
seaman" as well.

The *Spray's* good luck followed fast. I discovered, as she sailed along through a labyrinth of
islands, that she was in the Cockburn Channel,
which leads into the Strait of Magellan at a point
opposite Cape Froward, and that she was already
passing Thieves' Bay, suggestively named. And
at night, March 8, behold, she was at anchor in a
snug cove at the Turn! Every heart-beat on the
Spray now counted thanks.

Here I pondered on the events of the last few days, and, strangely enough, instead of feeling rested from sitting or lying down, I now began to feel jaded and worn; but a hot meal of venison stew soon put me right, so that I could sleep. As drowsiness came on I sprinkled the deck with tacks, and then I turned in, bearing in mind the advice of my old friend Samblich that I was not to step on them myself. I saw to it that not a few of them stood "business end" up; for when the *Spray* passed Thieves' Bay two canoes had put out and followed in her wake, and there was no disguising the fact any longer that I was alone.

Now, it is well known that one cannot step on a tack without saying something about it. A pretty good Christian will whistle when he steps on the "commercial end" of a carpet-tack; a savage will howl and claw the air, and that was just what happened that night about twelve o'clock, while I was asleep in the cabin, where the savages thought they "had me," sloop and all, but changed their minds when they stepped on deck, for then they thought that I or somebody else had them. I had no need of a dog; they howled like a pack of hounds. I had hardly use for a gun. They jumped pell-mell, some into their canoes and some into the sea, to cool off, I suppose, and there was a deal of free language over it as they went. I fired several guns when I came on deck, to let the rascals know that I was home, and then I turned in again, feeling sure I should not be disturbed any more by people who left in so great a hurry.

The Fuegians, being cruel, are naturally cowards;

they regard a rifle with superstitious fear. The only real danger one could see that might come from their quarter would be from allowing them to surround one within bow-shot, or to anchor within

"They howled like a pack of hounds."

range where they might lie in ambush. As for their coming on deck at night, even had I not put tacks about, I could have cleared them off by shots from the cabin and hold. I always kept a quantity of ammunition within reach in the hold and in the cabin and in the forepeak, so that retreating to any of these places I could "hold the fort" simply by shooting up through the deck.

Perhaps the greatest danger to be apprehended was from the use of fire. Every canoe carries fire; nothing is thought of that, for it is their custom to communicate by smoke-signals. The harmless brand that lies smoldering in the bottom of one of their canoes might be ablaze in one's cabin if he were not on the alert. The port captain of Sandy Point warned me particularly of this danger. Only a short time before they had fired a Chilean gunboat by throwing brands in through the stern windows of the cabin. The *Spray* had no openings in the cabin or deck, except two scuttles, and these were guarded by fastenings which could not be undone without waking me if I were asleep.

On the morning of the 9th, after a refreshing rest and a warm breakfast, and after I had swept the deck of tacks, I got out what spare canvas there was on board, and began to sew the pieces together in the shape of a peak for my square-mainsail, the tarpaulin. The day to all appearances promised fine weather and light winds, but appearances in Tierra del Fuego do not always count. While I was wondering why no trees grew on the slope abreast of the anchorage, half minded to lay by the sail-making and land with my gun for some game and to inspect a white boulder on the beach, near the brook, a williwaw came down with such terrific force as to carry the *Spray*, with two anchors down, like a feather out of the cove and away into deep water. No wonder trees did not grow on the side of that hill! Great Boreas! a tree would need to be all roots to hold on against such a furious wind.

From the cove to the nearest land to leeward was a long drift, however, and I had ample time to weigh both anchors before the sloop came near any danger, and so no harm came of it. I saw no more savages that day or the next; they probably had some sign by which they knew of the coming williwaws; at least, they were wise in not being afloat even on the second day, for I had no sooner gotten to work at sail-making again, after the anchor was down, than the wind, as on the day before, picked the sloop up and flung her seaward with a vengeance, anchor and all, as before. This fierce wind, usual to the Magellan country, continued on through the day, and swept the sloop by several miles of steep bluffs and precipices overhanging a bold shore of wild and uninviting appearance. I was not sorry to get away from it, though in doing so it was no Elysian shore to which I shaped my course. I kept on sailing in hope, since I had no choice but to go on, heading across for St. Nicholas Bay, where I had cast anchor February 19. It was now the 10th of March! Upon reaching the bay the second time I had circumnavigated the wildest part of desolate Tierra del Fuego. But the *Spray* had not yet arrived at St. Nicholas, and by the merest accident her bones were saved from resting there when she did arrive. The parting of a staysail-sheet in a williwaw, when the sea was turbulent and she was plunging into the storm, brought me forward to see instantly a dark cliff ahead and breakers so close under the bows that I felt surely lost, and in my thoughts cried, "Is the hand of fate against me, after all, leading me in the end to this dark spot?" I sprang aft again, unheeding the flapping sail, and threw the wheel over, expecting, as the sloop came down into the hollow of a wave, to feel her timbers smash under me on the rocks.

A glimpse of Sandy Point (Punta Arenas) in the Strait of Magellan.

But at the touch of her helm she swung clear of the danger, and in the next moment she was in the lee of the land.

It was the small island in the middle of the bay for which the sloop had been steering, and which she made with such unerring aim as nearly to run it down. Farther along in the bay was the anchorage, which I managed to reach, but before I could get the anchor down another squall caught the sloop and whirled her round like a top and carried her away, altogether to leeward of the bay. Still farther to leeward was a great headland, and I bore off for that. This was retracing my course toward Sandy Point, for the gale was from the southwest.

I had the sloop soon under good control, however, and in a short time rounded to under the lee of a mountain, where the sea was as smooth as a mill-pond, and the sails flapped and hung limp while she carried her way close in. Here I thought I would anchor and rest till morning, the depth being eight fathoms very close to the shore. But it was interesting to see, as I let go the anchor, that it did not reach the bottom before another williwaw struck down from this mountain and carried the sloop off faster than I could pay out cable. Instead of resting, I had to "man the windlass" and heave up the anchor and fifty fathoms of cable hanging up and down in deep water. This was in that part of the strait called Famine Reach. I could have wished it Jericho! On that little crab-windlass I worked the rest of the night, thinking how much easier it was for me when I could say, "Do that thing or the other," than to do it myself. But I hove away on the windlass and sang the old chants that I sang when I was a sailor, from "Blow, Boys, Blow for Californy, O" to "Sweet By and By."

It was daybreak when the anchor was at the hawse. By this time the wind had gone down, and cat's-paws took the place of williwaws. The sloop was then drifting slowly toward Sandy Point. She came within sight of ships at anchor in the roads, and I was more than half minded to put in for new sails, but the wind coming out from the northeast, which was fair for the other direction, I turned the prow of the *Spray* westward once more for the Pacific, to traverse a second time the second half of my first course through the strait.

CHAPTER IX

Repairing the *Spray's* sails — Savages and an obstreperous anchor —
A spider-fight — An encounter with Black Pedro — A visit to the
steamship *Colombia* — On the defensive against a fleet of canoes
— A record of voyages through the strait — A chance cargo of
tallow.

I WAS determined to rely on my own small
resources to repair the damages of the great
gale which drove me southward toward the
Horn, after I had passed from the Strait of Magellan out into the Pacific. So when I had got
back into the strait, by way of Cockburn Channel,
I did not proceed eastward for help at the Sandy
Point settlement, but turning again into the north-
westward reach of the strait, set to work with my
palm and needle at every opportunity, when at
anchor and when sailing. It was slow work; but
little by little the squaresail on the boom expanded
to the dimensions of a serviceable mainsail with a
peak to it and a leech besides. If it was not the
best-setting sail afloat, it was at least very strongly
made and would stand a hard blow. A ship, meeting the *Spray* long afterward, reported her as wearing a mainsail of some improved design and patent
reefer, but that was not the case.

The *Spray* for a few days after the storm enjoyed
fine weather, and made fair time through the strait

for the distance of twenty miles, which, in these
days of many adversities, I called a long run.   The
weather, I say, was fine for a few days; but it
brought little rest.   Care for the safety of my vessel, and even for my own life, was in no wise les-
sened by the absence of heavy weather.   Indeed,
the peril was even greater, inasmuch as the savages
on comparatively fine days ventured forth on their
marauding excursions, and in boisterous weather
disappeared from sight, their wretched canoes
being frail and undeserving the name of craft at all.
This being so, I now enjoyed gales of wind as never
before, and the *Spray* was never long without them
during her struggles about Cape Horn.   I became
in a measure inured to the life, and began to think
that one more trip through the strait, if perchance
the sloop should be blown off again, would make
me the aggressor, and put the Fuegians entirely on
the defensive.   This feeling was forcibly borne in
on me at Snug Bay, where I anchored at gray
morning after passing Cape Froward, to find, when
broad day appeared, that two canoes which I had
eluded by sailing all night were now entering the
same bay stealthily under the shadow of the high
headland.   They were well manned, and the savages were well armed with spears and bows.   At
a shot from my rifle across the bows, both turned
aside into a small creek out of range.   In danger
now of being flanked by the savages in the bush
close aboard, I was obliged to hoist the sails, which
I had barely lowered, and make across to the opposite side of the strait, a distance of six miles.
But now I was put to my wit's end as to how I

should weigh anchor, for through an accident to the windlass right here I could not budge it. However, I set all sail and filled away, first hauling short by hand. The sloop carried her anchor away, as though it was meant to be always towed in this way underfoot, and with it she towed a ton or more of kelp from a reef in the bay, the wind blowing a wholesale breeze.

Meanwhile I worked till blood started from my fingers, and with one eye over my shoulder for savages, I watched at the same time, and sent a bullet whistling whenever I saw a limb or a twig move; for I kept a gun always at hand, and an Indian appearing then within range would have been taken as a declaration of war. As it was, however, my own blood was all that was spilt—and from the trifling accident of sometimes breaking the flesh against a cleat or a pin which came in the way when I was in haste. Sea-cuts in my hands from pulling on hard, wet ropes were sometimes painful and often bled freely; but these healed when I finally got away from the strait into fine weather.

After clearing Snug Bay I hauled the sloop to the wind, repaired the windlass, and hove the anchor to the hawse, catted it, and then stretched across to a port of refuge under a high mountain about six miles away, and came to in nine fathoms close under the face of a perpendicular cliff. Here my own voice answered back, and I named the place "Echo Mountain." Seeing dead trees farther along where the shore was broken, I made a landing for fuel, taking, besides my ax, a rifle, which on these days I never left far from hand; but I saw no living thing here, except a small spider, which had nested in a dry log that I boated to the sloop. The conduct of this insect interested me now more than anything else around the wild place. In my cabin it met, oddly enough, a spider of its own size and species that had come all the way from Boston — a very civil little chap, too, but mighty spry. Well, the Fuegian threw up its antennæ for a fight; but my little Bostonian downed it at once, then broke its legs, and pulled them off, one by one, so dexterously that in less than three minutes from the time the battle began the Fuegian spider did n't know itself from a fly.

I made haste the following morning to be under way after a night of wakefulness on the weird shore. Before weighing anchor, however, I prepared a cup of warm coffee over a smart wood fire in my great Montevideo stove. In the same fire was cremated the Fuegian spider, slain the day before by the little warrior from Boston, which a Scots lady at Cape Town long after named "Bruce" upon hearing of its prowess at Echo Mountain. The *Spray* now reached away for Coffee Island, which I sighted on my birthday, February 20, 1896.

There she encountered another gale, that brought her in the lee of great Charles Island for shelter. On a bluff point on Charles were signal-fires, and a tribe of savages, mustered here since my first trip through the strait, manned their canoes to put off for the sloop. It was not prudent to come to, the anchorage being within bow-shot of the shore, which was thickly wooded; but I made signs that one canoe might come alongside, while the

" 'Yammerschooner!' "

sloop ranged about under sail in the lee of the
land. The others I motioned to keep off, and incidentally laid a smart Martini-Henry rifle in sight,
close at hand, on the top of the cabin. In the
canoe that came alongside, crying their never-ending begging word "yammerschooner," were two
squaws and one Indian, the hardest specimens of
humanity I had ever seen in any of my travels.
"Yammerschooner" was their plaint when they
pushed off from the shore, and "yammerschooner"
it was when they got alongside. The squaws beck-
oned for food, while the Indian, a black-visaged
savage, stood sulkily as if he took no interest at all
in the matter, but on my turning my back for some
biscuits and jerked beef for the squaws, the "buck"
sprang on deck and confronted me, saying in Spanish jargon that we had met before. I thought I
recognized the tone of his "yammerschooner," and
his full beard identified him as the Black Pedro
whom, it was true, I had met before. "Where are
the rest of the crew?" he asked, as he looked un-
easily around, expecting hands, maybe, to come
out of the fore-scuttle and deal him his just deserts
for many murders. "About three weeks ago,"
said he, "when you passed up here, I saw three
men on board. Where are the other two?" I answered him briefly that the same crew was still on
board. "But," said he, "I see you are doing all
the work," and with a leer he added, as he glanced
at the mainsail, "hombre valiente." I explained
that I did all the work in the day, while the rest
of the crew slept, so that they would be fresh to
watch for Indians at night. I was interested in

the subtle cunning of this savage, knowing him, as I did, better perhaps than he was aware. Even had I not been advised before I sailed from Sandy Point, I should have measured him for an arch-villain now. Moreover, one of the squaws, with that spark of kindliness which is somehow found in the breast of even the lowest savage, warned me by a sign to be on my guard, or Black Pedro would do me harm. There was no need of the warning, however, for I was on my guard from the first, and at that moment held a smart revolver in my hand ready for instant service.

"When you sailed through here before," he said, "you fired a shot at me," adding with some warmth that it was "muy malo." I affected not to understand, and said, "You have lived at Sandy Point, have you not?" He answered frankly, "Yes," and appeared delighted to meet one who had come from the dear old place. "At the mission?" I queried. "Why, yes," he replied, stepping forward as if to embrace an old friend. I motioned him back, for I did not share his flattering humor. "And you know Captain Pedro Samblich?" continued I. "Yes," said the villain, who had killed a kinsman of Samblich — "yes, indeed; he is a great friend of mine." "I know it," said I. Samblich had told me to shoot him on sight. Pointing to my rifle on the cabin, he wanted to know how many times it fired. "Cuantos?" said he. When I explained to him that that gun kept right on shooting, his jaw fell, and he spoke of getting away. I did not hinder him from going. I gave the squaws biscuits and beef, and one of them gave me several lumps of tallow in exchange, and I think it worth mentioning that she did not offer me the smallest pieces, but with some extra trouble handed me the largest of all the pieces in the canoe. No Christian could have done more. Before pushing off from the sloop the cunning savage asked for matches, and made as if to reach with the end of his spear the box I was about to give him; but I held it toward him on the muzzle of my rifle, the one that "kept on shooting." The chap picked the box off the gun gingerly enough, to be sure, but he jumped when I said, "Quedao [Look out]," at which the squaws laughed and seemed not at all displeased. Perhaps the wretch had clubbed them that morning for not gathering mussels enough for his breakfast. There was a good understanding among us all.

From Charles Island the *Spray* crossed over to Fortescue Bay, where she anchored and spent a comfortable night under the lee of high land, while the wind howled outside. The bay was deserted now. They were Fortescue Indians whom I had seen at the island, and I felt quite sure they could not follow the *Spray* in the present hard blow. Not to neglect a precaution, however, I sprinkled tacks on deck before I turned in.

On the following day the loneliness of the place was broken by the appearance of a great steamship, making for the anchorage with a lofty bearing. She was no Diego craft. I knew the sheer, the model, and the poise. I threw out my flag, and directly saw the Stars and Stripes flung to the breeze from the great ship.

The wind had then abated, and toward night the savages made their appearance from the island, going direct to the steamer to "yammerschooner." Then they came to the *Spray* to beg more, or to steal all, declaring that they got nothing from the steamer. Black Pedro here came alongside again. My own brother could not have been more delighted to see me, and he begged me to lend him my rifle to shoot a guanaco for me in the morning. I assured the fellow that if I remained there another day I would lend him the gun, but I had no mind to remain. I gave him a cooper's draw-knife and some other small implements which would be of service in canoe-making, and bade him be off.

Under the cover of darkness that night I went to the steamer, which I found to be the *Colombia*, Captain Henderson, from New York, bound for San Francisco. I carried all my guns along with me, in case it should be necessary to fight my way back. In the chief mate of the *Colombia*, Mr. Hannibal, I found an old friend, and he referred affectionately to days in Manila when we were there together, he in the *Southern Cross* and I in the *Northern Light*, both ships as beautiful as their names.

The *Colombia* had an abundance of fresh stores on board. The captain gave his steward some order, and I remember that the guileless young man asked me if I could manage, besides other things, a few cans of milk and a cheese. When I offered my Montevideo gold for the supplies, the captain roared like a lion and told me to put my money up. It was a glorious outfit of provisions of all kinds that I got.

Returning to the *Spray*, where I found all secure, I prepared for an early start in the morning. It was agreed that the steamer should blow her whistle for me if first on the move. I watched

A contrast in lighting — the electric lights of the *Colombia* and the canoe fires of the Fortescue Indians.

the steamer, off and on, through the night for the pleasure alone of seeing her electric lights, a pleasing sight in contrast to the ordinary Fuegian canoe with a brand of fire in it. The sloop was the first under way, but the *Colombia*, soon following, passed, and saluted as she went by. Had the captain given me his steamer, his company would have been no worse off than they were two or three months later. I read afterward, in a late California paper, "The *Colombia* will be a total loss." On her second trip to Panama she was wrecked on the rocks of the California coast.

The *Spray* was then beating against wind and current, as usual in the strait. At this point the tides from the Atlantic and the Pacific meet, and in the strait, as on the outside coast, their meeting makes a commotion of whirlpools and combers that in a gale of wind is dangerous to canoes and other frail craft.

A few miles farther along was a large steamer ashore, bottom up. Passing this place, the sloop ran into a streak of light wind, and then — a most remarkable condition for strait weather — it fell entirely calm. Signal-fires sprang up at once on all sides, and then more than twenty canoes hove in sight, all heading for the *Spray*. As they came within hail, their savage crews cried, "Amigo yammerschooner," "Anclas aqui," "Bueno puerto aqui," and like scraps of Spanish mixed with their own jargon. I had no thought of anchoring in their "good port." I hoisted the sloop's flag and fired a gun, all of which they might construe as a friendly salute or an invitation to come on. They drew up in a semicircle, but kept outside of eighty yards, which in self-defense would have been the death-line.

In their mosquito fleet was a ship's boat stolen probably from a murdered crew. Six savages paddled this rather awkwardly with the blades of oars which had been broken off. Two of the

savages standing erect wore sea-boots, and this
sustained the suspicion that they had fallen upon
some luckless ship's crew, and also added a hint
that they had already visited the *Spray's* deck, and
would now, if they could, try her again. Their
sea-boots, I have no doubt, would have protected
their feet and rendered carpet-tacks harmless.
Paddling clumsily, they passed down the strait
at a distance of a hundred yards from the sloop,
in an offhand manner and as if bound to Fortescue Bay. This I judged to be a piece of strategy,
and so kept a sharp lookout over a small island
which soon came in range between them and
the sloop, completely hiding them from view,
and toward which the *Spray* was now drifting
helplessly with the tide, and with every prospect of
going on the rocks, for there was no anchorage, at
least, none that my cables would reach. And, sure
enough, I soon saw a movement in the grass just
on top of the island, which is called Bonet Island
and is one hundred and thirty-six feet high. I
fired several shots over the place, but saw no other
sign of the savages. It was they that had moved
the grass, for as the sloop swept past the island,
the rebound of the tide carrying her clear, there on
the other side was the boat, surely enough ex-
posing their cunning and treachery. A stiff breeze,
coming up suddenly, now scattered the canoes
while it extricated the sloop from a dangerous
position, albeit the wind, though friendly, was still
ahead.

The *Spray*, flogging against current and wind,
made Borgia Bay on the following afternoon, and

cast anchor there for the second time. I would now, if I could, describe the moonlit scene on the strait at midnight after I had cleared the savages and Bonet Island. A heavy cloud-bank that had swept across the sky then cleared away, and the night became suddenly as light as day, or nearly so. A high mountain was mirrored in the channel ahead, and the *Spray* sailing along with her shadow was as two sloops on the sea.

Records of passages through the strait at the head of Borgia Bay.

NOTE.— On a small bush nearer the water there was a board bearing several other inscriptions, to which were added the words "Sloop *Spray*, March, 1896."

The sloop being moored, I threw out my skiff, and with ax and gun landed at the head of the cove, and filled a barrel of water from a stream. Then, as before, there was no sign of Indians at the place. Finding it quite deserted, I rambled about near the beach for an hour or more. The fine weather seemed, somehow, to add loneliness to the place, and when I came upon a spot where a grave was marked I went no farther. Returning to the head of the cove, I came to a sort of Calvary, it appeared to me, where navigators, carrying their cross, had each set one up as a beacon to others coming after. They had anchored here and gone on, all except the one under the little mound. One of the simple marks, curiously enough, had been left there by the steamship *Colimbia*, sister ship to the *Colombia*, my neighbor of that morning.

I read the names of many other vessels; some of them I copied in my journal, others were illegible. Many of the crosses had decayed and fallen, and many a hand that put them there I had known, many a hand now still. The air of depression was about the place, and I hurried back to the sloop to forget myself again in the voyage.

Early the next morning I stood out from Borgia Bay, and off Cape Quod, where the wind fell light, I moored the sloop by kelp in twenty fathoms of water, and held her there a few hours against a three-knot current. That night I anchored in Langara Cove, a few miles farther along, where on the following day I discovered wreckage and goods washed up from the sea. I worked all day now, salving and boating off a cargo to the sloop. The bulk of the goods was tallow in casks and in lumps from which the casks had broken away; and embedded in the seaweed was a barrel of wine, which I also towed alongside. I hoisted them all in with the throat-halyards, which I took to the windlass. The weight of some of the casks was a little over eight hundred pounds.

There were no Indians about Langara; evidently there had not been any since the great gale which had washed the wreckage on shore. Probably it

Salving wreckage.

was the same gale that drove the *Spray* off Cape
Horn, from March 3 to 8.   Hundreds of tons of
kelp had been torn from beds in deep water and
rolled up into ridges on the beach.   A specimen
stalk which I found entire, roots, leaves, and all,
measured one hundred and thirty-one feet in
length.   At this place I filled a barrel of water at
night, and on the following day sailed with a fair
wind at last.

I had not sailed far, however, when I came
abreast of more tallow in a small cove, where I
anchored, and boated off as before.   It rained and
snowed hard all that day, and it was no light work
carrying tallow in my arms over the boulders on
the beach.   But I worked on till the *Spray* was
loaded with a full cargo.   I was happy then in the
prospect of doing a good business farther along on
the voyage, for the habits of an old trader would
come to the surface.   I sailed from the cove about
noon, greased from top to toe, while my vessel was
tallowed from keelson to truck.   My cabin, as well
as the hold and deck, was stowed full of tallow,
and all were thoroughly smeared.

CHAPTER X

Running to Port Angosto in a snow-storm — A defective sheet-rope places the *Spray* in peril — The *Spray* as a target for a Fuegian arrow — The island of Alan Erric — Again in the open Pacific — The run to the island of Juan Fernandez — An absentee king — At Robinson Crusoe's anchorage.

ANOTHER gale had then sprung up, but the wind was still fair, and I had only twenty-six miles to run for Port Angosto, a dreary enough place, where, however, I would find a safe harbor in which to refit and stow cargo. I carried on sail to make the harbor before dark, and she fairly flew along, all covered with snow, which fell thick and fast, till she looked like a white winter bird. Between the storm-bursts I saw the headland of my port, and was steering for it when a flaw of wind caught the mainsail by the lee, jibed it over, and dear! dear! how nearly was this the cause of disaster; for the sheet parted and the boom unshipped, and it was then close upon night. I worked till the perspiration poured from my body to get things adjusted and in working order before dark, and, above all, to get it done before the sloop drove to leeward of the port of refuge. Even then I did not get the boom shipped in its saddle. I was at the entrance of the harbor before I could

126

get this done, and it was time to haul her to or lose the port; but in that condition, like a bird with a broken wing, she made the haven. The accident which so jeopardized my vessel and cargo came of a defective sheet-rope, one made from sisal, a treacherous fiber which has caused a deal of strong language among sailors.

I did not run the *Spray* into the inner harbor of Port Angosto, but came to inside a bed of kelp under a steep bluff on the port hand going in. It was an exceedingly snug nook, and to make doubly sure of holding on here against all williwaws I moored her with two anchors and secured her, besides, by cables to trees. However, no wind ever reached there except back flaws from the mountains on the opposite side of the harbor. There, as elsewhere in that region, the country was made up of mountains. This was the place where I was to refit and whence I was to sail direct, once more, for Cape Pillar and the Pacific.

I remained at Port Angosto some days, busily employed about the sloop. I stowed the tallow from the deck to the hold, arranged my cabin in better order, and took in a good supply of wood and water. I also mended the sloop's sails and rigging, and fitted a jigger, which changed the rig to a yawl, though I called the boat a sloop just the same, the jigger being merely a temporary affair.

I never forgot, even at the busiest time of my work there, to have my rifle by me ready for instant use; for I was of necessity within range of savages, and I had seen Fuegian canoes at this place when I anchored in the port, farther down

the reach, on the first trip through the strait. I
think it was on the second day, while I was busily
employed about decks, that I heard the swish of
something through the air close by my ear, and
heard a "zip"-like sound in the water, but saw
nothing. Presently, however, I suspected that it
was an arrow of some sort, for just then one passing not far from me struck the mainmast, where it
stuck fast, vibrating from the shock — a Fuegian
autograph. A savage was somewhere near, there
could be no doubt about that. I did not know but
he might be shooting at me, with a view to getting
my sloop and her cargo; and so I threw up my old
Martini-Henry, the rifle that kept on shooting, and
the first shot uncovered three Fuegians, who scam-
pered from a clump of bushes where they had been
concealed, and made over the hills. I fired away a
good many cartridges, aiming under their feet to
encourage their climbing. My dear old gun woke
up the hills, and at every report all three of the
savages jumped as if shot; but they kept on, and
put Fuego real estate between themselves and the
Spray as fast as their legs could carry them. I
took care then, more than ever before, that all my
firearms should be in order and that a supply of
ammunition should always be ready at hand. But
the savages did not return, and although I put
tacks on deck every night, I never discovered that
any more visitors came, and I had only to sweep
the deck of tacks carefully every morning after.

As the days went by, the season became more
favorable for a chance to clear the strait with a
fair wind, and so I made up my mind after six

"The first shot uncovered three Fuegians."

attempts, being driven back each time, to be in
no further haste to sail. The bad weather on my
last return to Port Angosto for shelter brought the
Chilean gunboat *Condor* and the Argentine cruiser

Azopardo into port.   As soon as the latter came to
anchor, Captain Mascarella, the commander, sent a
boat to the *Spray* with the message that he would
take me in tow for Sandy Point if I would give up
the voyage and return — the thing farthest from
my mind.   The officers of the *Azopardo* told me
that, coming up the strait after the *Spray* on her
first passage through, they saw Black Pedro and
learned that he had visited me.   The *Azopardo*,
being a foreign man-of-war, had no right to arrest
the Fuegian outlaw, but her captain blamed me for
not shooting the rascal when he came to my sloop.

I procured some cordage and other small supplies from these vessels, and the officers of each of
them mustered a supply of warm flannels, of which
I was most in need.   With these additions to my
outfit, and with the vessel in good trim, though
somewhat deeply laden, I was well prepared for
another bout with the Southern, misnamed Pacific,
Ocean.

In the first week in April southeast winds, such
as appear about Cape Horn in the fall and winter
seasons, bringing better weather than that experienced in the summer, began to disturb the upper
clouds; a little more patience, and the time would
come for sailing with a fair wind.

At Port Angosto I met Professor Dusen of the
Swedish scientific expedition to South America
and the Pacific Islands.   The professor was camped
by the side of a brook at the head of the harbor,
where there were many varieties of moss, in which
he was interested, and where the water was, as his
Argentine cook said, "muy rico."   The professor

had three well-armed Argentines along in his camp
to fight savages. They seemed disgusted when I
filled water at a small stream near the vessel, slight-
ing their advice to go farther up to the greater
brook, where it was " muy rico." But they were all
fine fellows, though it was a wonder that they did
not all die of rheumatic pains from living on wet
ground.

Of all the little haps and mishaps to the *Spray* at
Port Angosto, of the many attempts to put to sea,
and of each return for shelter, it is not my purpose
to speak. Of hindrances there were many to keep
her back, but on the thirteenth day of April, and for
the seventh and last time, she weighed anchor from
that port. Difficulties, however, multiplied all
about in so strange a manner that had I been given
to superstitious fears I should not have persisted
in sailing on a thirteenth day, notwithstanding
that a fair wind blew in the offing. Many of the
incidents were ludicrous. When I found myself,
for instance, disentangling the sloop's mast from
the branches of a tree after she had drifted three
times around a small island, against my will, it
seemed more than one's nerves could bear, and I
had to speak about it, so I thought, or die of lock-
jaw, and I apostrophized the *Spray* as an impatient
farmer might his horse or his ox. " Did n't you
know," cried I — " did n't you know that you
could n't climb a tree ? " But the poor old *Spray*
had essayed, and successfully too, nearly everything else in the Strait of Magellan, and my heart
softened toward her when I thought of what she
had gone through. Moreover, she had discovered

an island. On the charts this one that she had
sailed around was traced as a point of land. I
named it Alan Erric Island, after a worthy literary
friend whom I had met in strange by-places, and I
put up a sign, "Keep off the grass," which, as dis-
coverer, was within my rights.

Now at last the *Spray* carried me free of Tierra
del Fuego. If by a close shave only, still she carried me clear, though her boom actually hit the
beacon rocks to leeward as she lugged on sail to
clear the point. The thing was done on the 13th
of April, 1896. But a close shave and a narrow
escape were nothing new to the *Spray*.

The waves doffed their white caps beautifully to
her in the strait that day before the southeast
wind, the first true winter breeze of the season
from that quarter, and here she was out on the
first of it, with every prospect of clearing Cape
Pillar before it should shift. So it turned out;
the wind blew hard, as it always blows about Cape
Horn, but she had cleared the great tide-race off
Cape Pillar and the Evangelistas, the outermost
rocks of all, before the change came. I remained
at the helm, humoring my vessel in the cross seas,
for it was rough, and I did not dare to let her take
a straight course. It was necessary to change her
course in the combing seas, to meet them with
what skill I could when they rolled up ahead, and
to keep off when they came up abeam.

On the following morning, April 14, only the
tops of the highest mountains were in sight, and
the *Spray*, making good headway on a northwest
course, soon sank these out of sight. "Hurrah for

the *Spray !*" I shouted to seals, sea-gulls, and pen-
guins; for there were no other living creatures
about, and she had weathered all the dangers of
Cape Horn. Moreover, she had on her voyage
round the Horn salved a cargo of which she had
not jettisoned a pound. And why should not one
rejoice also in the main chance coming so of itself ?

I shook out a reef, and set the whole jib, for,
having sea-room, I could square away two points.
This brought the sea more on her quarter, and she
was the wholesomer under a press of sail. Occasionally an old southwest sea, rolling up, combed
athwart her, but did no harm. The wind freshened
as the sun rose half-mast or more, and the air, a bit
chilly in the morning, softened later in the day;
but I gave little thought to such things as these.

One wave, in the evening, larger than others that
had threatened all day,— one such as sailors call
" fine-weather seas,"— broke over the sloop fore
and aft. It washed over me at the helm, the last
that swept over the *Spray* off Cape Horn. It
seemed to wash away old regrets. All my troubles
were now astern ; summer was ahead ; all the world
was again before me. The wind was even literally fair. My "trick" at the wheel was now up,
and it was 5 P. M. I had stood at the helm since
eleven o'clock the morning before, or thirty hours.

Then was the time to uncover my head, for I
sailed alone with God. The vast ocean was again
around me, and the horizon was unbroken by land.
A few days later the *Spray* was under full sail, and
I saw her for the first time with a jigger spread.
This was indeed a small incident, but it was the

incident following a triumph. The wind was still southwest, but it had moderated, and roaring seas had turned to gossiping waves that rippled and pattered against her sides as she rolled among them, delighted with their story. Rapid changes went on, those days, in things all about while she headed for the tropics. New species of birds came around; albatrosses fell back and became scarcer and scarcer; lighter gulls came in their stead, and pecked for crumbs in the sloop's wake.

On the tenth day from Cape Pillar a shark came along, the first of its kind on this part of the voyage to get into trouble. I harpooned him and took out his ugly jaws. I had not till then felt inclined to take the life of any animal, but when John Shark hove in sight my sympathy flew to the winds. It is a fact that in Magellan I let pass many ducks that would have made a good stew, for I had no mind in the lonesome strait to take the life of any living thing.

From Cape Pillar I steered for Juan Fernandez, and on the 26th of April, fifteen days out, made that historic island right ahead.

The blue hills of Juan Fernandez, high among the clouds, could be seen about thirty miles off. A thousand emotions thrilled me when I saw the island, and I bowed my head to the deck. We may mock the Oriental salaam, but for my part I could find no other way of expressing myself.

The wind being light through the day, the *Spray* did not reach the island till night. With what wind there was to fill her sails she stood close in to shore on the northeast side, where it fell calm and remained so all night. I saw the twinkling of a small light farther along in a cove, and fired a gun, but got no answer, and soon the light disappeared altogether. I heard the sea booming against the cliffs all night, and realized that the ocean swell was still

great, although from the deck of my little ship it was apparently small. From the cry of animals in the hills, which sounded fainter and fainter through the night, I judged that a light current was drifting the sloop from the land, though she seemed all night

The *Spray* approaching Juan Fernandez, Robinson Crusoe's Island.

dangerously near the shore, for, the land being very high, appearances were deceptive.

Soon after daylight I saw a boat putting out toward me. As it pulled near, it so happened that I picked up my gun, which was on the deck, meaning only to put it below; but the people in the boat, seeing the piece in my hands, quickly turned and pulled back for shore, which was about four miles distant. There were six rowers in her, and I observed that they pulled with oars in oar-locks,

after the manner of trained seamen, and so I knew
they belonged to a civilized race; but their opinion
of me must have been anything but flattering
when they mistook my purpose with the gun and
pulled away with all their might. I made them
understand by signs, but not without difficulty,
that I did not intend to shoot, that I was simply
putting the piece in the cabin, and that I wished
them to return. When they understood my meaning they came back and were soon on board.

One of the party, whom the rest called "king,"
spoke English; the others spoke Spanish. They
had all heard of the voyage of the *Spray* through
the papers of Valparaiso, and were hungry for
news concerning it. They told me of a war between Chile and the Argentine, which I had not
heard of when I was there. I had just visited both
countries, and I told them that according to the
latest reports, while I was in Chile, their own
island was sunk. (This same report that Juan
Fernandez had sunk was current in Australia
when I arrived there three months later.)

I had already prepared a pot of coffee and a
plate of doughnuts, which, after some words of
civility, the islanders stood up to and discussed
with a will, after which they took the *Spray* in
tow of their boat and made toward the island
with her at the rate of a good three knots. The
man they called king took the helm, and with
whirling it up and down he so rattled the *Spray*
that I thought she would never carry herself
straight again. The others pulled away lustily
with their oars. The king, I soon learned, was

king only by courtesy. Having lived longer on
the island than any other man in the world,—
thirty years,— he was so dubbed. Juan Fernandez was then under the administration of a governor of Swedish nobility, so I was told. I was also
told that his daughter could ride the wildest goat
on the island. The governor, at the time of my
visit, was away at Valparaiso with his family, to
place his children at school. The king had been
away once for a year or two, and in Rio de Janeiro had married a Brazilian woman who followed
his fortunes to the far-off island. He was himself
a Portuguese and a native of the Azores. He had
sailed in New Bedford whale-ships and had steered
a boat. All this I learned, and more too, before we
reached the anchorage. The sea-breeze, coming in
before long, filled the *Spray's* sails, and the experienced Portuguese mariner piloted her to a safe
berth in the bay, where she was moored to a buoy
abreast the settlement.

CHAPTER XI

THE *Spray* being secured, the islanders returned
to the coffee and doughnuts, and I was more
than flattered when they did not slight my buns, as
the professor had done in the Strait of Magellan.
Between buns and doughnuts there was little
difference except in name. Both had been fried
in tallow, which was the strong point in both, for
there was nothing on the island fatter than a goat,
and a goat is but a lean beast, to make the best of
it. So with a view to business I hooked my steel-
yards to the boom at once, ready to weigh out
tallow, there being no customs officer to say, "Why
do you do so?" and before the sun went down the
islanders had learned the art of making buns and
doughnuts. I did not charge a high price for what
I sold, but the ancient and curious coins I got in
payment, some of them from the wreck of a galleon
sunk in the bay no one knows when, I sold afterward to antiquarians for more than face-value.
In this way I made a reasonable profit. I brought

away money of all denominations from the island, and nearly all there was, so far as I could find out.

Juan Fernandez, as a place of call, is a lovely spot. The hills are well wooded, the valleys fer-

The house of the king.

tile, and pouring down through many ravines are streams of pure water. There are no serpents on the island, and no wild beasts other than pigs and goats, of which I saw a number, with possibly a dog or two. The people lived without the use of rum or beer of any sort. There was not a police officer or a lawyer among them. The domestic economy of the island was simplicity itself. The fashions of Paris did not affect the inhabitants; each dressed according to his own taste. Although there was no doctor, the people were all healthy,

and the children were all beautiful. There were
about forty-five souls on the island all told. The
adults were mostly from the mainland of South

Robinson Crusoe's cave.

America. One lady there, from Chile, who made a
flying-jib for the *Spray*, taking her pay in tallow,
would be called a belle at Newport. Blessed island
of Juan Fernandez! Why Alexander Selkirk ever
left you was more than I could make out.

A large ship which had arrived some time before, on fire, had been stranded at the head of the
bay, and as the sea smashed her to pieces on the
rocks, after the fire was drowned, the islanders
picked up the timbers and utilized them in the

construction of houses, which naturally presented a ship-like appearance. The house of the king of Juan Fernandez, Manuel Carroza by name, besides resembling the ark, wore a polished brass knocker on its only door, which was painted green. In front of this gorgeous entrance was a flag-mast all ataunto, and near it a smart whale-boat painted red and blue, the delight of the king's old age.

I of course made a pilgrimage to the old lookout place at the top of the mountain, where Selkirk spent many days peering into the distance for the ship which came at last. From a tablet fixed into the face of the rock I copied these words, inscribed in Arabic capitals:

IN MEMORY

OF

ALEXANDER SELKIRK,

MARINER,

A native of Largo, in the county of Fife, Scotland, who lived on this island in complete solitude for four years and four months. He was landed from the *Cinque Ports* galley, 96 tons, 18 guns, A. D. 1704, and was taken off in the *Duke*, privateer, 12th February, 1709. He died Lieutenant of H. M. S. *Weymouth*, A. D. 1723,[1] aged 47. This tablet is erected near Selkirk's lookout, by Commodore Powell and the officers of H. M. S. *Topaze*, A. D. 1868.

The cave in which Selkirk dwelt while on the island is at the head of the bay now called Robin-

---

[1] Mr. J. Cuthbert Hadden, in the "Century Magazine" for July, 1899, shows that the tablet is in error as to the year of Selkirk's death. It should be 1721.

son Crusoe Bay. It is around a bold headland
west of the present anchorage and landing. Ships
have anchored there, but it affords a very indiffer-
ent berth. Both of these anchorages are exposed
to north winds, which, however, do not reach home
with much violence. The holding-ground being
good in the first-named bay to the eastward, the
anchorage there may be considered safe, although
the undertow at times makes it wild riding.

I visited Robinson Crusoe Bay in a boat, and
with some difficulty landed through the surf near
the cave, which I entered. I found it dry and in-
habitable. It is located in a beautiful nook sheltered by high mountains from all the severe storms
that sweep over the island, which are not many;
for it lies near the limits of the trade-wind regions,
being in latitude $35\frac{1}{2}°$ S. The island is about fourteen miles in length, east and west, and eight miles
in width; its height is over three thousand feet.
Its distance from Chile, to which country it be-
longs, is about three hundred and forty miles.

Juan Fernandez was once a convict station. A
number of caves in which the prisoners were kept,
damp, unwholesome dens, are no longer in use, and
no more prisoners are sent to the island.

The pleasantest day I spent on the island, if not
the pleasantest on my whole voyage, was my last
day on shore,— but by no means because it was the
last,— when the children of the little community,
one and all, went out with me to gather wild fruits
for the voyage. We found quinces, peaches, and
figs, and the children gathered a basket of each.
It takes very little to please children, and these

The man who called a cabra a goat.

little ones, never hearing a word in their lives except Spanish, made the hills ring with mirth at the sound of words in English. They asked me the names of all manner of things on the island. We came to a wild fig-tree loaded with fruit, of which I gave them the English name. "Figgies, figgies!" they cried, while they picked till their baskets were full. But when I told them that the

cabra they pointed out was only a goat, they
screamed with laughter, and rolled on the grass in
wild delight to think that a man had come to their
island who would call a cabra a goat.

The first child born on Juan Fernandez, I was
told, had become a beautiful woman and was now
a mother. Manuel Carroza and the good soul who
followed him here from Brazil had laid away their
only child, a girl, at the age of seven, in the little
churchyard on the point. In the same half-acre
were other mounds among the rough lava rocks,
some marking the burial-place of native-born children, some the resting-places of seamen from passing ships, landed here to end days of sickness and
get into a sailors' heaven.

The greatest drawback I saw in the island was
the want of a school. A class there would necessarily be small, but to some kind soul who loved
teaching and quietude life on Juan Fernandez
would, for a limited time, be one of delight.

On the morning of May 5, 1896, I sailed from
Juan Fernandez, having feasted on many things,
but on nothing sweeter than the adventure itself
of a visit to the home and to the very cave of Robinson Crusoe. From the island the *Spray* bore away
to the north, passing the island of St. Felix before
she gained the trade-winds, which seemed slow in
reaching their limits.

If the trades were tardy, however, when they did
come they came with a bang, and made up for lost
time; and the *Spray*, under reefs, sometimes one,
sometimes two, flew before a gale for a great many
days, with a bone in her mouth, toward the Mar-

quesas, in the west, which she made on the forty-third day out, and still kept on sailing. My time was all taken up those days — not by standing at the helm; no man, I think, could stand or sit and steer a vessel round the world: I did better than that; for I sat and read my books, mended my clothes, or cooked my meals and ate them in peace. I had already found that it was not good to be alone, and so I made companionship with what there was around me, sometimes with the universe and sometimes with my own insignificant self; but my books were always my friends, let fail all else. Nothing could be easier or more restful than my voyage in the trade-winds.

I sailed with a free wind day after day, marking the position of my ship on the chart with considerable precision; but this was done by intuition, I think, more than by slavish calculations. For one whole month my vessel held her course true; I had not, the while, so much as a light in the binnacle. The Southern Cross I saw every night abeam. The sun every morning came up astern; every evening it went down ahead. I wished for no other compass to guide me, for these were true. If I doubted my reckoning after a long time at sea I verified it by reading the clock aloft made by the Great Architect, and it was right.

There was no denying that the comical side of the strange life appeared. I awoke, sometimes, to find the sun already shining into my cabin. I heard water rushing by, with only a thin plank between me and the depths, and I said, "How is this?" But it was all right; it was my ship on her course, sailing

as no other ship had ever sailed before in the world.
The rushing water along her side told me that she
was sailing at full speed. I knew that no human
hand was at the helm; I knew that all was well with
"the hands" forward, and that there was no
mutiny on board.

The phenomena of ocean meteorology were interesting studies even here in the trade-winds. I
observed that about every seven days the wind
freshened and drew several points farther than
usual from the direction of the pole; that is, it went
round from east-southeast to south-southeast, while
at the same time a heavy swell rolled up from the
southwest. All this indicated that gales were
going on in the anti-trades. The wind then hauled
day after day as it moderated, till it stood again at
the normal point, east-southeast. This is more or
less the constant state of the winter trades in latitude 12° S., where I "ran down the longitude" for
weeks. The sun, we all know, is the creator of the
trade-winds and of the wind system over all the
earth. But ocean meteorology is, I think, the most
fascinating of all. From Juan Fernandez to the
Marquesas I experienced six changes of these great
palpitations of sea-winds and of the sea itself, the
effect of far-off gales. To know the laws that
govern the winds, and to know that you know
them, will give you an easy mind on your voyage
round the world; otherwise you may tremble at
the appearance of every cloud. What is true of
this in the trade-winds is much more so in the
variables, where changes run more to extremes.

To cross the Pacific Ocean, even under the most

favorable circumstances, brings you for many days close to nature, and you realize the vastness of the sea. Slowly but surely the mark of my little ship's course on the track-chart reached out on the ocean and across it, while at her utmost speed she marked with her keel still slowly the sea that carried her. On the forty-third day from land,— a long time to be at sea alone,— the sky being beautifully clear and the moon being "in distance" with the sun, I threw up my sextant for sights. I found from the result of three observations, after long wrestling with lunar tables, that her longitude by observation agreed within five miles of that by dead-reckoning.

This was wonderful; both, however, might be in error, but somehow I felt confident that both were nearly true, and that in a few hours more I should see land; and so it happened, for then I made the island of Nukahiva, the southernmost of the Marquesas group, clear-cut and lofty. The verified longitude when abreast was somewhere between the two reckonings; this was extraordinary. All navigators will tell you that from one day to another a ship may lose or gain more than five miles in her sailing-account, and again, in the matter of lunars, even expert lunarians are considered as doing clever work when they average within eight miles of the truth.

I hope I am making it clear that I do not lay claim to cleverness or to slavish calculations in my reckonings. I think I have already stated that I kept my longitude, at least, mostly by intuition. A rotator log always towed astern, but so much

has to be allowed for currents and for drift, which
the log never shows, that it is only an approxima-
tion, after all, to be corrected by one's own judgment from data of a thousand voyages; and even
then the master of the ship, if he be wise, cries out
for the lead and the lookout.

Unique was my experience in nautical astronomy
from the deck of the *Spray* — so much so that I
feel justified in briefly telling it here. The first set
of sights, just spoken of, put her many hundred
miles west of my reckoning by account. I knew
that this could not be correct. In about an hour's
time I took another set of observations with the
utmost care; the mean result of these was about
the same as that of the first set. I asked myself
why, with my boasted self-dependence, I had not
done at least better than this.   Then I went in
search of a discrepancy in the tables, and I found
it. In the tables I found that the column of figures
from which I had got an important logarithm was
in error. It was a matter I could prove beyond a
doubt, and it made the difference as already stated.
The tables being corrected, I sailed on with self-
reliance unshaken, and with my tin clock fast
asleep. The result of these observations naturally
tickled my vanity, for I knew that it was something to stand on a great ship's deck and with two
assistants take lunar observations approximately
near the truth. As one of the poorest of American
sailors, I was proud of the little achievement alone
on the sloop, even by chance though it may have
been.

I was *en rapport* now with my surroundings, and

was carried on a vast stream where I felt the buoyancy of His hand who made all the worlds. I realized the mathematical truth of their motions, so well known that astronomers compile tables of their positions through the years and the days, and the minutes of a day, with such precision that one coming along over the sea even five years later may, by their aid, find the standard time of any given meridian on the earth.

To find local time is a simpler matter. The difference between local and standard time is longitude expressed in time — four minutes, we all know, representing one degree. This, briefly, is the principle on which longitude is found independent of chronometers. The work of the lunarian, though seldom practised in these days of chronometers, is beautifully edifying, and there is nothing in the realm of navigation that lifts one's heart up more in adoration.

CHAPTER XII

Seventy-two days without a port—Whales and birds—A peep into the *Spray's* galley—Flying-fish for breakfast—A welcome at Apia—A visit from Mrs. Robert Louis Stevenson—At Vailima—Samoan hospitality—Arrested for fast riding—An amusing merry-go-round—Teachers and pupils of Papauta College—At the mercy of sea-nymphs.

TO be alone forty-three days would seem a long time, but in reality, even here, winged moments flew lightly by, and instead of my hauling in for Nukahiva, which I could have made as well as not, I kept on for Samoa, where I wished to make my next landing. This occupied twenty-nine days more, making seventy-two days in all. I was not distressed in any way during that time. There was no end of companionship; the very coral reefs kept me company, or gave me no time to feel lonely, which is the same thing, and there were many of them now in my course to Samoa.

First among the incidents of the voyage from Juan Fernandez to Samoa (which were not many) was a narrow escape from collision with a great whale that was absent-mindedly plowing the ocean at night while I was below. The noise from his startled snort and the commotion he made in the sea, as he turned to clear my vessel, brought me on deck in time to catch a wetting from the water he

threw up with his flukes. The monster was apparently frightened. He headed quickly for the east;
I kept on going west. Soon another whale passed,
evidently a companion, following in its wake. I

Meeting with the whale.

saw no more on this part of the voyage, nor did I
wish to.

Hungry sharks came about the vessel often
when she neared islands or coral reefs. I own to a
satisfaction in shooting them as one would a tiger.
Sharks, after all, are the tigers of the sea. Nothing is more dreadful to the mind of a sailor, I
think, than a possible encounter with a hungry
shark.

A number of birds were always about; occasionally one poised on the mast to look the *Spray*
over, wondering, perhaps, at her odd wings, for
she now wore her Fuego mainsail, which, like

Joseph's coat, was made of many pieces. Ships
are less common on the Southern seas than formerly. I saw not one in the many days crossing
the Pacific.

My diet on these long passages usually consisted
of potatoes and salt cod and biscuits, which I made
two or three times a week. I had always plenty of
coffee, tea, sugar, and flour. I carried usually a
good supply of potatoes, but before reaching Samoa
I had a mishap which left me destitute of this
highly prized sailors' luxury. Through meeting at
Juan Fernandez the Yankee Portuguese named
Manuel Carroza, who nearly traded me out of my
boots, I ran out of potatoes in mid-ocean, and was
wretched thereafter. I prided myself on being
something of a trader; but this Portuguese from
the Azores by way of New Bedford, who gave me
new potatoes for the older ones I had got from the
Colombia, a bushel or more of the best, left me no
ground for boasting. He wanted mine, he said, "for
changee the seed." When I got to sea I found that
his tubers were rank and unedible, and full of fine
yellow streaks of repulsive appearance. I tied the
sack up and returned to the few left of my old stock,
thinking that maybe when I got right hungry the
island potatoes would improve in flavor. Three
weeks later I opened the bag again, and out flew
millions of winged insects! Manuel's potatoes had
all turned to moths. I tied them up quickly and
threw all into the sea.

Manuel had a large crop of potatoes on hand,
and as a hint to whalemen, who are always eager
to buy vegetables, he wished me to report whales

off the island of Juan Fernandez, which I have
already done, and big ones at that, but they were
a long way off.

Taking things by and large, as sailors say, I got
on fairly well in the matter of provisions even on
the long voyage across the Pacific. I found always
some small stores to help the fare of luxuries;
what I lacked of fresh meat was made up in fresh
fish, at least while in the trade-winds, where flying-
fish crossing on the wing at night would hit the
sails and fall on deck, sometimes two or three of
them, sometimes a dozen. Every morning except
when the moon was large I got a bountiful supply
by merely picking them up from the lee scuppers.
All tinned meats went begging.

On the 16th of July, after considerable care and
some skill and hard work, the *Spray* cast anchor at
Apia, in the kingdom of Samoa, about noon. My
vessel being moored, I spread an awning, and instead of going at once on shore I sat under it till
late in the evening, listening with delight to the
musical voices of the Samoan men and women.

A canoe coming down the harbor, with three
young women in it, rested her paddles abreast the
sloop. One of the fair crew, hailing with the naïve
salutation, "Talofa lee" ("Love to you, chief"),
asked:

"Schoon come Melike?"

"Love to you," I answered, and said, "Yes."

"You man come 'lone?"

Again I answered, "Yes."

"I don't believe that. You had other mans, and
you eat 'em."

At this sally the others laughed. "What for you come long way?" they asked.

"To hear you ladies sing," I replied.

"Oh, talofa lee!" they all cried, and sang on. Their voices filled the air with music that rolled

First exchange of courtesies in Samoa.

across to the grove of tall palms on the other side of the harbor and back. Soon after this six young men came down in the United States consul-general's boat, singing in parts and beating time with their oars. In my interview with them I came off better than with the damsels in the canoe. They bore an invitation from General Churchill for me to come and dine at the consulate. There was a lady's hand in things about the consulate at Samoa. Mrs. Churchill picked the crew for the general's boat, and saw to it that they wore a smart uniform and that they could sing the Samoan boatsong, which in the first week Mrs. Churchill herself could sing like a native girl.

Next morning bright and early Mrs. Robert Louis Stevenson came to the *Spray* and invited me to Vailima the following day. I was of course thrilled when I found myself, after so many days of adventure, face to face with this bright woman, so lately the companion of the author who had delighted me on the voyage. The kindly eyes, that looked me through and through, sparkled when we compared notes of adventure. I marveled at some of her experiences and escapes. She told me that, along with her husband, she had voyaged in all manner of rickety craft among the islands of the Pacific, reflectively adding, "Our tastes were similar."

Following the subject of voyages, she gave me the four beautiful volumes of sailing directories for the Mediterranean, writing on the fly-leaf of the first:

To CAPTAIN SLOCUM. These volumes have been read and re-read many times by my husband, and I am very sure that he would be pleased that they should be passed on to the sort of seafaring man that he liked above all others.

FANNY V. DE G. STEVENSON.

Mrs. Stevenson also gave me a great directory of the Indian Ocean. It was not without a feeling of reverential awe that I received the books so nearly

direct from the hand of Tusitala, "who sleeps in
the forest." Aolele, the *Spray* will cherish your
gift.

The novelist's stepson, Mr. Lloyd Osbourne,
walked through the Vailima mansion with me

Vailima, the home of Robert Louis Stevenson.

and bade me write my letters at the old desk. I
thought it would be presumptuous to do that; it
was sufficient for me to enter the hall on the floor
of which the "Writer of Tales," according to the
Samoan custom, was wont to sit.

Coming through the main street of Apia one
day, with my hosts, all bound for the *Spray*, Mrs.
Stevenson on horseback, I walking by her side,
and Mr. and Mrs. Osbourne close in our wake on
bicycles, at a sudden turn in the road we found
ourselves mixed with a remarkable native proces-
sion, with a somewhat primitive band of music, in
front of us, while behind was a festival or a funeral,
we could not tell which. Several of the stoutest
men carried bales and bundles on poles. Some

were evidently bales of tapa-cloth. The burden of one set of poles, heavier than the rest, however, was not so easily made out. My curiosity was whetted to know whether it was a roast pig or something of a gruesome nature, and I inquired about it. "I don't know," said Mrs. Stevenson, "whether this is a wedding or a funeral. Whatever it is, though, captain, our place seems to be at the head of it."

The *Spray* being in the stream, we boarded her from the beach abreast, in the little razeed Gloucester dory, which had been painted a smart green. Our combined weight loaded it gunwale to the water, and I was obliged to steer with great care to avoid swamping. The adventure pleased Mrs. Stevenson greatly, and as we paddled along she sang, "They went to sea in a pea-green boat." I could understand her saying of her husband and herself, "Our tastes were similar."

As I sailed farther from the center of civilization I heard less and less of what would and what would not pay. Mrs. Stevenson, in speaking of my voyage, did not once ask me what I would make out of it. When I came to a Samoan village, the chief did not ask the price of gin, or say, "How much will you pay for roast pig?" but, "Dollar, dollar," said he; "white man know only dollar."

"Never mind dollar. The *tapo* has prepared ava; let us drink and rejoice." The tapo is the virgin hostess of the village; in this instance it was Taloa, daughter of the chief. "Our taro is good; let us eat. On the tree there is fruit. Let the day go by; why should we mourn over that? There are

millions of days coming. The breadfruit is yellow
in the sun, and from the cloth-tree is Taloa's gown.
Our house, which is good, cost but the labor of
building it, and there is no lock on the door."

While the days go thus in these Southern islands
we at the North are struggling for the bare necessi-
ties of life.

For food the islanders. have only to put out their
hand and take what nature has provided for them;
if they plant a banana-tree, their only care afterward is to see that too many trees do not grow.
They have great reason to love their country and
to fear the white man's yoke, for once harnessed to
the plow, their life would no longer be a poem.

The chief of the village of Caini, who was a tall
and dignified Tonga man, could be approached
only through an interpreter and talking man. It
was perfectly natural for him to inquire the
object of my visit, and I was sincere when I told
him that my reason for casting anchor in Samoa
was to see their fine men, and fine women, too.
After a considerable pause the chief said: "The
captain has come a long way to see so little; but,"
he added, "the tapo must sit nearer the captain."
"Yack," said Taloa, who had so nearly learned
to say yes in English, and suiting the action to
the word, she hitched a peg nearer, all hands
sitting in a circle upon mats. I was no less
taken with the chief's eloquence than delighted
with the simplicity of all he said. About him
there was nothing pompous; he might have been
taken for a great scholar or statesman, the least
assuming of the men I met on the voyage. As for

Taloa, a sort of Queen of the May, and the other tapo girls, well, it is wise to learn as soon as possible the manners and customs of these hospitable people, and meanwhile not to mistake for over-familiarity that which is intended as honor to a guest. I was fortunate in my travels in the islands, and saw nothing to shake one's faith in native virtue.

To the unconventional mind the punctilious etiquette of Samoa is perhaps a little painful. For instance, I found that in partaking of ava, the social bowl, I was supposed to toss a little of the beverage over my shoulder, or pretend to do so, and say, "Let the gods drink," and then drink it all myself; and the dish, invariably a cocoanut-shell, being empty, I might not pass it politely as we would do, but politely throw it twirling across the mats at the tapo.

My most grievous mistake while at the islands was made on a nag, which, inspired by a bit of good road, must needs break into a smart trot through a village. I was instantly hailed by the chief's deputy, who in an angry voice brought me to a halt. Perceiving that I was in trouble, I made signs for pardon, the safest thing to do, though I did not know what offense I had committed. My interpreter coming up, however, put me right, but not until a long palaver had ensued. The deputy's hail, liberally translated, was: "Ahoy, there, on the frantic steed! Know you not that it is against the law to ride thus through the village of our fathers?" I made what apologies I could, and offered to dismount

The Spray's course from the Strait of Magellan to Torres Strait.

The Spray's course from Australia to South Africa.

and, like my servant, lead my nag by the bridle.
This, the interpreter told me, would also be a
grievous wrong, and so I again begged for pardon.
I was summoned to appear before a chief; but my
interpreter, being a wit as well as a bit of a rogue,
explained that I was myself something of a chief,
and should not be detained, being on a most important mission. In my own behalf I could only
say that I was a stranger, but, pleading all this, I
knew I still deserved to be roasted, at which the
chief showed a fine row of teeth and seemed
pleased, but allowed me to pass on.

The chief of the Tongas and his family at Caini,
returning my visit, brought presents of tapa-cloth
and fruits. Taloa, the princess, brought a bottle
of cocoanut-oil for my hair, which another man
might have regarded as coming late.

It was impossible to entertain on the *Spray* after
the royal manner in which I had been received by
the chief. His fare had included all that the land
could afford, fruits, fowl, fishes, and flesh, a hog
having been roasted whole. I set before them
boiled salt pork and salt beef, with which I was
well supplied, and in the evening took them all to
a new amusement in the town, a rocking-horse
merry-go-round, which they called a "kee-kee,"
meaning theater; and in a spirit of justice they
pulled off the horses' tails, for the proprietors of
the show, two hard-fisted countrymen of mine, I
grieve to say, unceremoniously hustled them off
for a new set, almost at the first spin. I was not a
little proud of my Tonga friends; the chief, finest
of them all, carried a portentous club. As for the

theater, through the greed of the proprietors it was becoming unpopular, and the representatives of the three great powers, in want of laws which they could enforce, adopted a vigorous foreign policy, taxing it twenty-five per cent. on the gate-money. This was considered a great stroke of legislative reform!

It was the fashion of the native visitors to the *Spray* to come over the bows, where they could reach the head-gear and climb aboard with ease, and on going ashore to jump off the stern and swim away; nothing could have been more delightfully simple. The modest natives wore *lava-lava* bathing-dresses, a native cloth from the bark of the mulberry-tree, and they did no harm to the *Spray*. In summer-land Samoa their coming and going was only a merry every-day scene.

One day the head teachers of Papauta College, Miss Schultze and Miss Moore, came on board with their ninety-seven young women students. They were all dressed in white, and each wore a red rose, and of course came in boats or canoes in the cold-climate style. A merrier bevy of girls it would be difficult to find. As soon as they got on deck, by request of one of the teachers, they sang "The Watch on the Rhine," which I had never heard before. "And now," said they all, "let's up anchor and away." But I had no inclination to sail from Samoa so soon. On leaving the *Spray* these accomplished young women each seized a palm-branch or paddle, or whatever else would serve the purpose, and literally paddled her own canoe. Each could have swum as readily, and would have done so, I dare say, had it not been for the holiday muslin.

It was not uncommon at Apia to see a young woman swimming alongside a small canoe with a passenger for the *Spray*. Mr. Trood, an old Eton boy, came in this manner to see me, and he exclaimed, " Was ever king ferried in such state ? " Then, suiting his action to the sentiment, he gave the damsel pieces of silver till the natives watching on shore yelled with envy. My own canoe, a small dugout, one day when it had rolled over with me, was seized by a party of fair bathers, and before I could get my breath, almost, was towed around and around the *Spray*, while I sat in the bottom of it, wondering what they would do next. But in this case there were six of them, three on a side, and I could not help myself. One of the sprites, I remember, was a young English lady, who made more sport of it than any of the others.

CHAPTER XIII

AT Apia I had the pleasure of meeting Mr. A.
Young, the father of the late Queen Margaret,
who was Queen of Manua from 1891 to 1895. Her
grandfather was an English sailor who married a princess. Mr. Young is now the only sur-
vivor of the family, two of his children, the last of
them all, having been lost in an island trader which
a few months before had sailed, never to return.
Mr. Young was a Christian gentleman, and his
daughter Margaret was accomplished in graces
that would become any lady. It was with pain
that I saw in the newspapers a sensational account
of her life and death, taken evidently from a paper
in the supposed interest of a benevolent society,
but without foundation in fact. And the startling
head-lines saying, "Queen Margaret of Manua is
dead," could hardly be called news in 1898, the
queen having then been dead three years.

While hobnobbing, as it were, with royalty, I
called on the king himself, the late Malietoa. King

Malietoa was a great ruler; he never got less than forty-five dollars a month for the job, as he told me himself, and this amount had lately been raised, so that he could live on the fat of the land and not any longer be called " Tin-of-salmon Malietoa" by graceless beach-combers.

As my interpreter and I entered the front door of the palace, the king's brother, who was viceroy, sneaked in through a taro-patch by the back way, and sat cowering by the door while I told my story to the king. Mr. W—— of New York, a gentleman interested in missionary work, had charged me, when I sailed, to give his remembrance to the king of the Cannibal Islands, other islands of course being meant; but the good King Malietoa, notwithstanding that his people have not eaten a missionary in a hundred years, received the message himself, and seemed greatly pleased to hear so directly from the publishers of the " Missionary Review," and wished me to make his compliments in return. His Majesty then excused himself, while I talked with his daughter, the beautiful Faamu-Sami (a name signifying " To make the sea burn "), and soon reappeared in the full-dress uniform of the German commander-in-chief, Emperor William himself; for, stupidly enough, I had not sent my credentials ahead that the king might be in full regalia to receive me. Calling a few days later to say good-by to Faamu-Sami, I saw King Malietoa for the last time.

Of the landmarks in the pleasant town of Apia, my memory rests first on the little school just back of the London Missionary Society coffee-house and

reading-rooms, where Mrs. Bell taught English to
about a hundred native children, boys and girls.
Brighter children you will not find anywhere.

"Now, children," said Mrs. Bell, when I called
one day, "let us show the captain that we know
something about the Cape Horn he passed in the
Spray," at which a lad of nine or ten years stepped
nimbly forward and read Basil Hall's fine description of the great cape, and read it well. He afterward copied the essay for me in a clear hand.

Calling to say good-by to my friends at Vailima,
I met Mrs. Stevenson in her Panama hat, and
went over the estate with her. Men were at work
clearing the land, and to one of them she gave an
order to cut a couple of bamboo-trees for the
Spray from a clump she had planted four years
before, and which had grown to the height of sixty
feet. I used them for spare spars, and the butt of
one made a serviceable jib-boom on the homeward
voyage. I had then only to take ava with the
family and be ready for sea. This ceremony, important among Samoans, was conducted after the
native fashion. A Triton horn was sounded to
let us know when the beverage was ready, and in
response we all clapped hands. The bout being in
honor of the *Spray*, it was my turn first, after the
custom of the country, to spill a little over my
shoulder; but having forgotten the Samoan for
"Let the gods drink," I repeated the equivalent in
Russian and Chinook, as I remembered a word in
each, whereupon Mr. Osbourne pronounced me a
confirmed Samoan. Then I said "Tofah!" to my
good friends of Samoa, and all wishing the *Spray*

bon voyage, she stood out of the harbor August 20,
1896, and continued on her course. A sense of
loneliness seized upon me as the islands faded
astern, and as a remedy for it I crowded on sail
for lovely Australia, which was not a strange land
to me; but for long days in my dreams Vailima
stood before the prow.

The *Spray* had barely cleared the islands when a
sudden burst of the trades brought her down to
close reefs, and she reeled off one hundred and
eighty-four miles the first day, of which I counted
forty miles of current in her favor. Finding a
rough sea, I swung her off free and sailed north
of the Horn Islands, also north of Fiji instead of
south, as I had intended, and coasted down the west
side of the archipelago. Thence I sailed direct for
New South Wales, passing south of New Caledonia,
and arrived at Newcastle after a passage of forty-
two days, mostly of storms and gales.

One particularly severe gale encountered near
New Caledonia foundered the American clipper-
ship *Patrician* farther south. Again, nearer the
coast of Australia, when, however, I was not aware
that the gale was extraordinary, a French mail-
steamer from New Caledonia for Sydney, blown
considerably out of her course, on her arrival reported it an awful storm, and to inquiring friends
said: "Oh, my! we don't know what has become
of the little sloop *Spray*. We saw her in the thick
of the storm." The *Spray* was all right, lying to
like a duck. She was under a goose's wing mainsail,
and had had a dry deck while the passengers on
the steamer, I heard later, were up to their knees

in water in the saloon.   When their ship arrived at
Sydney they gave the captain a purse of gold for
his skill and seamanship in bringing them safe into
port.   The captain of the *Spray* got nothing of this
sort.   In this gale I made the land about Seal
Rocks, where the steamship *Catherton*, with many
lives, was lost a short time before.   I was many
hours off the rocks, beating back and forth, but
weathered them at last.

I arrived at Newcastle in the teeth of a gale of
wind.   It was a stormy season.   The government
pilot, Captain Cumming, met me at the harbor bar,
and with the assistance of a steamer carried my vessel to a safe berth.   Many visitors came on board,
the first being the United States consul, Mr. Brown.
Nothing was too good for the *Spray* here.   All
government dues were remitted, and after I had
rested a few days a port pilot with a tug carried
her to sea again, and she made along the coast
toward the harbor of Sydney, where she arrived on
the following day, October 10, 1896.

I came to in a snug cove near Manly for the
night, the Sydney harbor police-boat giving me a
pluck into anchorage while they gathered data
from an old scrap-book of mine, which seemed to
interest them.   Nothing escapes the vigilance of
the New South Wales police; their reputation is
known the world over.   They made a shrewd guess
that I could give them some useful information,
and they were the first to meet me.   Some one said
they came to arrest me, and — well, let it go at that.

Summer was approaching, and the harbor of
Sydney was blooming with yachts.   Some of them

The accident at Sydney.

came down to the weather-beaten *Spray* and sailed
round her at Shelcote, where she took a berth for a
few days.   At Sydney I was at once among friends.

The *Spray* remained at the various watering-places in the great port for several weeks, and was visited by many agreeable people, frequently by officers of H. M. S. *Orlando* and their friends. Captain Fisher, the commander, with a party of young ladies from the city and gentlemen belonging to his ship, came one day to pay me a visit in the midst of a deluge of rain. I never saw it rain harder even in Australia. But they were out for fun, and rain could not dampen their feelings, however hard it poured. But, as ill luck would have it, a young gentleman of another party on board, in the full uniform of a very great yacht club, with brass buttons enough to sink him, stepping quickly to get out of the wet, tumbled holus-bolus, head and heels, into a barrel of water I had been coopering, and being a short man, was soon out of sight, and nearly drowned before he was rescued. It was the nearest to a casualty on the *Spray* in her whole course, so far as I know. The young man having come on board with compliments made the mishap most embarrassing. It had been decided by his club that the *Spray* could not be officially recognized, for the reason that she brought no letters from yacht-clubs in America, and so I say it seemed all the more embarrassing and strange that I should have caught at least one of the members, in a barrel, and, too, when I was not fishing for yachtsmen.

The typical Sydney boat is a handy sloop of great beam and enormous sail-carrying power; but a capsize is not uncommon, for they carry sail like vikings. In Sydney I saw all manner of craft, from the smart steam-launch and sailing-cutter to

the smaller sloop and canoe pleasuring on the bay.
Everybody owned a boat. If a boy in Australia
has not the means to buy him a boat he builds one,
and it is usually one not to be ashamed of. The
Spray shed her Joseph's coat, the Fuego mainsail,
in Sydney, and wearing a new suit, the handsome
present of Commodore Foy, she was flagship of the
Johnstone's Bay Flying Squadron when the circumnavigators of Sydney harbor sailed in their
annual regatta. They "recognized" the *Spray* as
belonging to "a club of her own," and with more
Australian sentiment than fastidiousness gave her
credit for her record.

Time flew fast those days in Australia, and it
was December 6, 1896, when the *Spray* sailed from
Sydney. My intention was now to sail around
Cape Leeuwin direct for Mauritius on my way
home, and so I coasted along toward Bass Strait in
that direction.

There was little to report on this part of the
voyage, except changeable winds, "busters," and
rough seas. The 12th of December, however, was
an exceptional day, with a fine coast wind, northeast. The *Spray* early in the morning passed
Twofold Bay and later Cape Bundooro in a smooth
sea with land close aboard. The lighthouse on the
cape dipped a flag to the *Spray's* flag, and children
on the balconies of a cottage near the shore waved
handkerchiefs as she passed by. There were only
a few people all told on the shore, but the scene
was a happy one. I saw festoons of evergreen in
token of Christmas, near at hand. I saluted the
merrymakers, wishing them a "Merry Christmas,"

and could hear them say, "I wish you the same."

From Cape Bundooro I passed by Cliff Island in Bass Strait, and exchanged signals with the light-keepers while the *Spray* worked up under the island. The wind howled that day while the sea broke over their rocky home.

A few days later, December 17, the *Spray* came in close under Wilson's Promontory, again seeking shelter. The keeper of the light at that station, Mr. J. Clark, came on board and gave me directions for Waterloo Bay, about three miles to leeward, for which I bore up at once, finding good anchorage there in a sandy cove protected from all westerly and northerly winds.

Anchored here was the ketch *Secret*, a fisherman, and the *Mary* of Sydney, a steam ferry-boat fitted for whaling. The captain of the *Mary* was a genius, and an Australian genius at that, and smart. His crew, from a sawmill up the coast, had not one of them seen a live whale when they shipped; but they were boatmen after an Australian's own heart, and the captain had told them that to kill a whale was no more than to kill a rabbit. They believed him, and that settled it. As luck would have it, the very first one they saw on their cruise, although an ugly humpback, was a dead whale in no time, Captain Young, the master of the *Mary*, killing the monster at a single thrust of a harpoon. It was taken in tow for Sydney, where they put it on exhibition. Nothing but whales interested the crew of the gallant *Mary*, and they spent most of their time here gathering fuel along shore for a cruise on the grounds off Tasmania. Whenever the word "whale" was mentioned in the hearing of these men their eyes glistened with excitement.

Captain Slocum working the *Spray* out of the Yarrow River, a part of Melbourne harbor.

We spent three days in the quiet cove, listening to the wind outside. Meanwhile Captain Young and I explored the shores, visited abandoned miners' pits, and prospected for gold ourselves.

Our vessels, parting company the morning they sailed, stood away like sea-birds each on its own course. The wind for a few days was moderate,

and, with unusual luck of fine weather, the *Spray*
made Melbourne Heads on the 22d of December,
and, taken in tow by the steam-tug *Racer*, was
brought into port.

Christmas day was spent at a berth in the river
Yarrow, but I lost little time in shifting to St. Kilda,
where I spent nearly a month.

The *Spray* paid no port charges in Australia or
anywhere else on the voyage, except at Pernambuco,
till she poked her nose into the custom-house at
Melbourne, where she was charged tonnage dues; in
this instance, sixpence a ton on the gross. The collector exacted six shillings and sixpence, taking off
nothing for the fraction under thirteen tons, her
exact gross being 12.70 tons. I squared the matter
by charging people sixpence each for coming on
board, and when this business got dull I caught a
shark and charged them sixpence each to look at
that. The shark was twelve feet six inches in
length, and carried a progeny of twenty-six, not
one of them less than two feet in length. A slit
of a knife let them out in a canoe full of water,
which, changed constantly, kept them alive one
whole day. In less than an hour from the time I
heard of the ugly brute it was on deck and on exhibition, with rather more than the amount of the
Spray's tonnage dues already collected. Then I
hired a good Irishman, Tom Howard by name,—
who knew all about sharks, both on the land and
in the sea, and could talk about them,— to answer
questions and lecture. When I found that I could
not keep abreast of the questions I turned the re-
sponsibility over to him.

THOMAS FOGARTY.

The shark on the deck of the *Spray*.

Returning from the bank, where I had been to deposit money early in the day, I found Howard in the midst of a very excited crowd, telling imaginary habits of the fish. It was a good show; the people wished to see it, and it was my wish that they should; but owing to his over-stimulated enthusiasm, I was obliged to let Howard resign. The income from the show and the proceeds of the tallow I had gathered in the Strait of Magellan, the last of which I had disposed of to a German soap-boiler at Samoa, put me in ample funds.

January 24, 1897, found the *Spray* again in tow of the tug *Racer*, leaving Hobson's Bay after a pleasant time in Melbourne and St. Kilda, which had been protracted by a succession of southwest winds that seemed never-ending.

In the summer months, that is, December, January, February, and sometimes March, east winds are prevalent through Bass Strait and round Cape Leeuwin; but owing to a vast amount of ice drifting up from the Antarctic, this was all changed now and emphasized with much bad weather, so much so that I considered it impracticable to pursue the course farther. Therefore, instead of thrashing round cold and stormy Cape Leeuwin, I decided to spend a pleasanter and more profitable time in Tasmania, waiting for the season for favorable winds through Torres Strait, by way of the Great Barrier Reef, the route I finally decided on. To sail this course would be taking advantage of anticyclones, which never fail, and besides it would give me the chance to put foot on the shores of Tasmania, round which I had sailed years before.

I should mention that while I was at Melbourne there occurred one of those extraordinary storms sometimes called "rain of blood," the first of the kind in many years about Australia. The "blood" came from a fine brick-dust matter afloat in the air from the deserts. A rain-storm setting in brought down this dust simply as mud; it fell in such quantities that a bucketful was collected from the sloop's awnings, which were spread at the time. When the wind blew hard and I was obliged to furl awnings, her sails, unprotected on the booms, got mud-stained from clue to earing.

The phenomena of dust-storms, well understood by scientists, are not uncommon on the coast of Africa. Reaching some distance out over the sea, they frequently cover the track of ships, as in the case of the one through which the *Spray* passed in the earlier part of her voyage. Sailors no longer regard them with superstitious fear, but our credulous brothers on the land cry out "Rain of blood!" at the first splash of the awful mud.

The rip off Port Phillip Heads, a wild place, was rough when the *Spray* entered Hobson's Bay from the sea, and was rougher when she stood out. But, with sea-room and under sail, she made good weather immediately after passing it. It was only a few hours' sail to Tasmania across the strait, the wind being fair and blowing hard. I carried the St. Kilda shark along, stuffed with hay, and disposed of it to Professor Porter, the curator of the Victoria Museum of Launceston, which is at the

Larson, photo.

On board at St. Kilda. Retracing on the chart the course of the *Spray* from Boston.

head of the Tamar. For many a long day to come may be seen there the shark of St. Kilda. Alas! the good but mistaken people of St. Kilda, when the illustrated journals with pictures of my shark reached their news-stands, flew into a passion, and swept all papers containing mention of fish into the fire; for St. Kilda was a watering-place — and the idea of a shark *there!* But my show went on.

The *Spray* was berthed on the beach at a small jetty at Launceston while the tide driven in by the gale that brought her up the river was unusually high; and she lay there hard and fast, with not enough water around her at any time after to wet one's feet till she was ready to sail; then, to float her, the ground was dug from under her keel.

In this snug place I left her in charge of three children, while I made journeys among the hills and rested my bones, for the coming voyage, on the moss-covered rocks at the gorge hard by, and among the ferns I found wherever I went. My vessel was well taken care of. I never returned without finding that the decks had been washed and that one of the children, my nearest neighbor's little girl from across the road, was at the gangway attending to visitors, while the others, a brother and sister, sold marine curios such as were in the cargo, on "ship's account." They were a bright, cheerful crew, and people came a long way to hear them tell the story of the voyage, and of the monsters of the deep "the captain had slain." I had only to keep myself away to be a hero of the first water; and it suited me very well to do so and to rusticate in the forests and among the streams.

CHAPTER XIV

A testimonial from a lady — Cruising round Tasmania — The skipper
delivers his first lecture on the voyage — Abundant provisions —
An inspection of the *Spray* for safety at Devonport — Again at
Sydney — Northward bound for Torres Strait — An amateur ship-
wreck — Friends on the Australian coast — Perils of a coral sea.

FEBRUARY 1, 1897, on returning to my vessel
I found waiting for me the letter of sympathy
which I subjoin:

A lady sends Mr. Slocum the inclosed five-pound note
as a token of her appreciation of his bravery in crossing
the wide seas on so small a boat, and all alone, without
human sympathy to help when danger threatened. All
success to you.

To this day I do not know who wrote it or to
whom I am indebted for the generous gift it con-
tained. I could not refuse a thing so kindly meant,
but promised myself to pass it on with interest at
the first opportunity, and this I did before leaving
Australia.

The season of fair weather around the north of
Australia being yet a long way off, I sailed to other
ports in Tasmania, where it is fine the year round,
the first of these being Beauty Point, near which
are Beaconsfield and the great Tasmania gold-mine,
which I visited in turn. I saw much gray, unin-

teresting rock being hoisted out of the mine there, and hundreds of stamps crushing it into powder. People told me there was gold in it, and I believed what they said.

I remember Beauty Point for its shady forest and for the road among the tall gum-trees. While there the governor of New South Wales, Lord Hampden, and his family came in on a steam-yacht, sight-seeing. The *Spray*, anchored near the landing-pier, threw her bunting out, of course, and probably a more insignificant craft bearing the Stars and Stripes was never seen in those waters. However, the governor's party seemed to know why it floated there, and all about the *Spray*, and when I heard his Excellency say, "Introduce me to the captain," or "Introduce the captain to me," whichever it was, I found myself at once in the presence of a gentleman and a friend, and one greatly interested in my voyage. If any one of the party was more interested than the governor himself, it was the Honorable Margaret, his daughter. On leaving, Lord and Lady Hampden promised to rendezvous with me on board the *Spray* at the Paris Exposition in 1900. "If we live," they said, and I added, for my part, "Dangers of the seas excepted."

From Beauty Point the *Spray* visited George-town, near the mouth of the river Tamar. This little settlement, I believe, marks the place where the first footprints were made by whites in Tasmania, though it never grew to be more than a hamlet.

Considering that I had seen something of the

world, and finding people here interested in adventure, I talked the matter over before my first audience in a little hall by the country road. A piano having been brought in from a neighbor's, I was helped out by the severe thumping it got, and by a "Tommy Atkins" song from a strolling comedian. People came from a great distance, and the attendance all told netted the house about three pounds sterling. The owner of the hall, a kind lady from Scotland, would take no rent, and so my lecture from the start was a success.

From this snug little place I made sail for Devonport, a thriving place on the river Mersey, a few hours' sail westward along the coast, and fast becoming the most important port in Tasmania. Large steamers enter there now and carry away great cargoes of farm produce, but the *Spray* was the first vessel to bring the Stars and Stripes to the port, the harbor-master, Captain Murray, told me, and so it is written in the port records. For the great distinction the *Spray* enjoyed many civilities while she rode comfortably at anchor in her port-duster awning that covered her from stem to stern.

From the magistrate's house, "Malunnah," on the point, she was saluted by the Jack both on coming in and on going out, and dear Mrs. Aikenhead, the mistress of Malunnah, supplied the *Spray* with jams and jellies of all sorts, by the case, prepared from the fruits of her own rich garden — enough to last all the way home and to spare. Mrs. Wood, farther up the harbor, put up bottles of raspberry wine for me. At this point, more than ever before, I was in the land of good cheer. Mrs. Powell sent on board

chutney prepared " as we prepare it in India." Fish
and game were plentiful here, and the voice of the
gobbler was heard, and from Pardo, farther up the
country, came an enormous cheese; and yet people

The *Spray* in her port duster at Devonport, Tasmania,
February 22, 1897.

inquire: " What did you live on? What did you
eat?"

I was haunted by the beauty of the landscape all
about, of the natural ferneries then disappearing,
and of the domed forest-trees on the slopes, and
was fortunate in meeting a gentleman intent on

preserving in art the beauties of his country. He presented me with many reproductions from his collection of pictures, also many originals, to show to my friends.

By another gentleman I was charged to tell the glories of Tasmania in every land and on every occasion. This was Dr. McCall, M. L. C. The doctor gave me useful hints on lecturing. It was not without misgivings, however, that I filled away on this new course, and I am free to say that it is only by the kindness of sympathetic audiences that my oratorical bark was held on even keel. Soon after my first talk the kind doctor came to me with words of approval. As in many other of my enterprises, I had gone about it at once and without second thought. " Man, man," said he, " great nervousness is only a sign of brain, and the more brain a man has the longer it takes him to get over the affliction; but," he added reflectively, " you will get over it." However, in my own behalf I think it only fair to say that I am not yet entirely cured.

The *Spray* was hauled out on the marine railway at Devonport and examined carefully top and bottom, but was found absolutely free from the destructive teredo, and sound in all respects. To protect her further against the ravage of these insects the bottom was coated once more with copper paint, for she would have to sail through the Coral and Arafura seas before refitting again. Everything was done to fit her for all the known dangers. But it was not without regret that I looked forward to the day of sailing from a country of so many pleasant associations. If there was a moment in my voyage when I could have given it up, it was there and then; but no vacancies for a better post being open, I weighed anchor April 16, 1897, and again put to sea.

The season of summer was then over; winter was rolling up from the south, with fair winds for the north. A foretaste of winter wind sent the *Spray* flying round Cape Howe and as far as Cape Bundooro farther along, which she passed on the following day, retracing her course northward. This was a fine run, and boded good for the long voyage home from the antipodes. My old Christmas friends on Bundooro seemed to be up and moving when I came the second time by their cape, and we exchanged signals again, while the sloop sailed along as before in a smooth sea and close to the shore.

The weather was fine, with clear sky the rest of the passage to Port Jackson (Sydney), where the *Spray* arrived April 22, 1897, and anchored in Watson's Bay, near the heads, in eight fathoms of water. The harbor from the heads to Parramatta, up the river, was more than ever alive with boats and yachts of every class. It was, indeed, a scene of animation, hardly equaled in any other part of the world.

A few days later the bay was flecked with tempestuous waves, and none but stout ships carried sail. I was in a neighboring hotel then, nursing a neuralgia which I had picked up alongshore, and had only that moment got a glance of just the stern of a large, unmanageable steamship passing the range of my window as she forged in by the point, when the bell-boy burst into my room shouting that the *Spray* had "gone bung." I tumbled out quickly, to learn that "bung" meant that a large steamship had run into her, and that it was the one of which I saw the stern, the other end of her having hit the *Spray*. It turned out, however, that no damage was done beyond the loss of an anchor and chain, which from the shock of the collision had parted at the hawse. I had nothing at all to complain of, though, in the end, for the captain, after he clubbed his ship, took the *Spray* in tow up the harbor, clear of all dangers, and sent her back again, in charge of an officer and three men, to her anchorage in the bay, with a polite note saying he would repair any damages done. But what yawing about she made of it when she came with a stranger at the helm! Her old friend the pilot of the *Pinta* would not have been guilty of such lubberly work. But to my great delight they got her into a berth, and the neuralgia left me then, or was forgotten. The captain of the steamer, like a true seaman, kept his word, and his agent, Mr. Collishaw handed me on the very next day the price of the lost anchor and chain, with something over for anxiety of mind. I remember that he offered me twelve pounds at once; but my lucky number being thirteen, we made the amount thirteen pounds, which squared all accounts.

I sailed again, May 9, before a strong southwest wind, which sent the *Spray* gallantly on as far as Port Stevens, where it fell calm and then came up ahead; but the weather was fine, and so remained for many days, which was a great change from the state of the weather experienced here some months before.

Having a full set of admiralty sheet-charts of the coast and Barrier Reef, I felt easy in mind. Captain Fisher, R. N., who had steamed through the Barrier passages in H. M. S. *Orlando,* advised me from the first to take this route, and I did not regret coming back to it now.

The wind, for a few days after passing Port Stevens, Seal Rocks, and Cape Hawk, was light and dead ahead; but these points are photographed on my memory from the trial of beating round them some months before when bound the other way. But now, with a good stock of books on board, I fell to reading day and night, leaving this pleasant occupation merely to trim sails or tack, or to lie down and rest, while the *Spray* nibbled at the miles. I tried to compare my state with that of old circumnavigators, who sailed exactly over the route which I took from Cape Verde Islands or farther back to this point and beyond, but there was no comparison so far as I had got. Their hardships and romantic escapes — those of them who escaped death and worse sufferings — did not enter into my experience, sailing all alone around the world. For me is left to tell only of pleasant experiences, till finally my adventures are prosy and tame.

I had just finished reading some of the most interesting of the old voyages in woe-begone ships, and was already near Port Macquarie, on my own cruise, when I made out, May 13, a modern dandy craft in distress, anchored on the coast. Standing in for her, I found that she was the cutter-yacht *Akbar*,[1] which had sailed from Watson's Bay about

" ' Is it a-goin' to blow ? ' "

three days ahead of the *Spray*, and that she had run at once into trouble. No wonder she did so.

[1] *Akbar* was not her registered name, which need not be told.

It was a case of babes in the wood or butterflies at sea. Her owner, on his maiden voyage, was all duck trousers; the captain, distinguished for the enormous yachtsman's cap he wore, was a Murrumbidgee [1] whaler before he took command of the *Akbar;* and the navigating officer, poor fellow, was almost as deaf as a post, and nearly as stiff and immovable as a post in the ground. These three jolly tars comprised the crew. None of them knew more about the sea or about a vessel than a newly born babe knows about another world. They were bound for New Guinea, so they said; perhaps it was as well that three tenderfeet so tender as those never reached that destination.

The owner, whom I had met before he sailed, wanted to race the poor old *Spray* to Thursday Island en route. I declined the challenge, naturally, on the ground of the unfairness of three young yachtsmen in a clipper against an old sailor all alone in a craft of coarse build; besides that, I would not on any account race in the Coral Sea.

"*Spray* ahoy!" they all hailed now. "What 's the weather goin' t' be? Is it a-goin' to blow? And don't you think we 'd better go back t' r-r-refit?"

I thought, "If ever you get back, don't refit," but I said: "Give me the end of a rope, and I 'll tow you into yon port farther along; and on your lives," I urged, "do not go back round Cape Hawk, for it 's winter to the south of it."

They purposed making for Newcastle under jury-

[1] The Murrumbidgee is a small river winding among the mountains of Australia, and would be the last place in which to look for a whale.

sails; for their mainsail had been blown to ribbons, even the jigger had been blown away, and her rigging flew at loose ends. The *Akbar*, in a word, was a wreck.

"Up anchor," I shouted, "up anchor, and let me tow you into Port Macquarie, twelve miles north of this."

"No," cried the owner; "we 'll go back to Newcastle. We missed Newcastle on the way coming; we did n't see the light, and it was not thick, either." This he shouted very loud, ostensibly for my hearing, but closer even than necessary, I thought, to the ear of the navigating officer. Again I tried to persuade them to be towed into the port of refuge so near at hand. It would have cost them only the trouble of weighing their anchor and passing me a rope; of this I assured them, but they declined even this, in sheer ignorance of a rational course.

"What is your depth of water?" I asked.

"Don't know; we lost our lead. All the chain is out. We sounded with the anchor."

"Send your dinghy over, and I 'll give you a lead."

"We 've lost our dinghy, too," they cried.

"God is good, else you would have lost yourselves," and "Farewell" was all I could say.

The trifling service proffered by the *Spray* would have saved their vessel.

"Report us," they cried, as I stood on — "report us with sails blown away, and that we don't care a dash and are not afraid."

"Then there is no hope for you," and again "Farewell."

I promised I would report them, and did so at the first opportunity, and out of humane reasons I do so again. On the following day I spoke the steamship *Sherman*, bound down the coast, and reported the yacht in distress and that it would be an act of humanity to tow her somewhere away from her exposed position on an open coast. That she did not get a tow from the steamer was from no lack of funds to pay the bill; for the owner, lately heir to a few hundred pounds, had the money with him. The proposed voyage to New Guinea was to look that island over with a view to its purchase. It was about eighteen days before I heard of the *Akbar* again, which was on the 31st of May, when I reached Cooktown, on the Endeavor River, where I found this news:

May 31, the yacht *Akbar*, from Sydney for New Guinea, three hands on board, lost at Crescent Head; the crew saved.

So it took them several days to lose the yacht, after all.

After speaking the distressed *Akbar* and the *Sherman*, the voyage for many days was uneventful save in the pleasant incident on May 16 of a chat by signal with the people on South Solitary Island, a dreary stone heap in the ocean just off the coast of New South Wales, in latitude 30° 12′ south.

"What vessel is that?" they asked, as the sloop came abreast of their island. For answer I tried them with the Stars and Stripes at the peak. Down came their signals at once, and up went the

British ensign instead, which they dipped heartily. I understood from this that they made out my vessel and knew all about her, for they asked no more questions. They did n't even ask if the "voyage would pay," but they threw out this friendly message, "Wishing you a pleasant voyage," which at that very moment I was having.

May 19 the *Spray*, passing the Tweed River, was signaled from Danger Point, where those on shore seemed most anxious about the state of my health, for they asked if "all hands" were well, to which I could say, "Yes."

On the following day the *Spray* rounded Great Sandy Cape, and, what is a notable event in every voyage, picked up the trade-winds, and these winds followed her now for many thousands of miles, never ceasing to blow from a moderate gale to a mild summer breeze, except at rare intervals.

From the pitch of the cape was a noble light seen twenty-seven miles; passing from this to Lady Elliott Light, which stands on an island as a sentinel at the gateway of the Barrier Reef, the *Spray* was at once in the fairway leading north. Poets have sung of beacon-light and of pharos, but did ever poet behold a great light flash up before his path on a dark night in the midst of a coral sea? If so, he knew the meaning of his song.

The *Spray* had sailed for hours in suspense, evidently stemming a current. Almost mad with doubt, I grasped the helm to throw her head off shore, when blazing out of the sea was the light ahead. "Excalibur!" cried "all hands," and rejoiced, and sailed on. The *Spray* was now in a protected sea and smooth water, the first she had dipped her keel into since leaving Gibraltar, and a change it was from the heaving of the misnamed "Pacific" Ocean.

The Pacific is perhaps, upon the whole, no more boisterous than other oceans, though I feel quite safe in saying that it is not more pacific except in name. It is often wild enough in one part or another. I once knew a writer who, after saying beautiful things about the sea, passed through a Pacific hurricane, and he became a changed man. But where, after all, would be the poetry of the sea were there no wild waves? At last here was the *Spray* in the midst of a sea of coral. The sea itself might be called smooth indeed, but coral rocks are always rough, sharp, and dangerous. I trusted now to the mercies of the Maker of all reefs, keeping a good lookout at the same time for perils on every hand.

Lo! the Barrier Reef and the waters of many colors studded all about with enchanted islands! I behold among them after all many safe harbors, else my vision is astray. On the 24th of May, the sloop, having made one hundred and ten miles a day from Danger Point, now entered Whitsunday Pass, and that night sailed through among the islands. When the sun rose next morning I looked back and regretted having gone by while it was dark, for the scenery far astern was varied and charming.

CHAPTER XV

ON the morning of the 26th Gloucester Island was close aboard, and the *Spray* anchored in the evening at Port Denison, where rests, on a hill, the sweet little town of Bowen, the future watering place and health-resort of Queensland. The country all about here had a healthful appearance.

The harbor was easy of approach, spacious and safe, and afforded excellent holding-ground. It was quiet in Bowen when the *Spray* arrived, and the good people with an hour to throw away on the second evening of her arrival came down to the School of Arts to talk about the voyage, it being the latest event. It was duly advertised in the two little papers, "Boomerang" and "Nully Nully," in the one the day before the affair came off, and in the other the day after, which was all the same to the editor, and, for that matter, it was the same to me.

Besides this, circulars were distributed with a flourish, and the "best bellman" in Australia was employed. But I could have keelhauled the wretch, bell and all, when he came to the door of the little hotel where my prospective audience and I were dining, and with his clattering bell and fiendish yell made noises that would awake the dead, all over the voyage of the *Spray* from "Boston to Bowen, the two Hubs in the cart-wheels of creation," as the "Boomerang" afterward said.

Mr. Myles, magistrate, harbor-master, land commissioner, gold warden, etc., was chairman, and introduced me, for what reason I never knew, except to embarrass me with a sense of vain ostentation and embitter my life, for Heaven knows I had met every person in town the first hour ashore. I knew them all by name now, and they all knew me. However, Mr. Myles was a good talker. Indeed, I tried to induce him to go on and tell the story while I showed the pictures, but this he refused to do. I may explain that it was a talk illustrated by stereopticon. The views were good, but the lantern, a thirty-shilling affair, was wretched, and had only an oil-lamp in it.

I sailed early the next morning before the papers came out, thinking it best to do so. They each appeared with a favorable column, however, of what they called a lecture, so I learned afterward, and they had a kind word for the bellman besides.

From Port Denison the sloop ran before the constant trade-wind, and made no stop at all, night or day, till she reached Cooktown, on the Endeavor River, where she arrived Monday, May 31, 1897, before a furious blast of wind encountered that day fifty miles down the coast. On this parallel of latitude is the high ridge and backbone of the trade-winds, which about Cooktown amount often to a hard gale.

I had been charged to navigate the route with extra care, and to feel my way over the ground. The skilled officer of the royal navy who advised me to take the Barrier Reef passage wrote me that H. M. S. *Orlando* steamed nights as well as days through it, but that I, under sail, would jeopardize my vessel on coral reefs if I undertook to do so.

Confidentially, it would have been no easy matter finding anchorage every night. The hard work, too, of getting the sloop under way every morning was finished, I had hoped, when she cleared the Strait of Magellan. Besides that, the best of admiralty charts made it possible to keep on sailing night and day. Indeed, with a fair wind, and in the clear weather of that season, the way through the Barrier Reef Channel, in all sincerity, was clearer than a highway in a busy city, and by all odds less dangerous. But to any one contemplating the voyage I would say, beware of reefs day or night, or, remaining on the land, be wary still.

"The *Spray* came flying into port like a bird," said the longshore daily papers of Cooktown the morning after she arrived; "and it seemed strange," they added, "that only one man could be seen on board working the craft." The *Spray* was doing her best, to be sure, for it was near night, and she was in haste to find a perch before dark.

Tacking inside of all the craft in port, I moored her at sunset nearly abreast the Captain Cook monument, and next morning went ashore to

feast my eyes on the very stones the great navigator had seen, for I was now on a seaman's conse-
crated ground.   But there seemed a question in

The *Spray* leaving Sydney, Australia, in the new suit of sails given
by Commodore Foy of Australia.
(From a photograph.)

Cooktown's mind as to the exact spot where his
ship, the *Endeavor*, hove down for repairs on her
memorable voyage around the world.   Some said it
was not at all at the place where the monument

now stood. A discussion of the subject was going
on one morning where I happened to be, and a
young lady present, turning to me as one of some
authority in nautical matters, very flatteringly
asked my opinion. Well, I could see no reason why
Captain Cook, if he made up his mind to repair his
ship inland, could n't have dredged out a channel
to the place where the monument now stood, if he
had a dredging-machine with him, and afterward
fill it up again; for Captain Cook could do 'most
anything, and nobody ever said that he had n't a
dredger along. The young lady seemed to lean to
my way of thinking, and following up the story of
the historical voyage, asked if I had visited the
point farther down the harbor where the great circumnavigator was murdered. This took my breath,
but a bright school-boy coming along relieved my
embarrassment, for, like all boys, seeing that information was wanted, he volunteered to supply it.
Said he: "Captain Cook was n't murdered 'ere at
all, ma'am; 'e was killed in Hafrica: a lion et 'im."

Here I was reminded of distressful days gone
by. I think it was in 1866 that the old steamship
Soushay, from Batavia for Sydney, put in at Cooktown for scurvy-grass, as I always thought, and
"incidentally" to land mails. On her sick-list was
my fevered self; and so I did n't see the place till
I came back on the *Spray* thirty-one years later.
And now I saw coming into port the physical
wrecks of miners from New Guinea, destitute and
dying. Many had died on the way and had been
buried at sea. He would have been a hardened

wretch who could look on and not try to do something for them.

The sympathy of all went out to these sufferers, but the little town was already straitened from a long run on its benevolence. I thought of the matter, of the lady's gift to me at Tasmania, which I had promised myself I would keep only as a loan, but found now, to my embarrassment, that I had invested the money. However, the good Cooktown people wished to hear a story of the sea, and how the crew of the *Spray* fared when illness got aboard of her. Accordingly the little Presbyterian church on the hill was opened for a conversation; everybody talked, and they made a roaring success of it. Judge Chester, the magistrate, was at the head cf the gam, and so it was bound to succeed. He it was who annexed the island of New Guinea to Great Britain. "While I was about it," said he, "I annexed the blooming lot of it." There was a ring in the statement pleasant to the ear of an old voyager. However, the Germans made such a row over the judge's mainsail haul that they got a share in the venture.

Well, I was now indebted to the miners of Cooktown for the great privilege of adding a mite to a worthy cause, and to Judge Chester all the town was indebted for a general good time. The matter standing so, I sailed on June 6, 1897, heading away for the north as before.

Arrived at a very inviting anchorage about sundown, the 7th, I came to, for the night, abreast the Claremont light-ship. This was the only time

throughout the passage of the Barrier Reef Channel that the *Spray* anchored, except at Port Denison
and at Endeavor River. On the very night following this, however (the 8th), I regretted keenly, for
an instant, that I had not anchored before dark, as
I might have done easily under the lee of a coral
reef. It happened in this way. The *Spray* had
just passed M Reef light-ship, and left the light
dipping astern, when, going at full speed, with
sheets off, she hit the M Reef itself on the north
end, where I expected to see a beacon.

She swung off quickly on her heel, however, and
with one more bound on a swell cut across the shoal
point so quickly that I hardly knew how it was
done. The beacon was n't there; at least, I did n't
see it. I had n't time to look for it after she struck,
and certainly it did n't much matter then whether
I saw it or not.

But this gave her a fine departure for Cape
Greenville, the next point ahead. I saw the ugly
boulders under the sloop's keel as she flashed over
them, and I made a mental note of it that the letter
M, for which the reef was named, was the thirteenth
one in our alphabet, and that thirteen, as noted
years before, was still my lucky number. The natives of Cape Greenville are notoriously bad, and I
was advised to give them the go-by. Accordingly,
from M Reef I steered outside of the adjacent islands, to be on the safe side. Skipping along now,
the *Spray* passed Home Island, off the pitch of the
cape, soon after midnight, and squared away on a
westerly course. A short time later she fell in with
a steamer bound south, groping her way in the

dark and making the night dismal with her own black smoke.

From Home Island I made for Sunday Island, and bringing that abeam, shortened sail, not wishing to make Bird Island, farther along, before daylight, the wind being still fresh and the islands being low, with dangers about them. Wednesday, June 9, 1897, at daylight, Bird Island was dead ahead, distant two and a half miles, which I considered near enough. A strong current was pressing the sloop forward. I did not shorten sail too soon in the night! The first and only Australian canoe seen on the voyage was encountered here standing from the mainland, with a rag of sail set, bound for this island.

A long, slim fish that leaped on board in the night was found on deck this morning. I had it for breakfast. The spry chap was no larger around than a herring, which it resembled in every respect, except that it was three times as long; but that was so much the better, for I am rather fond of fresh herring, anyway. A great number of fisher-birds were about this day, which was one of the pleasantest on God's earth. The *Spray*, dancing over the waves, entered Albany Pass as the sun drew low in the west over the hills of Australia.

At 7:30 P.M. the *Spray*, now through the pass, came to anchor in a cove in the mainland, near a pearl-fisherman, called the *Tarawa*, which was at anchor, her captain from the deck of his vessel directing me to a berth. This done, he at once came on board to clasp hands. The *Tarawa* was a Californian, and Captain Jones, her master, was an American.

On the following morning Captain Jones brought on board two pairs of exquisite pearl shells, the most perfect ones I ever saw. They were probably the best he had, for Jones was the heart-yarn of a sailor. He assured me that if I would remain a few hours longer some friends from Somerset, near by, would pay us all a visit, and one of the crew, sorting shells on deck, " guessed " they would. The mate " guessed " so, too. The friends came, as even the second mate and cook had "guessed" they would. They were Mr. Jardine, stockman, famous throughout the land, and his family. Mrs. Jardine was the niece of King Malietoa, and cousin to the beautiful Faamu-Sami ("To make the sea burn "), who visited the *Spray* at Apia. Mr. Jardine was himself a fine specimen of a Scotsman. With his little family about him, he was content to live in this remote place, accumulating the comforts of life.

The fact of the *Tarawa* having been built in America accounted for the crew, boy Jim and all, being such good guessers. Strangely enough, though, Captain Jones himself, the only American aboard, was never heard to guess at all.

After a pleasant chat and good-by to the people of the *Tarawa*, and to Mr. and Mrs. Jardine, I again weighed anchor and stood across for Thursday Island, now in plain view, mid-channel in Torres Strait, where I arrived shortly after noon. Here the *Spray* remained over until June 24. Being the only American representative in port, this tarry

was imperative, for on the 22d was the Queen's
diamond jubilee. The two days over were, as sailors
say, for "coming up."

Meanwhile I spent pleasant days about the island.
Mr. Douglas, resident magistrate, invited me on a
cruise in his steamer one day among the islands in
Torres Strait. This being a scientific expedition
in charge of Professor Mason Bailey, botanist, we
rambled over Friday and Saturday islands, where
I got a glimpse of botany. Miss Bailey, the professor's daughter, accompanied the expedition, and
told me of many indigenous plants with long names.

The 22d was the great day on Thursday Island,
for then we had not only the jubilee, but a jubilee
with a grand corroboree in it, Mr. Douglas having
brought some four hundred native warriors and
their wives and children across from the mainland
to give the celebration the true native touch, for
when they do a thing on Thursday Island they do
it with a roar. The corroboree was, at any rate, a
howling success. It took place at night, and the
performers, painted in fantastic colors, danced or
leaped about before a blazing fire. Some were
rigged and painted like birds and beasts, in which
the emu and kangaroo were well represented. One
fellow leaped like a frog. Some had the human
skeleton painted on their bodies, while they jumped
about threateningly, spear in hand, ready to strike
down some imaginary enemy. The kangaroo
hopped and danced with natural ease and grace,
making a fine figure. All kept time to music, vocal
and instrumental, the instruments (save the mark!)
being bits of wood, which they beat one against

the other, and saucer-like bones, held in the palm
of the hands, which they knocked together, making
a dull sound. It was a show at once amusing,
spectacular, and hideous.

The warrior aborigines that I saw in Queensland
were for the most part lithe and fairly well built,
but they were stamped always with repulsive features, and their women were, if possible, still more
ill favored.

I observed that on the day of the jubilee no foreign flag was waving in the public grounds except
the Stars and Stripes, which along with the Union
Jack guarded the gateway, and floated in many
places, from the tiniest to the standard size. Speaking to Mr. Douglas, I ventured a remark on this
compliment to my country. "Oh," said he, "this
is a family affair, and we do not consider the Stars
and Stripes a foreign flag." The *Spray* of course
flew her best bunting, and hoisted the Jack as well
as her own noble flag as high as she could.

On June 24 the *Spray*, well fitted in every way,
sailed for the long voyage ahead, down the Indian
Ocean. Mr. Douglas gave her a flag as she was
leaving his island. The *Spray* had now passed
nearly all the dangers of the Coral Sea and Torres
Strait, which, indeed, were not a few; and all ahead
from this point was plain sailing and a straight
course. The trade-wind was still blowing fresh,
and could be safely counted on now down to the
coast of Madagascar, if not beyond that, for it was
still early in the season.

I had no wish to arrive off the Cape of Good
Hope before midsummer, and it was now early

winter. I had been off that cape once in July, which was, of course, midwinter there. The stout ship I then commanded encountered only fierce hurricanes, and she bore them ill. I wished for no winter gales now. It was not that I feared them more, being in the *Spray* instead of a large ship, but that I preferred fine weather in any case. It is true that one may encounter heavy gales off the Cape of Good Hope at any season of the year, but in the summer they are less frequent and do not continue so long. And so with time enough before me to admit of a run ashore on the islands en route, I shaped the course now for Keeling Cocos, atoll islands, distant twenty-seven hundred miles. Taking a departure from Booby Island, which the sloop passed early in the day, I decided to sight Timor on the way, an island of high mountains.

Booby Island I had seen before, but only once, however, and that was when in the steamship *Soushay*, onw hich I was "hove-down" in a fever. When she steamed along this way I was well enough to crawl on deck to look at Booby Island. Had I died for it, I would have seen that island. In those days passing ships landed stores in a cave on the island for shipwrecked and distressed wayfarers. Captain Airy of the *Soushay*, a good man, sent a boat to the cave with his contribution to the general store. The stores were landed in safety, and the boat, returning, brought back from the improvised post-office there a dozen or more letters, most of them left by whalemen, with the request that the first homeward-bound ship would carry them along and see to their mailing, which had been the cus-

tom of this strange postal service for many years.
Some of the letters brought back by our boat were
directed to New Bedford, and some to Fairhaven,
Massachusetts.

There is a light to-day on Booby Island, and
regular packet communication with the rest of the
world, and the beautiful uncertainty of the fate of
letters left there is a thing of the past. I made no
call at the little island, but standing close in, exchanged signals with the keeper of the light. Sailing on, the sloop was at once in the Arafura Sea,
where for days she sailed in water milky white and
green and purple. It was my good fortune to enter
the sea on the last quarter of the moon, the advantage being that in the dark nights I witnessed the
phosphorescent light effect at night in its greatest
splendor. The sea, where the sloop disturbed it,
seemed all ablaze, so that by its light I could see
the smallest articles on deck, and her wake was a
path of fire.

On the 25th of June the sloop was already clear
of all the shoals and dangers, and was sailing on a
smooth sea as steadily as before, but with speed
somewhat slackened. I got out the flying-jib made
at Juan Fernandez, and set it as a spinnaker from
the stoutest bamboo that Mrs. Stevenson had given
me at Samoa. The spinnaker pulled like a sodger,
and the bamboo holding its own, the *Spray* mended
her pace.

Several pigeons flying across to-day from Australia toward the islands bent their course over the
Spray. Smaller birds were seen flying in the opposite direction. In the part of the Arafura that I

came to first, where it was shallow, sea-snakes writhed about on the surface and tumbled over and over in the waves. As the sloop sailed farther on, where the sea became deep, they disappeared. In the ocean, where the water is blue, not one was ever seen.

In the days of serene weather there was not much to do but to read and take rest on the *Spray*, to make up as much as possible for the rough time off Cape Horn, which was not yet forgotten, and to forestall the Cape of Good Hope by a store of ease. My sea journal was now much the same from day to day — something like this of June 26 and 27, for example:

June 26, in the morning, it is a bit squally; later in the day blowing a steady breeze.

On the log at noon is	130	miles
Subtract correction for slip	10	"
	120	"
Add for current	10	"
	130	"

Latitude by observation at noon, 10° 23′ S.
Longitude as per mark on the chart.

There was n't much brain-work in that log, I 'm sure. June 27 makes a better showing, when all is told:

First of all, to-day, was. a flying-fish on deck; fried it in butter.

133 miles on the log.

For slip, off, and for current, on, as per guess, about equal — let it go at that.

Latitude by observation at noon, 10° 25′ S.

For several days now the *Spray* sailed west on
the parallel of 10° 25′ S., as true as a hair. If she
deviated at all from that, through the day or night,
— and this may have happened, — she was back,
strangely enough, at noon, at the same latitude.
But the greatest science was in reckoning the longitude. My tin clock and only timepiece had by this
time lost its minute-hand, but after I boiled her she
told the hours, and that was near enough on a long
stretch.

On the 2d of July the great island of Timor was
in view away to the nor'ard. On the following day
I saw Dana Island, not far off, and a breeze came
up from the land at night, fragrant of the spices or
what not of the coast.

On the 11th, with all sail set and with the spinnaker still abroad, Christmas Island, about noon,
came into view one point on the starboard bow.
Before night it was abeam and distant two and a
half miles. The surface of the island appeared
evenly rounded from the sea to a considerable
height in the center. In outline it was as smooth
as a fish, and a long ocean swell, rolling up, broke
against the sides, where it lay like a monster asleep,
motionless on the sea. It seemed to have the pro-
portions of a whale, and as the sloop sailed along
its side to the part where the head would be,
there was a nostril, even, which was a blow-hole
through a ledge of rock where every wave that
dashed threw up a shaft of water, lifelike and real.

It had been a long time since I last saw this
island; but I remember my temporary admiration
for the captain of the ship I was then in, the

Tanjore, when he sang out one morning from the quarter-deck, well aft, " Go aloft there, one of ye, with a pair of eyes, and see Christmas Island." Sure enough, there the island was in sight from the royal-yard. Captain M—— had thus made a great hit, and he never got over it. The chief mate, terror of us ordinaries in the ship, walking never to windward of the captain, now took himself very humbly to leeward altogether. When we arrived at Hong-Kong there was a letter in the ship's mail for me. I was in the boat with the captain some hours while he had it. But do you suppose he could hand a letter to a seaman? No, indeed; not even to an ordinary seaman. When we got to the ship he gave it to the first mate; the first mate gave it to the second mate, and he laid it, michingly, on the capstan-head, where I could get it!

CHAPTER XVI

TO the Keeling Cocos Islands was now only five hundred and fifty miles; but even in this short run it was necessary to be extremely careful in keeping a true course else I would miss the atoll.

On the 12th, some hundred miles southwest of Christmas Island, I saw anti-trade clouds flying up from the southwest very high over the regular winds, which weakened now for a few days, while a swell heavier than usual set in also from the southwest. A winter gale was going on in the direction of the Cape of Good Hope. Accordingly, I steered higher to windward, allowing twenty miles a day while this went on, for change of current; and it was not too much, for on that course I made the Keeling Islands right ahead. The first unmistakable sign of the land was a visit one morning from a white tern that fluttered very knowingly about the vessel, and then took itself off westward with a businesslike air in its wing. The tern is called by the islanders the "pilot of Keeling Cocos." Farther on I came among a great number of birds fishing, and fighting over whatever they caught. My reckoning was up, and springing aloft, I saw from half-way up the mast cocoanut-trees standing out of the water ahead. I expected to see this; still, it thrilled me as an electric shock might have done. I slid down the mast, trembling under the strangest sensations; and not able to resist the impulse, I sat on deck and gave way to my emotions. To folks in a parlor on shore this may seem weak indeed, but I am telling the story of a voyage alone.

I did n't touch the helm, for with the current and heave of the sea the sloop found herself at the end of the run absolutely in the fairway of the channel. You could n't have beaten it in the navy! Then I trimmed her sails by the wind, took the helm, and flogged her up the couple of miles or so abreast the harbor landing, where I cast anchor at 3:30 P. M., July 17, 1897, twenty-three days from Thursday Island. The distance run was twenty-seven hundred miles as the crow flies. This would have been a fair Atlantic voyage. It was a delightful sail! During those twenty-three days I had not spent altogether more than three hours at the helm, including the time occupied in beating into Keeling harbor. I just lashed the helm and let her go; whether the wind was abeam or dead aft, it was all the same: she always sailed on her course. No part of the voyage up to this point, taking it by and large, had been so finished as this.[1]

[1] Mr. Andrew J. Leach, reporting, July 21, 1897, through Governor Kynnersley of Singapore, to Joseph Chamberlain, Colonial Secretary,

The Keeling Cocos Islands, according to Admiral
Fitzroy, R. N., lie between the latitudes of 11° 50′
and 12° 12′ S., and the longitudes of 96° 51′ and
96° 58′ E. They were discovered in 1608–9 by
Captain William Keeling, then in the service of
the East India Company. The southern group
consists of seven or eight islands and islets on the
atoll, which is the skeleton of what some day, according to the history of coral reefs, will be a continuous island. North Keeling has no harbor, is
seldom visited, and is of no importance. The
South Keelings are a strange little world, with
a romantic history all their own. They have been
visited occasionally by the floating spar of some
hurricane-swept ship, or by a tree that has drifted
all the way from Australia, or by an ill-starred

said concerning the *Iphegenia's* visit to the atoll: " As we left the
ocean depths of deepest blue and entered the coral circle, the contrast was most remarkable. The brilliant colors of the waters,
transparent to a depth of over thirty feet, now purple, now of the
bluest sky-blue, and now green, with the white crests of the waves
flashing under a brilliant sun, the encircling . . . palm-clad
islands, the gaps between which were to the south undiscernible,
the white sand shores and the whiter gaps where breakers appeared,
and, lastly, the lagoon itself, seven or eight miles across from north
to south, and five to six from east to west, presented a sight never to
be forgotten. After some little delay, Mr. Sidney Ross, the eldest
son of Mr. George Ross, came off to meet us, and soon after, accompanied by the doctor and another officer, we went ashore.

" On reaching the landing-stage, we found, hauled up for cleaning,
etc., the *Spray* of Boston, a yawl of 12.70 tons gross, the property of
Captain Joshua Slocum. He arrived at the island on the 17th of July,
twenty-three days out from Thursday Island. This extraordinary
solitary traveler left Boston some two years ago single-handed,
crossed to Gibraltar, sailed down to Cape Horn, passed through the
Strait of Magellan to the Society Islands, thence to Australia, and
through the Torres Strait to Thursday Island."

ship cast away, and finally by man. Even a rock once drifted to Keeling, held fast among the roots of a tree.

After the discovery of the islands by Captain Keeling, their first notable visitor was Captain John Clunis-Ross, who in 1814 touched in the ship *Borneo* on a voyage to India. Captain Ross returned two years later with his wife and family and his mother-in-law, Mrs. Dymoke, and eight sailor-artisans, to take possession of the islands, but found there already one Alexander Hare, who meanwhile had marked the little atoll as a sort of Eden for a seraglio of Malay women which he moved over from the coast of Africa. It was Ross's own brother, oddly enough, who freighted Hare and his crowd of women to the islands, not knowing of Captain John's plans to occupy the little world. And so Hare was there with his outfit, as if he had come to stay.

On his previous visit, however, Ross had nailed the English Jack to a mast on Horsburg Island, one of the group. After two years shreds of it still fluttered in the wind, and his sailors, nothing loath, began at once the invasion of the new kingdom to take possession of it, women and all. The force of forty women, with only one man to command them, was not equal to driving eight sturdy sailors back into the sea.[1]

From this time on Hare had a hard time of it.

[1] In the accounts given in Findlay's " Sailing Directory" of some of the events there is a chronological discrepancy. I follow the accounts gathered from the old captain's grandsons and from records on the spot.

He and Ross did not get on well as neighbors. The
islands were too small and too near for characters
so widely different. Hare had "oceans of money,"
and might have lived well in London; but he had
been governor of a wild colony in Borneo, and
could not confine himself to the tame life that
prosy civilization affords. And so he hung on to
the atoll with his forty women, retreating little by
little before Ross and his sturdy crew, till at last
he found himself and his harem on the little island
known to this day as Prison Island, where, like
Bluebeard, he confined his wives in a castle. The
channel between the islands was narrow, the water
was not deep, and the eight Scotch sailors wore
long boots. Hare was now dismayed. He tried
to compromise with rum and other luxuries, but
these things only made matters worse. On the day
following the first St. Andrew's celebration on the
island, Hare, consumed with rage, and no longer
on speaking terms with the captain, dashed off a
note to him, saying: "DEAR ROSS: I thought when
I sent rum and roast pig to your sailors that they
would stay away from my flower-garden." In
reply to which the captain, burning with indigna-
tion, shouted from the center of the island, where
he stood, "Ahoy, there, on Prison Island! You
Hare, don't you know that rum and roast pig are not
a sailor's heaven?" Hare said afterward that one
might have heard the captain's roar across to Java.

The lawless establishment was soon broken up
by the women deserting Prison Island and putting
themselves under Ross's protection. Hare then
went to Batavia, where he met his death.

My first impression upon landing was that the crime of infanticide had not reached the islands of Keeling Cocos. "The children have all come to

The *Spray* ashore for "boot-topping" at the Keeling Islands.
(From a photograph.)

welcome you," explained Mr. Ross, as they mustered at the jetty by hundreds, of all ages and sizes. The people of this country were all rather shy, but, young or old, they never passed one or saw one passing

their door without a salutation. In their musical
voices they would say, "Are you walking?" ("Jalan,
jalan?") "Will you come along?" one would
answer.

For a long time after I arrived the children
regarded the "one-man ship" with suspicion and
fear. A native man had been blown away to sea
many years before, and they hinted to one another
that he might have been changed from black to
white, and returned in the sloop. For some time
every movement I made was closely watched.
They were particularly interested in what I ate.
One day, after I had been "boot-topping" the sloop
with a composition of coal-tar and other stuff, and
while I was taking my dinner, with the luxury of
blackberry jam, I heard a commotion, and then a
yell and a stampede, as the children ran away
yelling: "The captain is eating coal-tar! The
captain is eating coal-tar!" But they soon found
out that this same "coal-tar" was very good to eat,
and that I had brought a quantity of it. One day
when I was spreading a sea-biscuit thick with it for
a wide-awake youngster, I heard them whisper,
"Chut-chut!" meaning that a shark had bitten my
hand, which they observed was lame. Thenceforth
they regarded me as a hero, and I had not fingers
enough for the little bright-eyed tots that wanted
to cling to them and follow me about. Before this,
when I held out my hand and said, "Come!" they
would shy off for the nearest house, and say,
"Dingin" ("It's cold"), or "Ujan" ("It's going
to rain"). But it was now accepted that I was
not the returned spirit of the lost black, and I

had plenty of friends about the island, rain or shine.

One day after this, when I tried to haul the sloop and found her fast in the sand, the children all clapped their hands and cried that a *kpeting* (crab) was holding her by the keel; and little Ophelia, ten or twelve years of age, wrote in the *Spray's* log-book:

> A hundred men with might and main
>   On the windlass hove, yeo ho!
> The cable only came in twain;
>   The ship she would not go;
> For, child, to tell the strangest thing,
> The keel was held by a great kpeting.

This being so or not, it was decided that the Mohammedan priest, Sama the Emim, for a pot of jam, should ask Mohammed to bless the voyage and make the crab let go the sloop's keel, which it did, if it had hold, and she floated on the very next tide.

On the 22d of July arrived H. M. S. *Iphegenia*, with Mr. Justice Andrew J. Leech and court officers on board, on a circuit of inspection among the Straits Settlements, of which Keeling Cocos was a dependency, to hear complaints and try cases by law, if any there were to try. They found the *Spray* hauled ashore and tied to a cocoanut-tree. But at the Keeling Islands there had not been a grievance to complain of since the day that Hare migrated, for the Rosses have always treated the islanders as their own family.

If there is a paradise on this earth it is Keeling. There was not a case for a lawyer, but something had to be done, for here were two ships in port, a great man-of-war and the *Spray*. Instead of a lawsuit a dance was got up, and all the officers who could leave their ship came ashore. Everybody on the island came, old and young, and the governor's great hall was filled with people. All that could get on their feet danced, while the babies lay in heaps in the corners of the room, content to look on. My little friend Ophelia danced with the judge. For music two fiddles screeched over and over again the good old tune, " We won't go home till morning." And we did not.

The women at the Keelings do not do all the drudgery, as in many places visited on the voyage. It would cheer the heart of a Fuegian woman to see the Keeling lord of creation up a cocoanut-tree. Besides cleverly climbing the trees, the men of Keeling build exquisitely modeled canoes. By far the best workmanship in boat-building I saw on the voyage was here. Many finished mechanics dwelt under the palms at Keeling, and the hum of the band-saw and the ring of the anvil were heard from morning till night. The first Scotch settlers left there the strength of Northern blood and the inheritance of steady habits. No benevolent society has ever done so much for any islanders as the noble Captain Ross, and his sons, who have followed his example of industry and thrift.

Admiral Fitzroy of the *Beagle*, who visited here, where many things are reversed, spoke of " these singular though small islands, where crabs eat cocoanuts, fish eat coral, dogs catch fish, men ride on turtles, and shells are dangerous man-traps,"

adding that the greater part of the sea-fowl roost
on branches, and many rats make their nests in
the tops of palm-trees.

My vessel being refitted, I decided to load her
with the famous mammoth tridacna shell of Keeling, found in the bayou near by. And right here,
within sight of the village, I came near losing "the
crew of the *Spray*" — not from putting my foot in
a man-trap shell, however, but from carelessly
neglecting to look after the details of a trip across
the harbor in a boat. I had sailed over oceans; I
have since completed a course over them all, and
sailed round the whole world without so nearly
meeting a fatality as on that trip across a lagoon,
where I trusted all to some one else, and he, weak
mortal that he was, perhaps trusted all to me.
However that may be, I found myself with a
thoughtless African negro in a rickety bateau that
was fitted with a rotten sail, and this blew away in
mid-channel in a squall, that sent us drifting helplessly to sea, where we should have been incon-
tinently lost. With the whole ocean before us to
leeward, I was dismayed to see, while we drifted,
that there was not a paddle or an oar in the boat!
There was an anchor, to be sure, but not enough
rope to tie a cat, and we were already in deep
water. By great good fortune, however, there was
a pole. Plying this as a paddle with the utmost
energy, and by the merest accidental flaw in the
wind to favor us, the trap of a boat was worked
into shoal water, where we could touch bottom and
push her ashore. With Africa, the nearest coast
to leeward, three thousand miles away, with not so

much as a drop of water in the boat, and a lean
and hungry negro — well, cast the lot as one might,
the crew of the *Spray* in a little while would have

Captain Slocum drifting out to sea.

been hard to find.   It is needless to say that I took
no more such chances.   The tridacna were afterward procured in a safe boat, thirty of them taking

the place of three tons of cement ballast, which I threw overboard to make room and give buoyancy.

On August 22, the kpeting, or whatever else it was that held the sloop in the islands, let go its hold, and she swung out to sea under all sail, heading again for home. Mounting one or two heavy rollers on the fringe of the atoll, she cleared the flashing reefs. Long before dark Keeling Cocos, with its thousand souls, as sinless in their lives as perhaps it is possible for frail mortals to be, was left out of sight, astern. Out of sight, I say, except in my strongest affection.

The sea was rugged, and the *Spray* washed heavily when hauled on the wind, which course I took for the island of Rodriguez, and which brought the sea abeam. The true course for the island was west by south, one quarter south, and the distance was nineteen hundred miles; but I steered considerably to the windward of that to allow for the heave of the sea and other leeward effects. My sloop on this course ran under reefed sails for days together. I naturally tired of the never-ending motion of the sea, and, above all, of the wetting I got whenever I showed myself on deck. Under these heavy weather conditions the *Spray* seemed to lag behind on her course; at least, I attributed to these conditions a discrepancy in the log, which by the fifteenth day out from Keeling amounted to one hundred and fifty miles between the rotator and the mental calculations I had kept of what she should have gone, and so I kept an eye lifting for land. I could see about sundown this day a bunch of clouds that stood in one spot, right ahead,

while the other clouds floated on; this was a sign
of something. By midnight, as the sloop sailed on,
a black object appeared where I had seen the resting clouds. It was still a long way off, but there
could be no mistaking this: it was the high island
of Rodriguez. I hauled in the patent log, which I
was now towing more from habit than from necessity, for I had learned the *Spray* and her ways long
before this. If one thing was clearer than another in
her voyage, it was that she could be trusted to come
out right and in safety, though at the same time I always stood ready to give her the benefit of even the
least doubt. The officers who are over-sure, and
"know it all like a book," are the ones, I have observed, who wreck the most ships and lose the most
lives. The cause of the discrepancy in the log was
one often met with, namely, coming in contact with
some large fish; two out of the four blades of the
rotator were crushed or bent, the work probably of
a shark. Being sure of the sloop's position, I lay
down to rest and to think, and I felt better for it.
By daylight the island was abeam, about three
miles away. It wore a hard, weather-beaten appearance there, all alone, far out in the Indian Ocean,
like land adrift. The windward side was uninviting, but there was a good port to leeward, and I
hauled in now close on the wind for that. A pilot
came out to take me into the inner harbor, which
was reached through a narrow channel among coral
reefs.

It was a curious thing that at all of the islands
some reality was insisted on as unreal, while improb-
abilities were clothed as hard facts; and so it hap-

pened here that the good abbé, a few days before, had been telling his people about the coming of Antichrist, and when they saw the *Spray* sail into the harbor, all feather-white before a gale of wind, and run all standing upon the beach, and with only one man aboard, they cried, "May the Lord help us, it is he, and he has come in a boat!" which I say would have been the most improbable way of his coming. Nevertheless, the news went flying through the place. The governor of the island, Mr. Roberts, came down immediately to see what it was all about, for the little town was in a great commotion. One elderly woman, when she heard of my advent, made for her house and locked herself in. When she heard that I was actually coming up the street she barricaded her doors, and did not come out while I was on the island, a period of eight days. Governor Roberts and his family did not share the fears of their people, but came on board at the jetty, where the sloop was berthed, and their example induced others to come also. The governor's young boys took charge of the *Spray's* dinghy at once, and my visit cost his Excellency, besides great hospitality to me, the building of a boat for them like the one belonging to the *Spray*.

My first day at this Land of Promise was to me like a fairy-tale. For many days I had studied the charts and counted the time of my arrival at this spot, as one might his entrance to the Islands of the Blessed, looking upon it as the terminus of the last long run, made irksome by the want of many things with which, from this time on, I could keep well supplied. And behold, here was the sloop, arrived, and made securely fast to a pier in Rodriguez. On the first evening ashore, in the land of napkins and cut glass, I saw before me still the ghosts of hempen towels and of mugs with handles knocked off. Instead of tossing on the sea, however, as I might have been, here was I in a bright hall, surrounded by sparkling wit, and dining with the governor of the island! " Aladdin," I cried, " where is your lamp? My fisherman's lantern, which I got at Gloucester, has shown me better things than your smoky old burner ever revealed."

The second day in port was spent in receiving visitors. Mrs. Roberts and her children came first to " shake hands," they said, " with the *Spray*." No one was now afraid to come on board except the poor old woman, who still maintained that the *Spray* had Antichrist in the hold, if, indeed, he had not already gone ashore. The governor entertained that evening, and kindly invited the " destroyer of the world" to speak for himself. This he did, elaborating most effusively on the dangers of the sea (which, after the manner of many of our frailest mortals, he would have had smooth had he made it); also by contrivances of light and darkness he exhibited on the wall pictures of the places and countries visited on the voyage (nothing like the countries, however, that he would have made), and of the people seen, savage and other, frequently groaning, " Wicked world! Wicked world!" When this was finished his Excellency the governor, speaking words of thankfulness, distributed pieces of gold.

On the following day I accompanied his Excellency and family on a visit to San Gabriel, which was up the country among the hills. The good abbé of San Gabriel entertained us all royally at the convent, and we remained his guests until the following day. As I was leaving his place, the abbé said, "Captain, I embrace you, and of whatever religion you may be, my wish is that you succeed in making your voyage, and that our Saviour the Christ be always with you!" To this good man's words I could only say, "My dear abbé, had all religionists been so liberal there would have been less bloodshed in the world."

At Rodriguez one may now find every convenience for filling pure and wholesome water in any quantity, Governor Roberts having built a reservoir in the hills, above the village, and laid pipes to the jetty, where, at the time of my visit, there were five and a half feet at high tide. In former years well-water was used, and more or less sickness occurred from it. Beef may be had in any quantity on the island, and at a moderate price. Sweet potatoes were plentiful and cheap; the large sack of them that I bought there for about four shillings kept unusually well. I simply stored them in the sloop's dry hold. Of fruits, pomegranates were most plentiful; for two shillings I obtained a large sack of them, as many as a donkey could pack from the orchard, which, by the way, was planted by nature herself.

CHAPTER XVII

A clean bill of health at Mauritius — Sailing the voyage over again in the opera-house — A newly discovered plant named in honor of the *Spray's* skipper — A party of young ladies out for a sail — A bivouac on deck — A warm reception at Durban — A friendly cross-examination by Henry M. Stanley — Three wise Boers seek proof of the flatness of the earth — Leaving South Africa.

ON the 16th of September, after eight restful days at Rodriguez, the mid-ocean land of plenty, I set sail, and on the 19th arrived at Mauritius, anchoring at quarantine about noon. The sloop was towed in later on the same day by the doctor's launch, after he was satisfied that I had mustered all the crew for inspection. Of this he seemed in doubt until he examined the papers, which called for a crew of one all told from port to port, throughout the voyage. Then finding that I had been well enough to come thus far alone, he gave me pratique without further ado. There was still another official visit for the *Spray* to pass farther in the harbor. The governor of Rodriguez, who had most kindly given me, besides a regular mail, private letters of introduction to friends, told me I should meet, first of all, Mr. Jenkins of the postal service, a good man. "How do you do, Mr. Jenkins?" cried I, as his boat swung alongside. "You don't know me," he said. "Why not?" I

226

The *Spray* at Mauritius.

replied. "From where is the sloop?" "From
around the world," I again replied, very solemnly.
"And alone?" "Yes; why not?" "And you
know me?" "Three thousand years ago," cried
I, "when you and I had a warmer job than we
have now" (even this was hot). "You were then
Jenkinson, but if you have changed your name
I don't blame you for that." Mr. Jenkins, for-

bearing soul, entered into the spirit of the jest, which served the *Spray* a good turn, for on the strength of this tale it got out that if any one should go on board after dark the devil would get him at once. And so I could leave the *Spray* without the fear of her being robbed at night. The cabin, to be sure, was broken into, but it was done in daylight, and the thieves got no more than a box of smoked herrings before " Tom " Ledson, one of the port officials, caught them red-handed, as it were, and sent them to jail. This was discouraging to pilferers, for they feared Ledson more than they feared Satan himself. Even Mamode Hajee Ayoob, who was the day-watchman on board,— till an empty box fell over in the cabin and frightened him out of his wits,— could not be hired to watch nights, or even till the sun went down. " Sahib," he cried, " there is no need of it," and what he said was perfectly true.

At Mauritius, where I drew a long breath, the *Spray* rested her wings, it being the season of fine weather. The hardships of the voyage, if there had been any, were now computed by officers of experience as nine tenths finished, and yet somehow I could not forget that the United States was still a long way off.

The kind people of Mauritius, to make me richer and happier, rigged up the opera-house, which they had named the " Ship *Pantai*." [1] All decks and no bottom was this ship, but she was as stiff as a church. They gave me free use of it while I talked over the *Spray's* adventures. His Honor the mayor

---

[1] Guinea-hen.

introduced me to his Excellency the governor from the poop-deck of the *Pantai*. In this way I was also introduced again to our good consul, General John P. Campbell, who had already introduced me to his Excellency. I was becoming well acquainted, and was in for it now to sail the voyage over again. How I got through the story I hardly know. It was a hot night, and I could have choked the tailor who made the coat I wore for this occasion. The kind governor saw that I had done my part trying to rig like a man ashore, and he invited me to Government House at Reduit, where I found myself among friends.

It was winter still off stormy Cape of Good Hope, but the storms might whistle there. I determined to see it out in milder Mauritius, visiting Rose Hill, Curipepe, and other places on the island. I spent a day with the elder Mr. Roberts, father of Governor Roberts of Rodriguez, and with his friends the Very Reverend Fathers O'Loughlin and McCarthy. Returning to the *Spray* by way of the great flower conservatory near Moka, the proprietor, having only that morning discovered a new and hardy plant, to my great honor named it " Slocum," which he said Latinized it at once, saving him some trouble on the twist of a word; and the good botanist seemed pleased that I had come. How different things are in different countries! In Boston, Massachusetts, at that time, a gentleman, so I was told, paid thirty thousand dollars to have a flower named after his wife, and it was not a big flower either, while " Slocum," which came without the asking, was bigger than a mangel-wurzel!

I was royally entertained at Moka, as well as at
Reduit and other places — once by seven young
ladies, to whom I spoke of my inability to return
their hospitality except in my own poor way of
taking them on a sail in the sloop. "The very
thing! The very thing!" they all cried. "Then
please name the time," I said, as meek as Moses.
"To-morrow!" they all cried. "And, aunty, we
may go, may n't we, and we 'll be real good for a
whole week afterward, aunty! Say yes, aunty
dear!" All this after saying "To-morrow"; for
girls in Mauritius are, after all, the same as our
girls in America; and their dear aunt said "Me,
too" about the same as any really good aunt might
say in my own country.

I was then in a quandary, it having recurred to
me that on the very "to-morrow" I was to dine
with the harbor-master, Captain Wilson. However, I said to myself, "The *Spray* will run out
quickly into rough seas; these young ladies will
have *mal de mer* and a good time, and I 'll get in
early enough to be at the dinner, after all." But
not a bit of it. We sailed almost out of sight of
Mauritius, and they just stood up and laughed at
seas tumbling aboard, while I was at the helm
making the worst weather of it I could, and spin-
ning yarns to the aunt about sea-serpents and
whales. But she, dear lady, when I had finished
with stories of monsters, only hinted at a basket
of provisions they had brought along, enough to
last a week, for I had told them about my wretched
steward.

The more the *Spray* tried to make these young

ladies seasick, the more they all clapped their hands and said, "How lovely it is!" and "How beautifully she skims over the sea!" and "How beautiful our island appears from the distance!" and they still cried, "Go on!" We were fifteen miles or more at sea before they ceased the eager cry, "Go on!" Then the sloop swung round, I still hoping to be back to Port Louis in time to keep my appointment. The *Spray* reached the island quickly, and flew along the coast fast enough; but I made a mistake in steering along the coast on the way home, for as we came abreast of Tombo Bay it enchanted my crew. "Oh, let 's anchor here!" they cried. To this no sailor in the world would have said nay. The sloop came to anchor, ten minutes later, as they wished, and a young man on the cliff abreast, waving his hat, cried, "*Vive la Spray!*" My passengers said, "Aunty, may n't we have a swim in the surf along the shore?" Just then the harbor-master's launch hove in sight, coming out to meet us; but it was too late to get the sloop into Port Louis that night. The launch was in time, however, to land my fair crew for a swim; but they were determined not to desert the ship. Meanwhile I prepared a roof for the night on deck with the sails, and a Bengali man-servant arranged the evening meal. That night the *Spray* rode in Tombo Bay with her precious freight. Next morning bright and early, even before the stars were gone, I awoke to hear praying on deck.

The port officers' launch reappeared later in the morning, this time with Captain Wilson himself on board, to try his luck in getting the *Spray* into port, for he had heard of our predicament. It was worth something to hear a friend tell afterward how earnestly the good harbor-master of Mauritius said, "I'll find the *Spray* and I'll get her into port." A merry crew he discovered on her. They could hoist sails like old tars, and could trim them, too. They could tell all about the ship's "hoods," and one should have seen them clap a bonnet on the jib. Like the deepest of deep-water sailors, they could heave the lead, and — as I hope to see Mauritius again!— any of them could have put the sloop in stays. No ship ever had a fairer crew.

The voyage was the event of Port Louis; such a thing as young ladies sailing about the harbor, even, was almost unheard of before.

While at Mauritius the *Spray* was tendered the use of the military dock free of charge, and was thoroughly refitted by the port authorities. My sincere gratitude is also due other friends for many things needful for the voyage put on board, including bags of sugar from some of the famous old plantations.

The favorable season now set in, and thus well equipped, on the 26th of October, the *Spray* put to sea. As I sailed before a light wind the island receded slowly, and on the following day I could still see the Puce Mountain near Moka. The *Spray* arrived next day off Galets, Réunion, and a pilot came out and spoke her. I handed him a Mauritius paper and continued on my voyage; for rollers were running heavily at the time, and it was not practicable to make a landing. From Réunion

I shaped a course direct for Cape St. Mary, Madagascar.

The sloop was now drawing near the limits of the trade-wind, and the strong breeze that had carried her with free sheets the many thousands of miles from Sandy Cape, Australia, fell lighter each day until October 30, when it was altogether calm, and a motionless sea held her in a hushed world. I furled the sails at evening, sat down on deck, and enjoyed the vast stillness of the night.

October 31 a light east-northeast breeze sprang up, and the sloop passed Cape St. Mary about noon. On the 6th, 7th, 8th, and 9th of November, in the Mozambique Channel, she experienced a hard gale of wind from the southwest. Here the *Spray* suffered as much as she did anywhere, except off Cape Horn. The thunder and lightning preceding this gale were very heavy. From this point until the sloop arrived off the coast of Africa, she encountered a succession of gales of wind, which drove her about in many directions, but on the 17th of November she arrived at Port Natal.

This delightful place is the commercial center of the "Garden Colony," Durban itself, the city, being the continuation of a garden. The signalman from the bluff station reported the *Spray* fifteen miles off. The wind was freshening, and when she was within eight miles he said: "The *Spray* is shortening sail; the mainsail was reefed and set in ten minutes. One man is doing all the work."

This item of news was printed three minutes later in a Durban morning journal, which was handed to me when I arrived in port. I could not

verify the time it had taken to reef the sail, for, as
I have already said, the minute-hand of my timepiece was gone. I only knew that I reefed as
quickly as I could.

The same paper, commenting on the voyage, said:
"Judging from the stormy weather which has prevailed off this coast during the past few weeks, the
Spray must have had a very stormy voyage from
Mauritius to Natal." Doubtless the weather would
have been called stormy by sailors in any ship, but
it caused the *Spray* no more inconvenience than the
delay natural to head winds generally.

The question of how I sailed the sloop alone, often
asked, is best answered, perhaps, by a Durban news-
paper. I would shrink from repeating the editor's
words but for the reason that undue estimates have
been made of the amount of skill and energy required to sail a sloop of even the *Spray's* small tonnage. I heard a man who called himself a sailor
say that "it would require three men to do what it
was claimed" that I did alone, and what I found
perfectly easy to do over and over again; and I
have heard that others made similar nonsensical
remarks, adding that I would work myself to death.
But here is what the Durban paper said:

As briefly noted yesterday, the *Spray*, with a crew of
one man, arrived at this port yesterday afternoon on her
cruise round the world. The *Spray* made quite an auspi-
cious entrance to Natal. Her commander sailed his craft
right up the channel past the main wharf, and dropped
his anchor near the old *Forerunner* in the creek, before
any one had a chance to get on board. The *Spray* was
naturally an object of great curiosity to the Point people,

and her arrival was witnessed by a large crowd. The
skilful manner in which Captain Slocum steered his craft
about the vessels which were occupying the waterway was
a treat to witness.

The *Spray* was not sailing in among greenhorns
when she came to Natal. When she arrived off the
port the pilot-ship, a fine, able steam-tug, came out

Captain Joshua Slocum.

to meet her, and led the way in across the bar, for
it was blowing a smart gale and was too rough for
the sloop to be towed with safety. The trick of
going in I learned by watching the steamer; it
was simply to keep on the windward side of the
channel and take the combers end on.

I found that Durban supported two yacht-clubs,
both of them full of enterprise. I met all the members of both clubs, and sailed in the crack yacht
Florence of the Royal Natal, with Captain Spradbrow and the Right Honorable Harry Escombe,
premier of the colony. The yacht's center-board

plowed furrows through the mud-banks, which, according to Mr. Escombe, Spradbrow afterward planted with potatoes. The *Florence,* however, won races while she tilled the skipper's land. After our sail on the *Florence* Mr. Escombe offered to sail the *Spray* round the Cape of Good Hope for me, and hinted at his famous cribbage-board to while away the hours. Spradbrow, in retort, warned me of it. Said he, "You would be played out of the sloop before you could round the cape." By others it was not thought probable that the premier of Natal would play cribbage off the Cape of Good Hope to win even the *Spray.*

It was a matter of no small pride to me in South Africa to find that American humor was never at a discount, and one of the best American stories I ever heard was told by the premier. At Hotel Royal one day, dining with Colonel Saunderson, M. P., his son, and Lieutenant Tipping, I met Mr. Stanley. The great explorer was just from Pretoria, and had already as good as flayed President Krüger with his trenchant pen. But that did not signify, for everybody has a whack at Oom Paul, and no one in the world seems to stand the joke better than he, not even the Sultan of Turkey himself. The colonel introduced me to the explorer, and I hauled close to the wind, to go slow, for Mr. Stanley was a nautical man once himself,—on the Nyanza, I think,—and of course my desire was to appear in the best light before a man of his experience. He looked me over carefully, and said, "What an example of patience!" "Patience is all that is required," I ventured to reply. He then asked if my vessel had water-tight compartments. I explained that she was all water-tight and all compartment. " What if she should strike a rock?" he asked. " Compartments would not save her if she should hit the rocks lying along her course," said I; adding, "she must be kept away from the rocks." After a considerable pause Mr. Stanley asked, " What if a swordfish should pierce her hull with its sword?" Of course I had thought of that as one of the dangers of the sea, and also of the chance of being struck by lightning. In the case of the swordfish, I ventured to say that "the first thing would be to secure the sword." The colonel invited me to dine with the party on the following day, that we might go further into this matter, and so I had the pleasure of meeting Mr. Stanley a second time, but got no more hints in navigation from the famous explorer.

It sounds odd to hear scholars and statesmen say the world is flat; but it is a fact that three Boers favored by the opinion of President Krüger prepared a work to support that contention. While I was at Durban they came from Pretoria to obtain data from me, and they seemed annoyed when I told them that they could not prove it by my experience. With the advice to call up some ghost of the dark ages for research, I went ashore, and left these three wise men poring over the *Spray's* track on a chart of the world, which, however, proved nothing to them, for it was on Mercator's projection, and behold, it was " flat." The next morning I met one of the party in a clergyman's garb, carrying a large Bible, not different from the one I had read. He tackled me, saying, "If you respect the Word of God, you must admit that the world is flat." "If the Word of God stands on a flat world—" I began. "What!" cried he, losing himself in a passion, and making as if he would run me through with an assagai. "What!" he shouted in astonishment and rage, while I jumped aside to dodge the imaginary weapon. Had this good but misguided fanatic been armed with a real weapon, the crew of the *Spray* would have died a martyr there and then. The next day, seeing him across the street, I bowed and made curves with my hands. He responded with a level, swimming movement of his hands, meaning "the world is flat." A pamphlet by these Transvaal geographers, made up of arguments from sources high and low to prove their theory, was mailed to me before I sailed from Africa on my last stretch around the globe.

While I feebly portray the ignorance of these learned men, I have great admiration for their physical manhood. Much that I saw first and last of the Transvaal and the Boers was admirable. It is well known that they are the hardest of fighters, and as generous to the fallen as they are brave before the foe. Real stubborn bigotry with them is only found among old fogies, and will die a natural death, and that, too, perhaps long before we ourselves are entirely free from bigotry. Education in the Transvaal is by no means neglected, English as well as Dutch being taught to all that can afford both; but the tariff duty on English school-books is heavy, and from necessity the poorer people stick to the Transvaal Dutch and their flat world, just as in Samoa and other islands a mistaken policy has kept the natives down to Kanaka.

I visited many public schools at Durban, and had the pleasure of meeting many bright children.

But all fine things must end, and December 14, 1897, the "crew" of the *Spray*, after having a fine time in Natal, swung the sloop's dinghy in on deck, and sailed with a morning land-wind, which carried her clear of the bar, and again she was "off on her alone," as they say in Australia.

CHAPTER XVIII

Rounding the "Cape of Storms" in olden time — A rough Christmas
— The *Spray* ties up for a three months' rest at Cape Town — A
railway trip to the Transvaal — President Krüger's odd definition
of the *Spray's* voyage — His terse sayings — Distinguished guests
on the *Spray* — Cocoanut fiber as a padlock — Courtesies from
the admiral of the Queen's navy — Off for St. Helena — Land
in sight.

THE Cape of Good Hope was now the most prom-
inent point to pass. From Table Bay I could
count on the aid of brisk trades, and then the
Spray would soon be at home. On the first day out
from Durban it fell calm, and I sat thinking about
these things and the end of the voyage. The distance to Table Bay, where I intended to call, was
about eight hundred miles over what might prove
a rough sea. The early Portuguese navigators, en-
dowed with patience, were more than sixty-nine
years struggling to round this cape before they
got as far as Algoa Bay, and there the crew mutinied. They landed on a small island, now called
Santa Cruz, where they devoutly set up the cross,
and swore they would cut the captain's throat if
he attempted to sail farther. Beyond this they
thought was the edge of the world, which they too
believed was flat; and fearing that their ship
would sail over the brink of it, they compelled
Captain Diaz, their commander, to retrace his

course, all being only too glad to get home. A year later, we are told, Vasco da Gama sailed successfully round the "Cape of Storms," as the Cape of Good Hope was then called, and discovered Natal on Christmas or Natal day; hence the name. From this point the way to India was easy.

Gales of wind sweeping round the cape even now were frequent enough, one occurring, on an average, every thirty-six hours; but one gale was much the same as another, with no more serious result than to blow the Spray along on her course when it was fair, or to blow her back somewhat when it was ahead. On Christmas, 1897, I came to the pitch of the cape. On this day the Spray was trying to stand on her head, and she gave me every reason to believe that she would accomplish the feat before night. She began very early in the morning to pitch and toss about in a most unusual manner, and I have to record that, while I was at the end of the bowsprit reefing the jib, she ducked me under water three times for a Christmas box. I got wet and did not like it a bit: never in any other sea was I put under more than once in the same short space of time, say three minutes. A large English steamer passing ran up the signal, "Wishing you a Merry Christmas." I think the captain was a humorist; his own ship was throwing her propeller out of water.

Two days later, the Spray, having recovered the distance lost in the gale, passed Cape Agulhas in company with the steamship Scotsman, now with a fair wind. The keeper of the light on Agulhas exchanged signals with the Spray as she passed, and

afterward wrote me at New York congratulations
on the completion of the voyage. He seemed to
think the incident of two ships of so widely different types passing his cape together worthy of a
place on canvas, and he went about having the
picture made. So I gathered from his letter. At
lonely stations like this hearts grow responsive
and sympathetic, and even poetic. This feeling
was shown toward the *Spray* along many a rugged
coast, and reading many a kind signal thrown
out to her gave one a grateful feeling for all the
world.

One more gale of wind came down upon the
Spray from the west after she passed Cape Agulhas, but that one she dodged by getting into
Simons Bay. When it moderated she beat around
the Cape of Good Hope, where they say the *Flying
Dutchman* is still sailing. The voyage then seemed
as good as finished; from this time on I knew that
all, or nearly all, would be plain sailing.

Here I crossed the dividing-line of weather. To
the north it was clear and settled, while south it
was humid and squally, with, often enough, as I
have said, a treacherous gale. From the recent
hard weather the *Spray* ran into a calm under
Table Mountain, where she lay quietly till the generous sun rose over the land and drew a breeze in
from the sea.

The steam-tug *Alert*, then out looking for ships,
came to the *Spray* off the Lion's Rump, and in lieu
of a larger ship towed her into port. The sea being
smooth, she came to anchor in the bay off the city
of Cape Town, where she remained a day, simply

to rest clear of the bustle of commerce. The good harbor-master sent his steam-launch to bring the sloop to a berth in dock at once, but I preferred to remain for one day alone, in the quiet of a smooth sea, enjoying the retrospect of the passage of the two great capes. On the following morning the *Spray* sailed into the Alfred Dry-docks, where she remained for about three months in the care of the port authorities, while I traveled the country over from Simons Town to Pretoria, being accorded by the colonial government a free railroad pass over all the land.

The trip to Kimberley, Johannesburg, and Pretoria was a pleasant one. At the last-named place I met Mr. Krüger, the Transvaal president. His Excellency received me cordially enough; but my friend Judge Beyers, the gentleman who presented me, by mentioning that I was on a voyage around the world, unwittingly gave great offense to the venerable statesman, which we both regretted deeply. Mr. Krüger corrected the judge rather sharply, reminding him that the world is flat. "You don't mean *round* the world," said the president; "it is impossible! You mean *in* the world. Impossible!" he said, "impossible!" and not another word did he utter either to the judge or to me. The judge looked at me and I looked at the judge, who should have known his ground, so to speak, and Mr. Krüger glowered at us both. My friend the judge seemed embarrassed, but I was delighted; the incident pleased me more than anything else that could have happened. It was a nugget of information quarried out of Oom Paul, some of

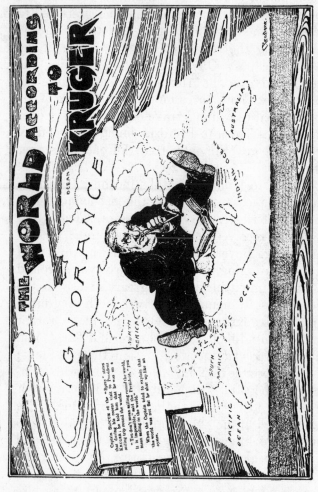

Cartoon printed in the Cape Town "Owl" of March 5, 1898, in connection with an item about Captain Slocum's trip to Pretoria.

whose sayings are famous.   Of the English he said, "They took first my coat and then my trousers."   He also said, "Dynamite is the corner-stone of the South African Republic."   Only unthinking people call President Krüger dull.

Soon after my arrival at the cape, Mr. Krüger's friend Colonel Saunderson,[1] who had arrived from Durban some time before, invited me to Newlands Vineyard, where I met many agreeable people. His Excellency Sir Alfred Milner, the governor, found time to come aboard with a party.   The governor, after making a survey of the deck, found a seat on a box in my cabin; Lady Muriel sat on a keg, and Lady Saunderson sat by the skipper at the wheel, while the colonel, with his kodak, away in the dinghy, took snap shots of the sloop and her distinguished visitors.   Dr. David Gill, astronomer royal, who was of the party, invited me the next day to the famous Cape Observatory.   An hour with Dr. Gill was an hour among the stars.   His discoveries in stellar photography are well known.   He showed me the great astronomical clock of the observatory, and I showed him the tin clock on the *Spray*, and we went over the subject of standard time at sea, and how it was found from the deck of the little sloop without the aid of a clock of any kind.   Later it was advertised that Dr. Gill would preside at a talk about the voyage of the *Spray*: that alone secured for me a full house.   The hall was packed, and many were not able to get in.   This success

---

[1] Colonel Saunderson was Mr. Krüger's very best friend, inasmuch as he advised the president to avast mounting guns.

brought me sufficient money for all my needs in port and for the homeward voyage.

After visiting Kimberley and Pretoria, and finding the *Spray* all right in the docks, I returned to Worcester and Wellington, towns famous for colleges and seminaries, passed coming in, still traveling as the guest of the colony. The ladies of all these institutions of learning wished to know how one might sail round the world alone, which I thought augured of sailing-mistresses in the future instead of sailing-masters. It will come to that yet if we men-folk keep on saying we " can't."

On the plains of Africa I passed through hundreds of miles of rich but still barren land, save for scrub-bushes, on which herds of sheep were browsing. The bushes grew about the length of a sheep apart, and they, I thought, were rather long of body; but there was still room for all. My longing for a foothold on land seized upon me here, where so much of it lay waste; but instead of remaining to plant forests and reclaim vegetation, I returned again to the *Spray* at the Alfred Docks, where I found her waiting for me, with everything in order, exactly as I had left her.

I have often been asked how it was that my vessel and all appurtenances were not stolen in the various ports where I left her for days together without a watchman in charge. This is just how it was: The *Spray* seldom fell among thieves. At the Keeling Islands, at Rodriguez, and at many such places, a wisp of cocoanut fiber in the door-latch, to indicate that the owner was away, secured the

goods against even a longing glance. But when I
came to a great island nearer home, stout locks
were needed; the first night in port things which

Captain Slocum, Sir Alfred Milner (with the tall hat), and Colonel
Saunderson, M. P., on the bow of the *Spray* at Cape Town.

I had always left uncovered disappeared, as if the
deck on which they were stowed had been swept
by a sea.

A pleasant visit from Admiral Sir Harry Raw-

son of the Royal Navy and his family brought
to an end the *Spray's* social relations with the
Cape of Good Hope. The admiral, then commanding the South African Squadron, and now in
command of the great Channel fleet, evinced the
greatest interest in the diminutive *Spray* and her
behavior off Cape Horn, where he was not an entire
stranger. I have to admit that I was delighted
with the trend of Admiral Rawson's questions, and
that I profited by some of his suggestions, notwithstanding the wide difference in our respective
commands.

On March 26, 1898, the *Spray* sailed from South
Africa, the land of distances and pure air, where
she had spent a pleasant and profitable time. The
steam-tug *Tigre* towed her to sea from her wonted
berth at the Alfred Docks, giving her a good offing.
The light morning breeze, which scantily filled her
sails when the tug let go the tow-line, soon died
away altogether, and left her riding over a heavy
swell, in full view of Table Mountain and the high
peaks of the Cape of Good Hope. For a while
the grand scenery served to relieve the monotony.
One of the old circumnavigators (Sir Francis Drake,
I think), when he first saw this magnificent pile,
sang, "'T is the fairest thing and the grandest cape
I 've seen in the whole circumference of the earth."

The view was certainly fine, but one has no wish
to linger long to look in a calm at anything, and
I was glad to note, finally, the short heaving sea,
precursor of the wind which followed on the second
day. Seals playing about the *Spray* all day, before
the breeze came, looked with large eyes when, at

evening, she sat no longer like a lazy bird with folded wings. They parted company now, and the *Spray* soon sailed the highest peaks of the mountains out of sight, and the world changed from a mere

" Reading day and night."

panoramic view to the light of a homeward-bound voyage. Porpoises and dolphins, and such other fishes as did not mind making a hundred and fifty miles a day, were her companions now for several days. The wind was from the southeast; this suited the *Spray* well, and she ran along steadily at her best speed, while I dipped into the new books given me at the cape, reading day and night. March 30 was for me a fast-day in honor of them. I read on, oblivious of hunger or wind or sea, thinking that all was going well, when suddenly a comber rolled over the stern and slopped saucily into the cabin, wetting the very book I was reading. Evidently it was time to put in a reef, that she might not wallow on her course.

March 31 the fresh southeast wind had come to stay. The *Spray* was running under a single-reefed mainsail, a whole jib, and a flying-jib besides, set on the Vailima bamboo, while I was reading Stevenson's delightful "Inland Voyage." The sloop was again doing her work smoothly, hardly rolling at all, but just leaping along among the white horses, a thousand gamboling porpoises keeping her company on all sides. She was again among her old friends the flying-fish, interesting denizens of the sea. Shooting out of the waves like arrows, and with outstretched wings, they sailed on the wind in graceful curves; then falling till again they touched the crest of the waves to wet their delicate wings and renew the flight. They made merry the livelong day. One of the joyful sights on the ocean of a bright day is the continual flight of these interesting fish.

One could not be lonely in a sea like this. Moreover, the reading of delightful adventures enhanced the scene. I was now in the *Spray* and on the Oise in the *Arethusa* at one and the same time.

And so the *Spray* reeled off the miles, showing a
good run every day till April 11, which came almost before I knew it. Very early that morning I
was awakened by that rare bird, the booby, with
its harsh quack, which I recognized at once as
a call to go on deck; it was as much as to say,
"Skipper, there 's land in sight." I tumbled out
quickly, and sure enough, away ahead in the dim
twilight, about twenty miles off, was St. Helena.

My first impulse was to call out, "Oh, what a
speck in the sea!" It is in reality nine miles in
length and two thousand eight hundred and
twenty-three feet in height. I reached for a bottle
of port-wine out of the locker, and took a long pull
from it to the health of my invisible helmsman—
the pilot of the *Pinta*.

CHAPTER XIX

IT was about noon when the *Spray* came to anchor off Jamestown, and "all hands" at once went ashore to pay respects to his Excellency the governor of the island, Sir R. A. Sterndale. His Excellency, when I landed, remarked that it was not often, nowadays, that a circumnavigator came his way, and he cordially welcomed me, and arranged that I should tell about the voyage, first at Garden Hall to the people of Jamestown, and then at Plantation House — the governor's residence, which is in the hills a mile or two back — to his Excellency and the officers of the garrison and their friends. Mr. Poole, our worthy consul, introduced me at the castle, and in the course of his remarks asserted that the sea-serpent was a Yankee.

Most royally was the crew of the *Spray* entertained by the governor. I remained at Plantation House a couple of days, and one of the rooms in the mansion, called the "west room," being haunted, the butler, by command of his Excellency, put me

up in that — like a prince. Indeed, to make sure
that no mistake had been made, his Excellency
came later to see that I was in the right room, and
to tell me all about the ghosts he had seen or heard
of. He had discovered all but one, and wishing
me pleasant dreams, he hoped I might have the
honor of a visit from the unknown one of the west
room. For the rest of the chilly night I kept the
candle burning, and often looked from under the
blankets, thinking that maybe I should meet the
great Napoleon face to face; but I saw only furniture, and the horseshoe that was nailed over the
door opposite my bed.

St. Helena has been an island of tragedies —
tragedies that have been lost sight of in wailing
over the Corsican. On the second day of my visit
the governor took me by carriage-road through the
turns over the island. At one point of our journey
the road, in winding around spurs and ravines,
formed a perfect W within the distance of a few
rods. The roads, though tortuous and steep, were
fairly good, and I was struck with the amount of
labor it must have cost to build them. The air on
the heights was cool and bracing. It is said that,
since hanging for trivial offenses went out of
fashion, no one has died there, except from falling
over the cliffs in old age, or from being crushed by
stones rolling on them from the steep mountains!
Witches at one time were persistent at St. Helena,
as with us in America in the days of Cotton Mather.
At the present day crime is rare in the island.
While I was there, Governor Sterndale, in token
of the fact that not one criminal case had come to

court within the year, was presented with a pair of white gloves by the officers of justice.

Returning from the governor's house to Jamestown, I drove with Mr. Clark, a countryman of mine, to "Longwood," the home of Napoleon. M. Morilleau, French consular agent in charge, keeps the place respectable and the buildings in good repair. His family at Longwood, consisting of wife and grown daughters, are natives of courtly and refined manners, and spend here days, months, and years of contentment, though they have never seen the world beyond the horizon of St. Helena.

On the 20th of April the *Spray* was again ready for sea. Before going on board I took luncheon with the governor and his family at the castle. Lady Sterndale had sent a large fruit-cake, early in the morning, from Plantation House, to be taken along on the voyage. It was a great high-decker, and I ate sparingly of it, as I thought, but it did not keep as I had hoped it would. I ate the last of it along with my first cup of coffee at Antigua, West Indies, which, after all, was quite a record. The one my own sister made me at the little island in the Bay of Fundy, at the first of the voyage, kept about the same length of time, namely, forty-two days.

After luncheon a royal mail was made up for Ascension, the island next on my way. Then Mr. Poole and his daughter paid the *Spray* a farewell visit, bringing me a basket of fruit. It was late in the evening before the anchor was up, and I bore off for the west, loath to leave my new friends. But fresh winds filled the sloop's sails once more, and I watched the beacon-light at Plantation House, the governor's parting signal for the *Spray*, till the island faded in the darkness astern and became one with the night, and by midnight the light itself had disappeared below the horizon.

When morning came there was no land in sight, but the day went on the same as days before, save for one small incident. Governor Sterndale had given me a bag of coffee in the husk, and Clark, the American, in an evil moment, had put a goat on board, "to butt the sack and hustle the coffee-beans out of the pods." He urged that the animal, besides being useful, would be as companionable as a dog. I soon found that my sailing-companion, this sort of dog with horns, had to be tied up entirely. The mistake I made was that I did not chain him to the mast instead of tying him with grass ropes less securely, and this I learned to my cost. Except for the first day, before the beast got his sea-legs on, I had no peace of mind. After that, actuated by a spirit born, maybe, of his pasturage, this incarnation of evil threatened to devour everything from flying-jib to stern-davits. He was the worst pirate I met on the whole voyage. He began depredations by eating my chart of the West Indies, in the cabin, one day, while I was about my work for'ard, thinking that the critter was securely tied on deck by the pumps. Alas! there was not a rope in the sloop proof against that goat's awful teeth!

It was clear from the very first that I was having no luck with animals on board. There was the tree-crab from the Keeling Islands. No sooner

had it got a claw through its prison-box than my
sea-jacket, hanging within reach, was torn to ribbons. Encouraged by this success, it smashed the
box open and escaped into my cabin, tearing up
things generally, and finally threatening my life in
the dark. I had hoped to bring the creature home
alive, but this did not prove feasible. Next the
goat devoured my straw hat, and so when I arrived in port I had nothing to wear ashore on my
head. This last unkind stroke decided his fate.
On the 27th of April the *Spray* arrived at Ascension, which is garrisoned by a man-of-war crew,
and the boatswain of the island came on board.
As he stepped out of his boat the mutinous goat
climbed into it, and defied boatswain and crew. I
hired them to land the wretch at once, which they
were only too willing to do, and there he fell into
the hands of a most excellent Scotchman, with the
chances that he would never get away. I was des-
tined to sail once more into the depths of solitude,
but these experiences had no bad effect upon me;
on the contrary, a spirit of charity and even benevolence grew stronger in my nature through the
meditations of these supreme hours on the sea.

In the loneliness of the dreary country about
Cape Horn I found myself in no mood to make one
life less in the world, except in self-defense, and as
I sailed this trait of the hermit character grew till
the mention of killing food-animals was revolting
to me. However well I may have enjoyed a chicken
stew afterward at Samoa, a new self rebelled at the
thought suggested there of carrying chickens to be
slain for my table on the voyage, and Mrs. Steven-

son, hearing my protest, agreed with me that to kill the companions of my voyage and eat them would be indeed next to murder and cannibalism.

As to pet animals, there was no room for a noble large dog on the *Spray* on so long a voyage, and a small cur was for many years associated in my mind with hydrophobia. I witnessed once the death of a sterling young German from that dreadful disease, and about the same time heard of the death, also by hydrophobia, of the young gentleman who had just written a line of insurance in his company's books for me. I have seen the whole crew of a ship scamper up the rigging to avoid a dog racing about the decks in a fit. It would never do, I thought, for the crew of the *Spray* to take a canine risk, and with these just prejudices indelibly stamped on my mind, I have, I am afraid, answered impatiently too often the query, "Did n't you have a dog?" with, "I and the dog would n't have been very long in the same boat, in any sense." A cat would have been a harmless animal, I dare say, but there was nothing for puss to do on board, and she is an unsociable animal at best. True, a rat got into my vessel at the Keeling Cocos Islands, and another at Rodriguez, along with a centiped stowed away in the hold; but one of them I drove out of the ship, and the other I caught. This is how it was: for the first one with infinite pains I made a trap, looking to its capture and destruction; but the wily rodent, not to be deluded, took the hint and got ashore the day the thing was completed.

It is, according to tradition, a most reassuring

sign to find rats coming to a ship, and I had a mind to abide the knowing one of Rodriguez; but a breach of discipline decided the matter against him. While I slept one night, my ship sailing on, he undertook to walk over me, beginning at the crown of my head, concerning which I am always sensitive. I sleep lightly. Before his impertinence had got him even to my nose I cried "Rat!" had him by the tail, and threw him out of the companionway into the sea.

As for the centiped, I was not aware of its presence till the wretched insect, all feet and venom, beginning, like the rat, at my head, wakened me by a sharp bite on the scalp. This also was more than I could tolerate. After a few applications of kerosene the poisonous bite, painful at first, gave me no further inconvenience.

From this on for a time no living thing disturbed my solitude; no insect even was present in my vessel, except the spider and his wife, from Boston, now with a family of young spiders. Nothing, I say, till sailing down the last stretch of the Indian Ocean, where mosquitos came by hundreds from rain-water poured out of the heavens. Simply a barrel of rain-water stood on deck five days, I think, in the sun, then music began. I knew the sound at once; it was the same as heard from Alaska to New Orleans.

Again at Cape Town, while dining out one day, I was taken with the song of a cricket, and Mr. Branscombe, my host, volunteered to capture a pair of them for me. They were sent on board next day in a box labeled, "Pluto and Scamp."

Stowing them away in the binnacle in their own snug box, I left them there without food till I got to sea—a few days. I had never heard of a cricket eating anything. It seems that Pluto was a cannibal, for only the wings of poor Scamp were visible when I opened the lid, and they lay broken on the floor of the prison-box. Even with Pluto it had gone hard, for he lay on his back stark and stiff, never to chirrup again.

Ascension Island, where the goat was marooned, is called the Stone Frigate, R. N., and is rated "tender" to the South African Squadron. It lies in 7° 55′ south latitude and 14° 25′ west longitude, being in the very heart of the southeast trade-winds and about eight hundred and forty miles from the coast of Liberia. It is a mass of volcanic matter, thrown up from the bed of the ocean to the height of two thousand eight hundred and eighteen feet at the highest point above sea-level. It is a strategic point, and belonged to Great Britain before it got cold. In the limited but rich soil at the top of the island, among the clouds, vegetation has taken root, and a little scientific farming is carried on under the supervision of a gentleman from Canada. Also a few cattle and sheep are pastured there for the garrison mess. Water storage is made on a large scale. In a word, this heap of cinders and lava rock is stored and fortified, and would stand a siege.

Very soon after the *Spray* arrived I received a note from Captain Blaxland, the commander of the island, conveying his thanks for the royal mail brought from St. Helena, and inviting me to luncheon with him and his wife and sister at headquarters, not far away. It is hardly necessary to say that I availed myself of the captain's hospitality at once. A carriage was waiting at the jetty when I landed, and a sailor, with a broad grin, led the horse carefully up the hill to the captain's house, as if I were a lord of the admiralty, and a governor besides; and he led it as carefully down again when I returned. On the following day I visited the summit among the clouds, the same team being provided, and the same old sailor leading the horse. There was probably not a man on the island at that moment better able to walk than I. The sailor knew that. I finally suggested that we change places. "Let me take the bridle," I said, "and keep the horse from bolting." "Great Stone Frigate!" he exclaimed, as he burst into a laugh, "this 'ere 'oss would n't bolt no faster nor a turtle. If I did n't tow 'im 'ard we 'd never get into port." I walked most of the way over the steep grades, whereupon my guide, every inch a sailor, became my friend. Arriving at the summit of the island, I met Mr. Schank, the farmer from Canada, and his sister, living very cozily in a house among the rocks, as snug as conies, and as safe. He showed me over the farm, taking me through a tunnel which led from one field to the other, divided by an inaccessible spur of mountain. Mr. Schank said that he had lost many cows and bullocks, as well as sheep, from breakneck over the steep cliffs and precipices. One cow, he said, would sometimes hook another right over a precipice to destruction, and go on feeding unconcernedly. It seemed that the ani-

mals on the island farm, like mankind in the wide
world, found it all too small.

On the 26th of April, while I was ashore, rollers
came in which rendered launching a boat impossible. However, the sloop being securely moored to
a buoy in deep water outside of all breakers, she
was safe, while I, in the best of quarters, listened
to well-told stories among the officers of the Stone
Frigate. On the evening of the 29th, the sea having gone down, I went on board and made preparations to start again on my voyage early next day,
the boatswain of the island and his crew giving me
a hearty handshake as I embarked at the jetty.

For reasons of scientific interest, I invited in
mid-ocean the most thorough investigation concerning the crew-list of the *Spray*. Very few had
challenged it, and perhaps few ever will do so
henceforth; but for the benefit of the few that may,
I wished to clench beyond doubt the fact that it
was not at all necessary in the expedition of a
sloop around the world to have more than one man
for the crew, all told, and that the *Spray* sailed
with only one person on board. And so, by appointment, Lieutenant Eagles, the executive officer,
in the morning, just as I was ready to sail, fumigated the sloop, rendering it impossible for a person
to live concealed below, and proving that only one
person was on board when she arrived. A certificate to this effect, besides the official documents
from the many consulates, health offices, and custom-
houses, will seem to many superfluous; but this
story of the voyage may find its way into hands
unfamiliar with the business of these offices and of

their ways of seeing that a vessel's papers, and, above all, her bills of health, are in order.

The lieutenant's certificate being made out, the *Spray*, nothing loath, now filled away clear of the sea-beaten rocks, and the trade-winds, comfortably cool and bracing, sent her flying along on her course. On May 8, 1898, she crossed the track, homeward bound, that she had made October 2, 1895, on the voyage out. She passed Fernando de Noronha at night, going some miles south of it, and so I did not see the island. I felt a contentment in knowing that the *Spray* had encircled the globe, and even as an adventure alone I was in no way discouraged as to its utility, and said to myself, "Let what will happen, the voyage is now on record." A period was made.

CHAPTER XX

ON May 10 there was a great change in the condition of the sea; there could be no doubt of my longitude now, if any had before existed in my mind. Strange and long-forgotten current ripples pattered against the sloop's sides in grateful music; the tune arrested the ear, and I sat quietly listening to it while the *Spray* kept on her course. By these current ripples I was assured that she was now off St. Roque and had struck the current which sweeps around that cape. The trade-winds, we old sailors say, produce this current, which, in its course from this point forward, is governed by the coast-line of Brazil, Guiana, Venezuela, and, as some would say, by the Monroe Doctrine.

The trades had been blowing fresh for some time, and the current, now at its height, amounted to forty miles a day. This, added to the sloop's run by the log, made the handsome day's work of one hundred and eighty miles on several consecutive days. I saw nothing of the coast of Brazil, though

I was not many leagues off and was always in the Brazil current.

I did not know that war with Spain had been declared, and that I might be liable, right there, to meet the enemy and be captured. Many had told me at Cape Town that, in their opinion, war was inevitable, and they said: "The Spaniard will get you! The Spaniard will get you!" To all this I could only say that, even so, he would not get much. Even in the fever-heat over the disaster to the *Maine* I did not think there would be war; but I am no politician. Indeed, I had hardly given the matter a serious thought when, on the 14th of May, just north of the equator, and near the longitude of the river Amazon, I saw first a mast, with the Stars and Stripes floating from it, rising astern as if poked up out of the sea, and then rapidly appearing on the horizon, like a citadel, the *Oregon!* As she came near I saw that the great ship was flying the signals "C B T," which read, "Are there any men-of-war about?" Right under these flags, and larger than the *Spray's* mainsail, so it appeared, was the yellowest Spanish flag I ever saw. It gave me nightmare some time after when I reflected on it in my dreams.

I did not make out the *Oregon's* signals till she passed ahead, where I could read them better, for she was two miles away, and I had no binoculars. When I had read her flags I hoisted the signal "No," for I had not seen any Spanish men-of-war; I had not been looking for any. My final signal, "Let us keep together for mutual protection," Captain Clark did not seem to regard as necessary. Per-

THOMAS FOGARTY.

The *Spray* passed by the *Oregon*.

haps my small flags were not made out; anyhow,
the *Oregon* steamed on with a rush, looking for
Spanish men-of-war, as I learned afterward.   The
Oregon's great flag was dipped beautifully three
times to the *Spray's* lowered flag as she passed on.
Both had crossed the line only a few hours before.
I pondered long that night over the probability of
a war risk now coming upon the *Spray* after she
had cleared all, or nearly all, the dangers of the sea,
but finally a strong hope mastered my fears.

On the 17th of May, the *Spray*, coming out of a
storm at daylight, made Devil's Island, two points
on the lee bow, not far off.   The wind was still
blowing a stiff breeze on shore.   I could clearly see
the dark-gray buildings on the island as the sloop
brought it abeam.   No flag or sign of life was seen
on the dreary place.

Later in the day a French bark on the port tack,
making for Cayenne, hove in sight, close-hauled
on the wind.   She was falling to leeward fast.
The *Spray* was also closed-hauled, and was lugging
on sail to secure an offing on the starboard tack, a
heavy swell in the night having thrown her too
near the shore, and now I considered the matter of
supplicating a change of wind.   I had already enjoyed my share of favoring breezes over the great
oceans, and I asked myself if it would be right to
have the wind turned now all into my sails while
the Frenchman was bound the other way.   A head
current, which he stemmed, together with a scant
wind, was bad enough for him.   And so I could
only say, in my heart, " Lord, let matters stand as
they are, but do not help the Frenchman any more

just now, for what would suit him well would ruin me!"

I remembered that when a lad I heard a captain often say in meeting that in answer to a prayer of his own the wind changed from southeast to northwest, entirely to his satisfaction. He was a good man, but did this glorify the Architect — the Ruler of the winds and the waves? Moreover, it was not a trade-wind, as I remember it, that changed for him, but one of the variables which will change when you ask it, if you ask long enough. Again, this man's brother maybe was not bound the opposite way, well content with a fair wind himself, which made all the difference in the world.[1]

On May 18, 1898, is written large in the *Spray's* log-book: "To-night, in latitude 7° 13' N., for the first time in nearly three years I see the north star." The *Spray* on the day following logged one hundred and forty-seven miles. To this I add thirty-five miles for current sweeping her onward. On the 20th of May, about sunset, the island of Tobago, off the Orinoco, came into view, bearing west by north, distant twenty-two miles. The *Spray* was drawing rapidly toward her home destination. Later at night, while running free along the coast of Tobago, the wind still blowing fresh, I was startled by the sudden flash of breakers on the port bow and not far off. I luffed instantly offshore, and then tacked, heading in for the island. Find-

---

[1] The Bishop of Melbourne (commend me to his teachings) refused to set aside a day of prayer for rain, recommending his people to husband water when the rainy season was on. In like manner, a navigator husbands the wind, keeping a weather-gage where practicable.

ing myself, shortly after, close in with the land, I
tacked again offshore, but without much altering
the bearings of the danger. Sail whichever way I
would, it seemed clear that if the sloop weathered
the rocks at all it would be a close shave, and I
watched with anxiety, while beating against the
current, always losing ground. So the matter stood
hour after hour, while I watched the flashes of light
thrown up as regularly as the beats of the long
ocean swells, and always they seemed just a little
nearer. It was evidently a coral reef,— of this I
had not the slightest doubt,— and a bad reef at
that. Worse still, there might be other reefs ahead
forming a bight into which the current would
sweep me, and where I should be hemmed in and
finally wrecked. I had not sailed these waters since
a lad, and lamented the day I had allowed on
board the goat that ate my chart. I taxed my
memory of sea lore, of wrecks on sunken reefs, and
of pirates harbored among coral reefs where other
ships might not come, but nothing that I could
think of applied to the island of Tobago, save the
one wreck of Robinson Crusoe's ship in the fiction,
and that gave me little information about reefs.
I remembered only that in Crusoe's case he kept
his powder dry. "But there she booms again," I
cried, "and how close the flash is now! Almost
aboard was that last breaker! But you 'll go by,
Spray, old girl! 'T is abeam now! One surge
more! and oh, one more like that will clear your
ribs and keel!" And I slapped her on the tran-
som, proud of her last noble effort to leap clear
of the danger, when a wave greater than the rest

threw her higher than before, and, behold, from the crest of it was revealed at once all there was of the reef. I fell back in a coil of rope, speechless and amazed, not distressed, but rejoiced. Aladdin's lamp! My fisherman's own lantern! It was the great revolving light on the island of Trinidad, thirty miles away, throwing flashes over the waves, which had deceived me! The orb of the light was now dipping on the horizon, and how glorious was the sight of it! But, dear Father Neptune, as I live, after a long life at sea, and much among corals, I would have made a solemn declaration to that reef! Through all the rest of the night I saw imaginary reefs, and not knowing what moment the sloop might fetch up on a real one, I tacked off and on till daylight, as nearly as possible in the same track, all for the want of a chart. I could have nailed the St. Helena goat's pelt to the deck.

My course was now for Grenada, to which I carried letters from Mauritius. About midnight of the 22d of May I arrived at the island, and cast anchor in the roads off the town of St. George, entering the inner harbor at daylight on the morning of the 23d, which made forty-two days' sailing from the Cape of Good Hope. It was a good run, and I doffed my cap again to the pilot of the *Pinta*.

Lady Bruce, in a note to the *Spray* at Port Louis, said Grenada was a lovely island, and she wished the sloop might call there on the voyage home. When the *Spray* arrived, I found that she had been fully expected. "How so?" I asked. "Oh, we heard that you were at Mauritius," they said, "and from Mauritius, after meeting Sir Charles

Bruce, our old governor, we knew you would come to Grenada." This was a charming introduction, and it brought me in contact with people worth knowing.

The *Spray* sailed from Grenada on the 28th of May, and coasted along under the lee of the Antilles, arriving at the island of Dominica on the 30th, where, for the want of knowing better, I cast anchor at the quarantine ground; for I was still without a chart of the islands, not having been able to get one even at Grenada. Here I not only met with further disappointment in the matter, but was threatened with a fine for the mistake I made in the anchorage. There were no ships either at the quarantine or at the commercial roads, and I could not see that it made much difference where I anchored. But a negro chap, a sort of deputy harbormaster, coming along, thought it did, and he ordered me to shift to the other anchorage, which, in truth, I had already investigated and did not like, because of the heavier roll there from the sea. And so instead of springing to the sails at once to shift, I said I would leave outright as soon as I could procure a chart, which I begged he would send and get for me. "But I say you mus' move befo' you gets anyt'ing 't all," he insisted, and raising his voice so that all the people alongshore could hear him, he added, "An' jes now!" Then he flew into a towering passion when they on shore snickered to see the crew of the *Spray* sitting calmly by the bulwark instead of hoisting sail. "I tell you dis am quarantine," he shouted, very much louder than before. "That's all right, general," I replied; "I want to be quarantined anyhow." "That 's right, boss," some one on the beach cried, "that's right; you get quarantined," while others shouted to the deputy to "make de white trash move 'long out o' dat." They were about equally divided on the island for and against me. The man who had made so much fuss over the matter gave it up when he found that I wished to be quarantined, and sent for an all-important half-white, who soon came alongside, starched from clue to earing. He stood in the boat as straight up and down as a fathom of pump-water — a marvel of importance. "Charts!" cried I, as soon as his shirt-collar appeared over the sloop's rail; "have you any charts?" "No, sah," he replied with much-stiffened dignity; "no, sah; cha'ts do's n't grow on dis island." Not doubting the information, I tripped anchor immediately, as I had intended to do from the first, and made all sail for St. John, Antigua, where I arrived on the 1st of June, having sailed with great caution in midchannel all the way.

The *Spray*, always in good company, now fell in with the port officers' steam-launch at the harbor entrance, having on board Sir Francis Fleming, governor of the Leeward Islands, who, to the delight of "all hands," gave the officer in charge instructions to tow my ship into port. On the following day his Excellency and Lady Fleming, along with Captain Burr, R. N., paid me a visit. The court-house was tendered free to me at Antigua, as was done also at Grenada, and at each place a highly intelligent audience filled the hall to listen to a talk about the seas the *Spray* had crossed, and the countries she had visited.

CHAPTER XXI

ON the 4th of June, 1898, the *Spray* cleared from the United States consulate, and her license to sail single-handed, even round the world, was returned to her for the last time. The United States consul, Mr. Hunt, before handing the paper to me, wrote on it, as General Roberts had done at Cape Town, a short commentary on the voyage. The document, by regular course, is now lodged in the Treasury Department at Washington, D. C.

On June 5, 1898, the *Spray* sailed for a home port, heading first direct for Cape Hatteras. On the 8th of June she passed under the sun from south to north; the sun's declination on that day was 22° 54', and the latitude of the *Spray* was the same just before noon. Many think it is excessively hot right under the sun. It is not necessarily so. As a matter of fact the thermometer stands at a bearable point whenever there is a breeze and a ripple on the sea, even exactly under the sun. It is often hotter in cities and on sandy shores in higher latitudes.

The *Spray* was booming joyously along for home now, making her usual good time, when of a sudden she struck the horse latitudes, and her sail flapped limp in a calm. I had almost forgotten this calm belt, or had come to regard it as a myth. I now found it real, however, and difficult to cross. This was as it should have been, for, after all of the dangers of the sea, the dust-storm on the coast of Africa, the "rain of blood" in Australia, and the war risk when nearing home, a natural experience would have been missing had the calm of the horse latitudes been left out. Anyhow, a philosophical turn of thought now was not amiss, else one's patience would have given out almost at the harbor entrance. The term of her probation was eight days. Evening after evening during this time I read by the light of a candle on deck. There was no wind at all, and the sea became smooth and monotonous. For three days I saw a full-rigged ship on the horizon, also becalmed.

Sargasso, scattered over the sea in bunches, or trailed curiously along down the wind in narrow lanes, now gathered together in great fields, strange sea-animals, little and big, swimming in and out, the most curious among them being a tiny sea-horse which I captured and brought home preserved in a bottle. But on the 18th of June a gale began to blow from the southwest, and the sargasso was dispersed again in windrows and lanes.

On this day there was soon wind enough and to spare. The same might have been said of the sea The *Spray* was in the midst of the turbulent Gulf Stream itself. She was jumping like a porpoise

over the uneasy waves. As if to make up for lost
time, she seemed to touch only the high places.
Under a sudden shock and strain her rigging began
to give out. First the main-sheet strap was carried
away, and then the peak halyard-block broke from
the gaff. It was time to reef and refit, and so when
"all hands" came on deck I went about doing that.

The 19th of June was fine, but on the morning
of the 20th another gale was blowing, accompanied
by cross-seas that tumbled about and shook things
up with great confusion. Just as I was thinking
about taking in sail the jibstay broke at the masthead, and fell, jib and all, into the sea. It gave me
the strangest sensation to see the bellying sail fall,
and where it had been suddenly to see only space.
However, I was at the bows, with presence of mind
to gather it in on the first wave that rolled up, before it was torn or trailed under the sloop's bottom.
I found by the amount of work done in three minutes' or less time that I had by no means grown
stiff-jointed on the voyage; anyhow, scurvy had
not set in, and being now within a few degrees
of home, I might complete the voyage, I thought,
without the aid of a doctor. Yes, my health was
still good, and I could skip about the decks in a
lively manner, but could I climb? The great King
Neptune tested me severely at this time, for the
stay being gone, the mast itself switched about like
a reed, and was not easy to climb; but a gun-tackle
purchase was got up, and the stay set taut from
the masthead, for I had spare blocks and rope on
board with which to rig it, and the jib, with a reef
in it, was soon pulling again like a "sodger" for

home. Had the *Spray's* mast not been well stepped, however, it would have been "John Walker" when the stay broke. Good work in the building of my vessel stood me always in good stead.

On the 23d of June I was at last tired, tired, tired of baffling squalls and fretful cobble-seas. I had not seen a vessel for days and days, where I had expected the company of at least a schooner now and then. As to the whistling of the wind through the rigging, and the slopping of the sea against the sloop's sides, that was well enough in its way, and we could not have got on without it, the *Spray* and I; but there was so much of it now, and it lasted so long! At noon of that day a winterish storm was upon us from the nor'west. In the Gulf Stream, thus late in June, hailstones were pelting the *Spray*, and lightning was pouring down from the clouds, not in flashes alone, but in almost continuous streams. By slants, however, day and night I worked the sloop in toward the coast, where, on the 25th of June, off Fire Island, she fell into the tornado which, an hour earlier, had swept over New York city with lightning that wrecked buildings and sent trees flying about in splinters; even ships at docks had parted their moorings and smashed into other ships, doing great damage. It was the climax storm of the voyage, but I saw the unmistakable character of it in time to have all snug aboard and receive it under bare poles. Even so, the sloop shivered when it struck her, and she heeled over unwillingly on her beam ends; but rounding to, with a sea-anchor ahead, she righted and faced out the storm. In the midst of the gale I could do no more than look on, for what is a man in a storm like this ? I had seen one electric storm on the voyage, off the coast of Madagascar, but it was unlike this one. Here the lightning kept on longer, and thunderbolts fell in the sea all about. Up to this time I was bound for New York; but when all was over I rose, made sail, and hove the sloop round from starboard to port tack, to make for a quiet harbor to think the matter over; and so, under short sail, she reached in for the coast of Long Island, while I sat thinking and watching the lights of coasting-vessels which now began to appear in sight. Reflections of the voyage so nearly finished stole in upon me now; many tunes I had hummed again and again came back once more. I found myself repeating fragments of a hymn often sung by a dear Christian woman of Fairhaven when I was rebuilding the *Spray*. I was to hear once more and only once, in profound solemnity, the metaphorical hymn:

> By waves and wind I 'm tossed and driven.

And again :

> But still my little ship outbraves
> The blust'ring winds and stormy waves.

After this storm I saw the pilot of the *Pinta* no more.

The experiences of the voyage of the *Spray*, reaching over three years, had been to me like reading a book, and one that was more and more interesting as I turned the pages, till I had come now to the last page of all, and the one more interesting than any of the rest.

When daylight came I saw that the sea had changed color from dark green to light. I threw the lead and got soundings in thirteen fathoms. I made the land soon after, some miles east of Fire Island, and sailing thence before a pleasant breeze along the coast, made for Newport. The weather after the furious gale was remarkably fine. The *Spray* rounded Montauk Point early in the afternoon; Point Judith was abeam at dark; she fetched in at Beavertail next. Sailing on, she had one more danger to pass — Newport harbor was mined. The *Spray* hugged the rocks along where neither friend nor foe could come if drawing much water, and where she would not disturb the guard-ship in the channel. It was close work, but it was safe enough so long as she hugged the rocks close, and not the mines. Flitting by a low point abreast of the guard-ship, the dear old *Dexter*, which I knew well, some one on board of her sang out, "There goes a craft!" I threw up a light at once and heard the hail, "*Spray*, ahoy!" It was the voice of a friend, and I knew that a friend would not fire on the *Spray*. I eased off the main-sheet now, and the *Spray* swung off for the beacon-lights of the inner harbor. At last she reached port in safety, and there at 1 A. M. on June 27, 1898, cast anchor, after the cruise of more than forty-six thousand miles round the world, during an absence of three years and two months, with two days over for coming up.

Was the crew well? Was I not? I had profited in many ways by the voyage. I had even gained flesh, and actually weighed a pound more than when I sailed from Boston. As for aging, why, the dial of my life was turned back till my friends all said, "Slocum is young again." And so I was, at least ten years younger than the day I felled the first tree for the construction of the *Spray*.

My ship was also in better condition than when she sailed from Boston on her long voyage. She was still as sound as a nut, and as tight as the best ship afloat. She did not leak a drop — not one drop! The pump, which had been little used before reaching Australia, had not been rigged since that at all.

The first name on the *Spray's* visitors' book in the home port was written by the one who always said, "The *Spray* will come back." The *Spray* was not quite satisfied till I sailed her around to her birthplace, Fairhaven, Massachusetts, farther along. I had myself a desire to return to the place of the very beginning whence I had, as I have said, renewed my age. So on July 3, with a fair wind, she waltzed beautifully round the coast and up the Acushnet River to Fairhaven, where I secured her to the cedar spile driven in the bank to hold her when she was launched. I could bring her no nearer home.

If the *Spray* discovered no continents on her voyage, it may be that there were no more continents to be discovered; she did not seek new worlds, or sail to powwow about the dangers of the seas. The sea has been much maligned. To

Again tied to the old stake at Fairhaven.

find one's way to lands already discovered is a good thing, and the *Spray* made the discovery that even the worst sea is not so terrible to a well-appointed ship. No king, no country, no treasury at all, was taxed for the voyage of the *Spray*, and she accomplished all that she undertook to do.

To succeed, however, in anything at all, one should go understandingly about his work and be prepared for every emergency. I see, as I look back over my own small achievement, a kit of not too elaborate carpenters' tools, a tin clock, and some carpet-tacks, not a great many, to facilitate the enterprise as already mentioned in the story. But above all to be taken into account were some years of schooling, where I studied with diligence Neptune's laws, and these laws I tried to obey when I sailed overseas; it was worth the while.

And now, without having wearied my friends, I hope, with detailed scientific accounts, theories, or deductions, I will only say that I have endeavored to tell just the story of the adventure itself. This, in my own poor way, having been done, I now moor ship, weather-bitt cables, and leave the sloop *Spray*, for the present, safe in port.

APPENDIX

APPENDIX

FROM a feeling of diffidence toward sailors of great experience, I refrained, in the preceding chapters as prepared for serial publication in the "Century Magazine," from entering fully into the details of the *Spray's* build, and of the primitive methods employed to sail her. Having had no yachting experience at all, I had no means of knowing that the trim vessels seen in our harbors and near the land could not all do as much, or even more, than the *Spray*, sailing, for example, on a course with the helm lashed.

I was aware that no other vessel had sailed in this manner around the globe, but would have been loath to say that another could not do it, or that many men had not sailed vessels of a certain rig in that manner as far as they wished to go. I was greatly amused, therefore, by the flat assertions of an expert that it could not be done.

The *Spray*, as I sailed her, was entirely a new boat, built over from a sloop which bore the same name, and which, tradition said, had first served as

an oysterman, about a hundred years ago, on the
coast of Delaware. There was no record in the
custom-house of where she was built. She was once
owned at Noank, Connecticut, afterward in New
Bedford and when Captain Eben Pierce presented

Plan of the after cabin of the *Spray*.

her to me, at the end of her natural life, she stood, as
I have already described, propped up in a field at
Fairhaven. Her lines were supposed to be those
of a North Sea fisherman. In rebuilding timber
by timber and plank by plank, I added to her free-

board twelve inches amidships, eighteen inches forward, and fourteen inches aft, thereby increasing
her sheer, and making her, as I thought, a better
deep-water ship. I will not repeat the history of
the rebuilding of the *Spray*, which I have detailed
in my first chapter, except to say that, when finished, her dimensions were thirty-six feet nine
inches over all, fourteen feet two inches wide, and
four feet two inches deep in the hold, her tonnage
being nine tons net, and twelve and seventy one-
hundredths tons gross.

I gladly produce the lines of the *Spray*, with such
hints as my really limited fore-and-aft sailing will
allow, my seafaring life having been spent mostly
in barks and ships. No pains have been spared to
give them accurately. The *Spray* was taken from
New York to Bridgeport, Connecticut, and, under
the supervision of the Park City Yacht Club, was
hauled out of water and very carefully measured
in every way to secure a satisfactory result. Captain Robins produced the model. Our young
yachtsmen, pleasuring in the "lilies of the sea,"
very naturally will not think favorably of my craft.
They have a right to their opinion, while I stick to
mine. They will take exceptions to her short ends,
the advantage of these being most apparent in a
heavy sea.

Some things about the *Spray's* deck might be
fashioned differently without materially affecting
the vessel. I know of no good reason why for
a party-boat a cabin trunk might not be built
amidships instead of far aft, like the one on her,
which leaves a very narrow space between the

wheel and the line of the companionway. Some
even say that I might have improved the shape
of her stern. I do not know about that. The
water leaves her run sharp after bearing her to
the last inch, and no suction is formed by undue
cutaway.

Smooth-water sailors say, "Where is her overhang?" They never crossed the Gulf Stream in
a nor'easter, and they do not know what is best
in all weathers. For your life, build no fantail
overhang on a craft going offshore. As a sailor
judges his prospective ship by a "blow of the
eye" when he takes interest enough to look her
over at all, so I judged the *Spray*, and I was not
deceived.

In a sloop-rig the *Spray* made that part of her
voyage reaching from Boston through the Strait of
Magellan, during which she experienced the greatest variety of weather conditions. The yawl-rig
then adopted was an improvement only in that it
reduced the size of a rather heavy mainsail and
slightly improved her steering qualities on the
wind. When the wind was aft the jigger was not
in use; invariably it was then furled. With her
boom broad off and with the wind two points on
the quarter the *Spray* sailed her truest course. It
never took long to find the amount of helm, or
angle of rudder, required to hold her on her course,
and when that was found I lashed the wheel with
it at that angle. The mainsail then drove her,
and the main-jib, with its sheet boused flat amidships or a little to one side or the other, added
greatly to the steadying power. Then if the wind
was even strong or squally I would sometimes set

Deck-plan of the Spray.

a flying-jib also, on a pole rigged out on the bowsprit, with the sheets hauled flat amidships, which was a safe thing to do, even in a gale of wind. A stout downhaul on the gaff was a necessity, because without it the mainsail might not have come down when I wished to lower it in a breeze. The amount of helm required varied according to the amount of wind and its direction. These points are quickly gathered from practice.

Briefly I have to say that when close-hauled in a light wind under all sail she required little or no weather helm. As the wind increased I would go

SCALE OF FEET
1 2 3 4 5 6 7 8 9 10

41 FT

19 FT

22 FT. 6 IN.

34 FT

Sail-plan of the *Spray*.

The solid lines represent the sail-plan of the *Spray* on starting for the long voyage. With it she crossed the Atlantic to Gibraltar, and then crossed again southwest to Brazil. In South American waters the bowsprit and boom were shortened and the jigger-sail added to form the yawl-rig with which the rest of the trip was made, the sail-plan of which is indicated by the dotted lines. The extreme sail forward is a flying jib occasionally used, set to a bamboo stick fastened to the bowsprit. The manner of setting and bracing the jigger-mast is not indicated in this drawing, but may be partly observed in the plans on pages 287 and 289.

on deck, if below, and turn the wheel up a spoke
more or less, relash it, or, as sailors say, put it in a
becket, and then leave it as before.

To answer the questions that might be asked to
meet every contingency would be a pleasure, but
it would overburden my book. I can only say
here that much comes to one in practice, and
that, with such as love sailing, mother-wit is the

Steering-gear of the *Spray*.

The dotted lines are the ropes used to lash the wheel. In practice the loose ends were belayed, one
over the other, around the top spokes of the wheel.

best teacher, after experience. Labor-saving appli-
ances? There were none. The sails were hoisted
by hand; the halyards were rove through ordinary
ships' blocks with common patent rollers. Of
course the sheets were all belayed aft.

The windlass used was in the shape of a winch,
or crab, I think it is called. I had three anchors,

weighing forty pounds, one hundred pounds, and one hundred and eighty pounds respectively. The windlass and the forty-pound anchor, and the "fiddle-head," or carving, on the end of the cutwater, belonged to the original *Spray*. The ballast, concrete cement, was stanchioned down securely. There was no iron or lead or other weight on the keel.

If I took measurements by rule I did not set them down, and after sailing even the longest voyage in her I could not tell offhand the length of her mast, boom, or gaff. I did not know the center of effort in her sails, except as it hit me in practice at sea, nor did I care a rope yarn about it. Mathematical calculations, however, are all right in a good boat, and the *Spray* could have stood them. She was easily balanced and easily kept in trim.

Some of the oldest and ablest shipmasters have asked how it was possible for her to hold a true course before the wind, which was just what the *Spray* did for weeks together. One of these gentlemen, a highly esteemed shipmaster and friend, testified as government expert in a famous murder trial in Boston, not long since, that a ship would not hold her course long enough for the steersman to leave the helm to cut the captain's throat. Ordinarily it would be so. One might say that with a square-rigged ship it would always be so. But the *Spray*, at the moment of the tragedy in question, was sailing around the globe with no one at the helm, except at intervals more or less rare. However, I may say here that this would have had no bearing on the murder case in Boston. In all probability Justice laid her hand on the true rogue. In other words, in the case of a model and rig similar to that of the tragedy ship, I should myself testify as did the nautical experts at the trial.

But see the run the *Spray* made from Thursday Island to the Keeling Cocos Islands, twenty-seven hundred miles distant, in twenty-three days, with no one at the helm in that time, save for about one hour, from land to land. No other ship in the

Body-plan of the *Spray*.

history of the world ever performed, under similar circumstances, the feat on so long and continuous a voyage. It was, however, a delightful midsummer sail. No one can know the pleasure of sailing free over the great oceans save those who have had the experience. It is not necessary, in order to realize the utmost enjoyment of going around the globe, to sail alone, yet for once and the first time there was a great deal of fun in it. My friend the government expert, and saltest of salt sea-captains, standing only yesterday on the deck of the *Spray*, was convinced of her famous qualities, and he spoke enthusiastically of selling his farm on Cape Cod and putting to sea again.

To young men contemplating a voyage I would say go. The tales of rough usage are for the most part exaggerations, as also are the stories of sea danger. I had a fair schooling in the so-called "hard ships" on the hard Western Ocean, and in the years there I do not remember having once been "called out of my name." Such recollections have endeared the sea to me. I owe it further to the officers of all the ships I ever sailed in as boy and man to say that not one ever lifted so much as a finger to me. I did not live among angels, but among men who could be roused. My wish was, though, to please the officers of my ship wherever I was, and so I got on. Dangers there are, to be sure, on the sea as well as on the land, but the intelligence and skill God gives to man reduce these to a minimum. And here comes in again the skilfully modeled ship worthy to sail the seas.

To face the elements is, to be sure, no light matter when the sea is in its grandest mood. You must then know the sea, and know that you know it, and not forget that it was made to be sailed over.

I have given in the plans of the *Spray* the dimensions of such a ship as I should call seaworthy in all conditions of weather and on all seas. It is only right to say, though, that to insure a reasonable measure of success, experience should sail with

—Scale—

Lines of the *Spray*.

the ship.   But in order to be a successful navigator or sailor it is not necessary to hang a tar-bucket about one's neck.   On the other hand, much thought concerning the brass buttons one should wear adds nothing to the safety of the ship.

I may some day see reason to modify the model of the dear old *Spray*, but out of my limited experience I strongly recommend her wholesome lines over those of pleasure-fliers for safety.   Practice in a craft such as the *Spray* will teach young sailors and fit them for the more important vessels.   I myself learned more seamanship, I think, on the *Spray* than on any other ship I ever sailed, and as for patience, the greatest of all the virtues, even while sailing through the reaches of the Strait of Magellan, between the bluff mainland and dismal Fuego, where through intricate sailing I was obliged to steer, I learned to sit by the wheel, content to make ten miles a day beating against the tide, and when a month at that was all lost, I could find some old tune to hum while I worked the route all over again, beating as before.   Nor did thirty hours at the wheel, in storm, overtax my human endurance, and to clap a hand to an oar and pull into or out of port in a calm was no strange experience for the crew of the *Spray*.   The days passed happily with me wherever my ship sailed.

A CATALOGUE OF SELECTED DOVER BOOKS
IN ALL FIELDS OF INTEREST

A CATALOGUE OF SELECTED DOVER BOOKS
IN ALL FIELDS OF INTEREST

AMERICA'S OLD MASTERS, James T. Flexner. Four men emerged unexpectedly from provincial 18th century America to leadership in European art: Benjamin West, J. S. Copley, C. R. Peale, Gilbert Stuart. Brilliant coverage of lives and contributions. Revised, 1967 edition. 69 plates. 365pp. of text.
21806-6 Paperbound $3.00

FIRST FLOWERS OF OUR WILDERNESS: AMERICAN PAINTING, THE COLONIAL PERIOD, James T. Flexner. Painters, and regional painting traditions from earliest Colonial times up to the emergence of Copley, West and Peale Sr., Foster, Gustavus Hesselius, Feke, John Smibert and many anonymous painters in the primitive manner. Engaging presentation, with 162 illustrations. xxii + 368pp.
22180-6 Paperbound $3.50

THE LIGHT OF DISTANT SKIES: AMERICAN PAINTING, 1760-1835, James T. Flexner. The great generation of early American painters goes to Europe to learn and to teach: West, Copley, Gilbert Stuart and others. Allston, Trumbull, Morse; also contemporary American painters—primitives, derivatives, academics—who remained in America. 102 illustrations. xiii + 306pp.
22179-2 Paperbound $3.50

A HISTORY OF THE RISE AND PROGRESS OF THE ARTS OF DESIGN IN THE UNITED STATES, William Dunlap. Much the richest mine of information on early American painters, sculptors, architects, engravers, miniaturists, etc. The only source of information for scores of artists, the major primary source for many others. Unabridged reprint of rare original 1834 edition, with new introduction by James T. Flexner, and 394 new illustrations. Edited by Rita Weiss. 6⅝ x 9⅝.
21695-0, 21696-9, 21697-7 Three volumes, Paperbound $15.00

EPOCHS OF CHINESE AND JAPANESE ART, Ernest F. Fenollosa. From primitive Chinese art to the 20th century, thorough history, explanation of every important art period and form, including Japanese woodcuts; main stress on China and Japan, but Tibet, Korea also included. Still unexcelled for its detailed, rich coverage of cultural background, aesthetic elements, diffusion studies, particularly of the historical period. 2nd, 1913 edition. 242 illustrations. lii + 439pp. of text.
20364-6, 20365-4 Two volumes, Paperbound $6.00

THE GENTLE ART OF MAKING ENEMIES, James A. M. Whistler. Greatest wit of his day deflates Oscar Wilde, Ruskin, Swinburne; strikes back at inane critics, exhibitions, art journalism; aesthetics of impressionist revolution in most striking form. Highly readable classic by great painter. Reproduction of edition designed by Whistler. Introduction by Alfred Werner. xxxvi + 334pp.
21875-9 Paperbound $3.00

VISUAL ILLUSIONS: THEIR CAUSES, CHARACTERISTICS, AND APPLICATIONS, Matthew Luckiesh. Thorough description and discussion of optical illusion, geometric and perspective, particularly; size and shape distortions, illusions of color, of motion; natural illusions; use of illusion in art and magic, industry, etc. Most useful today with op art, also for classical art. Scores of effects illustrated. Introduction by William H. Ittleson. 100 illustrations. xxi + 252pp.

21530-X Paperbound $2.00

A HANDBOOK OF ANATOMY FOR ART STUDENTS, Arthur Thomson. Thorough, virtually exhaustive coverage of skeletal structure, musculature, etc. Full text, supplemented by anatomical diagrams and drawings and by photographs of undraped figures. Unique in its comparison of male and female forms, pointing out differences of contour, texture, form. 211 figures, 40 drawings, 86 photographs. xx + 459pp. 5⅜ x 8⅜.

21163-0 Paperbound $3.50

150 MASTERPIECES OF DRAWING, Selected by Anthony Toney. Full page reproductions of drawings from the early 16th to the end of the 18th century, all beautifully reproduced: Rembrandt, Michelangelo, Dürer, Fragonard, Urs, Graf, Wouwerman, many others. First-rate browsing book, model book for artists. xviii + 150pp. 8⅜ x 11¼.

21032-4 Paperbound $3.50

THE LATER WORK OF AUBREY BEARDSLEY, Aubrey Beardsley. Exotic, erotic, ironic masterpieces in full maturity: Comedy Ballet, Venus and Tannhauser, Pierrot, Lysistrata, Rape of the Lock, Savoy material, Ali Baba, Volpone, etc. This material revolutionized the art world, and is still powerful, fresh, brilliant. With *The Early Work,* all Beardsley's finest work. 174 plates, 2 in color. xiv + 176pp. 8⅛ x 11.

21817-1 Paperbound $3.75

DRAWINGS OF REMBRANDT, Rembrandt van Rijn. Complete reproduction of fabulously rare edition by Lippmann and Hofstede de Groot, completely reedited, updated, improved by Prof. Seymour Slive, Fogg Museum. Portraits, Biblical sketches, landscapes, Oriental types, nudes, episodes from classical mythology—All Rembrandt's fertile genius. Also selection of drawings by his pupils and followers. "Stunning volumes," *Saturday Review.* 550 illustrations. lxxviii + 552pp. 9⅛ x 12¼.

21485-0, 21486-9 Two volumes, Paperbound $10.00

THE DISASTERS OF WAR, Francisco Goya. One of the masterpieces of Western civilization—83 etchings that record Goya's shattering, bitter reaction to the Napoleonic war that swept through Spain after the insurrection of 1808 and to war in general. Reprint of the first edition, with three additional plates from Boston's Museum of Fine Arts. All plates facsimile size. Introduction by Philip Hofer, Fogg Museum. v + 97pp. 9⅜ x 8¼.

21872-4 Paperbound $2.50

GRAPHIC WORKS OF ODILON REDON. Largest collection of Redon's graphic works ever assembled: 172 lithographs, 28 etchings and engravings, 9 drawings. These include some of his most famous works. All the plates from *Odilon Redon: oeuvre graphique complet,* plus additional plates. New introduction and caption translations by Alfred Werner. 209 illustrations. xxvii + 209pp. 9⅛ x 12¼.

21966-8 Paperbound $5.00

DESIGN BY ACCIDENT; A BOOK OF "ACCIDENTAL EFFECTS" FOR ARTISTS AND DESIGNERS, James F. O'Brien. Create your own unique, striking, imaginative effects by "controlled accident" interaction of materials: paints and lacquers, oil and water based paints, splatter, crackling materials, shatter, similar items. Everything you do will be different; first book on this limitless art, so useful to both fine artist and commercial artist. Full instructions. 192 plates showing "accidents," 8 in color. viii + 215pp. 8⅜ x 11¼. 21942-9 Paperbound $3.75

THE BOOK OF SIGNS, Rudolf Koch. Famed German type designer draws 493 beautiful symbols: religious, mystical, alchemical, imperial, property marks, runes, etc. Remarkable fusion of traditional and modern. Good for suggestions of timelessness, smartness, modernity. Text. vi + 104pp. 6⅛ x 9¼. 20162-7 Paperbound $1.25

HISTORY OF INDIAN AND INDONESIAN ART, Ananda K. Coomaraswamy. An unabridged republication of one of the finest books by a great scholar in Eastern art. Rich in descriptive material, history, social backgrounds; Sunga reliefs, Rajput paintings, Gupta temples, Burmese frescoes, textiles, jewelry, sculpture, etc. 400 photos. viii + 423pp. 6⅜ x 9¾. 21436-2 Paperbound $5.00

PRIMITIVE ART, Franz Boas. America's foremost anthropologist surveys textiles, ceramics, woodcarving, basketry, metalwork, etc.; patterns, technology, creation of symbols, style origins. All areas of world, but very full on Northwest Coast Indians. More than 350 illustrations of baskets, boxes, totem poles, weapons, etc. 378 pp. 20025-6 Paperbound $3.00

THE GENTLEMAN AND CABINET MAKER'S DIRECTOR, Thomas Chippendale. Full reprint (third edition, 1762) of most influential furniture book of all time, by master cabinetmaker. 200 plates, illustrating chairs, sofas, mirrors, tables, cabinets, plus 24 photographs of surviving pieces. Biographical introduction by N. Bienenstock. vi + 249pp. 9⅞ x 12¾. 21601-2 Paperbound $4.00

AMERICAN ANTIQUE FURNITURE, Edgar G. Miller, Jr. The basic coverage of all American furniture before 1840. Individual chapters cover type of furniture— clocks, tables, sideboards, etc.—chronologically, with inexhaustible wealth of data. More than 2100 photographs, all identified, commented on. Essential to all early American collectors. Introduction by H. E. Keyes. vi + 1106pp. 7⅞ x 10¾. 21599-7, 21600-4 Two volumes, Paperbound $11.00

PENNSYLVANIA DUTCH AMERICAN FOLK ART, Henry J. Kauffman. 279 photos, 28 drawings of tulipware, Fraktur script, painted tinware, toys, flowered furniture, quilts, samplers, hex signs, house interiors, etc. Full descriptive text. Excellent for tourist, rewarding for designer, collector. Map. 146pp. 7⅞ x 10¾. 21205-X Paperbound $2.50

EARLY NEW ENGLAND GRAVESTONE RUBBINGS, Edmund V. Gillon, Jr. 43 photographs, 226 carefully reproduced rubbings show heavily symbolic, sometimes macabre early gravestones, up to early 19th century. Remarkable early American primitive art, occasionally strikingly beautiful; always powerful. Text. xxvi + 207pp. 8⅜ x 11¼. 21380-3 Paperbound $3.50

CATALOGUE OF DOVER BOOKS

ALPHABETS AND ORNAMENTS, Ernst Lehner. Well-known pictorial source for decorative alphabets, script examples, cartouches, frames, decorative title pages, calligraphic initials, borders, similar material. 14th to 19th century, mostly European. Useful in almost any graphic arts designing, varied styles. 750 illustrations. 256pp. 7 x 10. 21905-4 Paperbound $4.00

PAINTING: A CREATIVE APPROACH, Norman Colquhoun. For the beginner simple guide provides an instructive approach to painting: major stumbling blocks for beginner; overcoming them, technical points; paints and pigments; oil painting; watercolor and other media and color. New section on "plastic" paints. Glossary. Formerly *Paint Your Own Pictures*. 221pp. 22000-1 Paperbound $1.75

THE ENJOYMENT AND USE OF COLOR, Walter Sargent. Explanation of the relations between colors themselves and between colors in nature and art, including hundreds of little-known facts about color values, intensities, effects of high and low illumination, complementary colors. Many practical hints for painters, references to great masters. 7 color plates, 29 illustrations. x + 274pp. 20944-X Paperbound $2.75

THE NOTEBOOKS OF LEONARDO DA VINCI, compiled and edited by Jean Paul Richter. 1566 extracts from original manuscripts reveal the full range of Leonardo's versatile genius: all his writings on painting, sculpture, architecture, anatomy, astronomy, geography, topography, physiology, mining, music, etc., in both Italian and English, with 186 plates of manuscript pages and more than 500 additional drawings. Includes studies for the Last Supper, the lost Sforza monument, and other works. Total of xlvii + 866pp. 7⅞ x 10¾. 22572-0, 22573-9 Two volumes, Paperbound $11.00

MONTGOMERY WARD CATALOGUE OF 1895. Tea gowns, yards of flannel and pillow-case lace, stereoscopes, books of gospel hymns, the New Improved Singer Sewing Machine, side saddles, milk skimmers, straight-edged razors, high-button shoes, spittoons, and on and on . . . listing some 25,000 items, practically all illustrated. Essential to the shoppers of the 1890's, it is our truest record of the spirit of the period. Unaltered reprint of Issue No. 57, Spring and Summer 1895. Introduction by Boris Emmet. Innumerable illustrations. xiii + 624pp. 8½ x 11⅝. 22377-9 Paperbound $6.95

THE CRYSTAL PALACE EXHIBITION ILLUSTRATED CATALOGUE (LONDON, 1851). One of the wonders of the modern world—the Crystal Palace Exhibition in which all the nations of the civilized world exhibited their achievements in the arts and sciences—presented in an equally important illustrated catalogue. More than 1700 items pictured with accompanying text—ceramics, textiles, cast-iron work, carpets, pianos, sleds, razors, wall-papers, billiard tables, beehives, silverware and hundreds of other artifacts—represent the focal point of Victorian culture in the Western World. Probably the largest collection of Victorian decorative art ever assembled—indispensable for antiquarians and designers. Unabridged republication of the Art-Journal Catalogue of the Great Exhibition of 1851, with all terminal essays. New introduction by John Gloag, F.S.A. xxxiv + 426pp. 9 x 12. 22503-8 Paperbound $5.00

CATALOGUE OF DOVER BOOKS

A History of Costume, Carl Köhler. Definitive history, based on surviving pieces of clothing primarily, and paintings, statues, etc. secondarily. Highly readable text, supplemented by 594 illustrations of costumes of the ancient Mediterranean peoples, Greece and Rome, the Teutonic prehistoric period; costumes of the Middle Ages, Renaissance, Baroque, 18th and 19th centuries. Clear, measured patterns are provided for many clothing articles. Approach is practical throughout. Enlarged by Emma von Sichart. 464pp. 21030-8 Paperbound $3.50.

Oriental Rugs, Antique and Modern, Walter A. Hawley. A complete and authoritative treatise on the Oriental rug—where they are made, by whom and how, designs and symbols, characteristics in detail of the six major groups, how to distinguish them and how to buy them. Detailed technical data is provided on periods, weaves, warps, wefts, textures, sides, ends and knots, although no technical background is required for an understanding. 11 color plates, 80 halftones, 4 maps. vi + 320pp. 6⅛ x 9⅛. 22366-3 Paperbound $5.00

Ten Books on Architecture, Vitruvius. By any standards the most important book on architecture ever written. Early Roman discussion of aesthetics of building, construction methods, orders, sites, and every other aspect of architecture has inspired, instructed architecture for about 2,000 years. Stands behind Palladio, Michelangelo, Bramante, Wren, countless others. Definitive Morris H. Morgan translation. 68 illustrations. xii + 331pp. 20645-9 Paperbound $3.00

The Four Books of Architecture, Andrea Palladio. Translated into every major Western European language in the two centuries following its publication in 1570, this has been one of the most influential books in the history of architecture. Complete reprint of the 1738 Isaac Ware edition. New introduction by Adolf Placzek, Columbia Univ. 216 plates. xxii + 110pp. of text. 9½ x 12¾. 21308-0 Clothbound $12.50

Sticks and Stones: A Study of American Architecture and Civilization, Lewis Mumford.One of the great classics of American cultural history. American architecture from the medieval-inspired earliest forms to the early 20th century; evolution of structure and style, and reciprocal influences on environment. 21 photographic illustrations. 238pp. 20202-X Paperbound $2.00

The American Builder's Companion, Asher Benjamin. The most widely used early 19th century architectural style and source book, for colonial up into Greek Revival periods. Extensive development of geometry of carpentering, construction of sashes, frames, doors, stairs; plans and elevations of domestic and other buildings. Hundreds of thousands of houses were built according to this book, now invaluable to historians, architects, restorers, etc. 1827 edition. 59 plates. 114pp. 7⅞ x 10¾. 22236-5 Paperbound $3.50

Dutch Houses in the Hudson Valley Before 1776, Helen Wilkinson Reynolds. The standard survey of the Dutch colonial house and outbuildings, with constructional features, decoration, and local history associated with individual homesteads. Introduction by Franklin D. Roosevelt. Map. 150 illustrations. 469pp. 6⅝ x 9¼. 21469-9 Paperbound $5.00

CATALOGUE OF DOVER BOOKS

THE ARCHITECTURE OF COUNTRY HOUSES, Andrew J. Downing. Together with Vaux's *Villas and Cottages* this is the basic book for Hudson River Gothic architecture of the middle Victorian period. Full, sound discussions of general aspects of housing, architecture, style, decoration, furnishing, together with scores of detailed house plans, illustrations of specific buildings, accompanied by full text. Perhaps the most influential single American architectural book. 1850 edition. Introduction by J. Stewart Johnson. 321 figures, 34 architectural designs. xvi + 560pp.
22003-6 Paperbound $4.00

LOST EXAMPLES OF COLONIAL ARCHITECTURE, John Mead Howells. Full-page photographs of buildings that have disappeared or been so altered as to be denatured, including many designed by major early American architects. 245 plates. xvii + 248pp. 7⅞ x 10¾. 21143-6 Paperbound $3.50

DOMESTIC ARCHITECTURE OF THE AMERICAN COLONIES AND OF THE EARLY REPUBLIC, Fiske Kimball. Foremost architect and restorer of Williamsburg and Monticello covers nearly 200 homes between 1620-1825. Architectural details, construction, style features, special fixtures, floor plans, etc. Generally considered finest work in its area. 219 illustrations of houses, doorways, windows, capital mantels. xx + 314pp. 7⅞ x 10¾. 21743-4 Paperbound $4.00

EARLY AMERICAN ROOMS: 1650-1858, edited by Russell Hawes Kettell. Tour of 12 rooms, each representative of a different era in American history and each furnished, decorated, designed and occupied in the style of the era. 72 plans and elevations, 8-page color section, etc., show fabrics, wall papers, arrangements, etc. Full descriptive text. xvii + 200pp. of text. 8⅜ x 11¼.
21633-0 Paperbound $5.00

THE FITZWILLIAM VIRGINAL BOOK, edited by J. Fuller Maitland and W. B. Squire. Full modern printing of famous early 17th-century ms. volume of 300 works by Morley, Byrd, Bull, Gibbons, etc. For piano or other modern keyboard instrument; easy to read format. xxxvi + 938pp. 8⅜ x 11.
21068-5, 21069-3 Two volumes, Paperbound $10.00

KEYBOARD MUSIC, Johann Sebastian Bach. Bach Gesellschaft edition. A rich selection of Bach's masterpieces for the harpsichord: the six English Suites, six French Suites, the six Partitas (Clavierübung part I), the Goldberg Variations (Clavierübung part IV), the fifteen Two-Part Inventions and the fifteen Three-Part Sinfonias. Clearly reproduced on large sheets with ample margins; eminently playable. vi + 312pp. 8⅛ x 11. 22360-4 Paperbound $5.00

THE MUSIC OF BACH: AN INTRODUCTION, Charles Sanford Terry. A fine, nontechnical introduction to Bach's music, both instrumental and vocal. Covers organ music, chamber music, passion music, other types. Analyzes themes, developments, innovations. x + 114pp. 21075-8 Paperbound $1.50

BEETHOVEN AND HIS NINE SYMPHONIES, Sir George Grove. Noted British musicologist provides best history, analysis, commentary on symphonies. Very thorough, rigorously accurate; necessary to both advanced student and amateur music lover. 436 musical passages. vii + 407 pp. 20334-4 Paperbound $2.75

JOHANN SEBASTIAN BACH, Philipp Spitta. One of the great classics of musicology, this definitive analysis of Bach's music (and life) has never been surpassed. Lucid, nontechnical analyses of hundreds of pieces (30 pages devoted to St. Matthew Passion, 26 to B Minor Mass). Also includes major analysis of 18th-century music. 450 musical examples. 40-page musical supplement. Total of xx + 1799pp.

(EUK) 22278-0, 22279-9 Two volumes, Clothbound $17.50

MOZART AND HIS PIANO CONCERTOS, Cuthbert Girdlestone. The only full-length study of an important area of Mozart's creativity. Provides detailed analyses of all 23 concertos, traces inspirational sources. 417 musical examples. Second edition. 509pp.

21271-8 Paperbound $3.50

THE PERFECT WAGNERITE: A COMMENTARY ON THE NIBLUNG'S RING, George Bernard Shaw. Brilliant and still relevant criticism in remarkable essays on Wagner's Ring cycle, Shaw's ideas on political and social ideology behind the plots, role of Leitmotifs, vocal requisites, etc. Prefaces. xxi + 136pp.

(USO) 21707-8 Paperbound $1.75

DON GIOVANNI, W. A. Mozart. Complete libretto, modern English translation; biographies of composer and librettist; accounts of early performances and critical reaction. Lavishly illustrated. All the material you need to understand and appreciate this great work. Dover Opera Guide and Libretto Series; translated and introduced by Ellen Bleiler. 92 illustrations. 209pp.

21134-7 Paperbound $2.00

BASIC ELECTRICITY, U. S. Bureau of Naval Personel. Originally a training course, best non-technical coverage of basic theory of electricity and its applications. Fundamental concepts, batteries, circuits, conductors and wiring techniques, AC and DC, inductance and capacitance, generators, motors, transformers, magnetic amplifiers, synchros, servomechanisms, etc. Also covers blue-prints, electrical diagrams, etc. Many questions, with answers. 349 illustrations. x + 448pp. 6½ x 9¼.

20973-3 Paperbound $3.50

REPRODUCTION OF SOUND, Edgar Villchur. Thorough coverage for laymen of high fidelity systems, reproducing systems in general, needles, amplifiers, preamps, loudspeakers, feedback, explaining physical background. "A rare talent for making technicalities vividly comprehensible," R. Darrell, *High Fidelity*. 69 figures. iv + 92pp.

21515-6 Paperbound $1.35

HEAR ME TALKIN' TO YA: THE STORY OF JAZZ AS TOLD BY THE MEN WHO MADE IT, Nat Shapiro and Nat Hentoff. Louis Armstrong, Fats Waller, Jo Jones, Clarence Williams, Billy Holiday, Duke Ellington, Jelly Roll Morton and dozens of other jazz greats tell how it was in Chicago's South Side, New Orleans, depression Harlem and the modern West Coast as jazz was born and grew. xvi + 429pp.

21726-4 Paperbound $3.00

FABLES OF AESOP, translated by Sir Roger L'Estrange. A reproduction of the very rare 1931 Paris edition; a selection of the most interesting fables, together with 50 imaginative drawings by Alexander Calder. v + 128pp. 6½x9¼.

21780-9 Paperbound $1.50

AGAINST THE GRAIN (A REBOURS), Joris K. Huysmans. Filled with weird images, evidences of a bizarre imagination, exotic experiments with hallucinatory drugs, rich tastes and smells and the diversions of its sybarite hero Duc Jean des Esseintes, this classic novel pushed 19th-century literary decadence to its limits. Full unabridged edition. Do not confuse this with abridged editions generally sold. Introduction by Havelock Ellis. xlix + 206pp. 22190-3 Paperbound $2.50

VARIORUM SHAKESPEARE: HAMLET. Edited by Horace H. Furness; a landmark of American scholarship. Exhaustive footnotes and appendices treat all doubtful words and phrases, as well as suggested critical emendations throughout the play's history. First volume contains editor's own text, collated with all Quartos and Folios. Second volume contains full first Quarto, translations of Shakespeare's sources (Belleforest, and Saxo Grammaticus), Der Bestrafte Brudermord, and many essays on critical and historical points of interest by major authorities of past and present. Includes details of staging and costuming over the years. By far the best edition available for serious students of Shakespeare. Total of xx + 905pp. 21004-9, 21005-7, 2 volumes, Paperbound $7.00

A LIFE OF WILLIAM SHAKESPEARE, Sir Sidney Lee. This is the standard life of Shakespeare, summarizing everything known about Shakespeare and his plays. Incredibly rich in material, broad in coverage, clear and judicious, it has served thousands as the best introduction to Shakespeare. 1931 edition. 9 plates. xxix + 792pp. 21967-4 Paperbound $4.50

MASTERS OF THE DRAMA, John Gassner. Most comprehensive history of the drama in print, covering every tradition from Greeks to modern Europe and America, including India, Far East, etc. Covers more than 800 dramatists, 2000 plays, with biographical material, plot summaries, theatre history, criticism, etc. "Best of its kind in English," New Republic. 77 illustrations. xxii + 890pp. 20100-7 Clothbound $10.00

THE EVOLUTION OF THE ENGLISH LANGUAGE, George McKnight. The growth of English, from the 14th century to the present. Unusual, non-technical account presents basic information in very interesting form: sound shifts, change in grammar and syntax, vocabulary growth, similar topics. Abundantly illustrated with quotations. Formerly Modern English in the Making. xii + 590pp. 21932-1 Paperbound $4.00

AN ETYMOLOGICAL DICTIONARY OF MODERN ENGLISH, Ernest Weekley. Fullest, richest work of its sort, by foremost British lexicographer. Detailed word histories, including many colloquial and archaic words; extensive quotations. Do not confuse this with the Concise Etymological Dictionary, which is much abridged. Total of xxvii + 830pp. 6½ x 9¼. 21873-2, 21874-0 Two volumes, Paperbound $7.90

FLATLAND: A ROMANCE OF MANY DIMENSIONS, E. A. Abbott. Classic of science-fiction explores ramifications of life in a two-dimensional world, and what happens when a three-dimensional being intrudes. Amusing reading, but also useful as introduction to thought about hyperspace. Introduction by Banesh Hoffmann. 16 illustrations. xx + 103pp. 20001-9 Paperbound $1.25

POEMS OF ANNE BRADSTREET, edited with an introduction by Robert Hutchinson. A new selection of poems by America's first poet and perhaps the first significant woman poet in the English language. 48 poems display her development in works of considerable variety—love poems, domestic poems, religious meditations, formal elegies, "quaternions," etc. Notes, bibliography. viii + 222pp.

22160-1 Paperbound $2.50

THREE GOTHIC NOVELS: THE CASTLE OF OTRANTO BY HORACE WALPOLE; VATHEK BY WILLIAM BECKFORD; THE VAMPYRE BY JOHN POLIDORI, WITH FRAGMENT OF A NOVEL BY LORD BYRON, edited by E. F. Bleiler. The first Gothic novel, by Walpole; the finest Oriental tale in English, by Beckford; powerful Romantic supernatural story in versions by Polidori and Byron. All extremely important in history of literature; all still exciting, packed with supernatural thrills, ghosts, haunted castles, magic, etc. xl + 291pp.

21232-7 Paperbound $2.50

THE BEST TALES OF HOFFMANN, E. T. A. Hoffmann. 10 of Hoffmann's most important stories, in modern re-editings of standard translations: Nutcracker and the King of Mice, Signor Formica, Automata, The Sandman, Rath Krespel, The Golden Flowerpot, Master Martin the Cooper, The Mines of Falun, The King's Betrothed, A New Year's Eve Adventure. 7 illustrations by Hoffmann. Edited by E. F. Bleiler. xxxix + 419pp.

21793-0 Paperbound $3.00

GHOST AND HORROR STORIES OF AMBROSE BIERCE, Ambrose Bierce. 23 strikingly modern stories of the horrors latent in the human mind: The Eyes of the Panther, The Damned Thing, An Occurrence at Owl Creek Bridge, An Inhabitant of Carcosa, etc., plus the dream-essay, Visions of the Night. Edited by E. F. Bleiler. xxii + 199pp.

20767-6 Paperbound $1.50

BEST GHOST STORIES OF J. S. LeFANU, J. Sheridan LeFanu. Finest stories by Victorian master often considered greatest supernatural writer of all. Carmilla, Green Tea, The Haunted Baronet, The Familiar, and 12 others. Most never before available in the U. S. A. Edited by E. F. Bleiler. 8 illustrations from Victorian publications. xvii + 467pp.

20415-4 Paperbound $3.00

MATHEMATICAL FOUNDATIONS OF INFORMATION THEORY, A. I. Khinchin. Comprehensive introduction to work of Shannon, McMillan, Feinstein and Khinchin, placing these investigations on a rigorous mathematical basis. Covers entropy concept in probability theory, uniqueness theorem, Shannon's inequality, ergodic sources, the E property, martingale concept, noise, Feinstein's fundamental lemma, Shanon's first and second theorems. Translated by R. A. Silverman and M. D. Friedman. iii + 120pp.

60434-9 Paperbound $2.00

SEVEN SCIENCE FICTION NOVELS, H. G. Wells. The standard collection of the great novels. Complete, unabridged. *First Men in the Moon, Island of Dr. Moreau, War of the Worlds, Food of the Gods, Invisible Man, Time Machine, In the Days of the Comet.* Not only science fiction fans, but every educated person owes it to himself to read these novels. 1015pp. (USO) 20264-X Clothbound $6.00

LAST AND FIRST MEN AND STAR MAKER, TWO SCIENCE FICTION NOVELS, Olaf Stapledon. Greatest future histories in science fiction. In the first, human intelligence is the "hero," through strange paths of evolution, interplanetary invasions, incredible technologies, near extinctions and reemergences. Star Maker describes the quest of a band of star rovers for intelligence itself, through time and space: weird inhuman civilizations, crustacean minds, symbiotic worlds, etc. Complete, unabridged. v + 438pp. (USO) 21962-3 Paperbound $2.50

THREE PROPHETIC NOVELS, H. G. WELLS. Stages of a consistently planned future for mankind. *When the Sleeper Wakes,* and *A Story of the Days to Come,* anticipate *Brave New World* and *1984,* in the 21st Century; *The Time Machine,* only complete version in print, shows farther future and the end of mankind. All show Wells's greatest gifts as storyteller and novelist. Edited by E. F. Bleiler. x + 335pp. (USO) 20605-X Paperbound $2.50

THE DEVIL'S DICTIONARY, Ambrose Bierce. America's own Oscar Wilde— Ambrose Bierce—offers his barbed iconoclastic wisdom in over 1,000 definitions hailed by H. L. Mencken as "some of the most gorgeous witticisms in the English language." 145pp. 20487-1 Paperbound $1.25

MAX AND MORITZ, Wilhelm Busch. Great children's classic, father of comic strip, of two bad boys, Max and Moritz. Also Ker and Plunk (Plisch und Plumm), Cat and Mouse, Deceitful Henry, Ice-Peter, The Boy and the Pipe, and five other pieces. Original German, with English translation. Edited by H. Arthur Klein; translations by various hands and H. Arthur Klein. vi + 216pp.
20181-3 Paperbound $2.00

PIGS IS PIGS AND OTHER FAVORITES, Ellis Parker Butler. The title story is one of the best humor short stories, as Mike Flannery obfuscates biology and English. Also included, That Pup of Murchison's, The Great American Pie Company, and Perkins of Portland. 14 illustrations. v + 109pp. 21532-6 Paperbound $1.25

THE PETERKIN PAPERS, Lucretia P. Hale. It takes genius to be as stupidly mad as the Peterkins, as they decide to become wise, celebrate the "Fourth," keep a cow, and otherwise strain the resources of the Lady from Philadelphia. Basic book of American humor. 153 illustrations. 219pp. 20794-3 Paperbound $2.00

PERRAULT'S FAIRY TALES, translated by A. E. Johnson and S. R. Littlewood, with 34 full-page illustrations by Gustave Doré. All the original Perrault stories— Cinderella, Sleeping Beauty, Bluebeard, Little Red Riding Hood, Puss in Boots, Tom Thumb, etc.—with their witty verse morals and the magnificent illustrations of Doré. One of the five or six great books of European fairy tales. viii + 117pp. 8⅛ x 11. 22311-6 Paperbound $2.00

OLD HUNGARIAN FAIRY TALES, Baroness Orczy. Favorites translated and adapted by author of the *Scarlet Pimpernel.* Eight fairy tales include "The Suitors of Princess Fire-Fly," "The Twin Hunchbacks," "Mr. Cuttlefish's Love Story," and "The Enchanted Cat." This little volume of magic and adventure will captivate children as it has for generations. 90 drawings by Montagu Barstow. 96pp.
(USO) 22293-4 Paperbound $1.95

THE RED FAIRY BOOK, Andrew Lang. Lang's color fairy books have long been children's favorites. This volume includes Rapunzel, Jack and the Bean-stalk and 35 other stories, familiar and unfamiliar. 4 plates, 93 illustrations x + 367pp.

21673-X Paperbound $2.50

THE BLUE FAIRY BOOK, Andrew Lang. Lang's tales come from all countries and all times. Here are 37 tales from Grimm, the Arabian Nights, Greek Mythology, and other fascinating sources. 8 plates, 130 illustrations. xi + 390pp.

21437-0 Paperbound $2.75

HOUSEHOLD STORIES BY THE BROTHERS GRIMM. Classic English-language edition of the well-known tales — Rumpelstiltskin, Snow White, Hansel and Gretel, The Twelve Brothers, Faithful John, Rapunzel, Tom Thumb (52 stories in all). Translated into simple, straightforward English by Lucy Crane. Ornamented with headpieces, vignettes, elaborate decorative initials and a dozen full-page illustrations by Walter Crane. x + 269pp.

21080-4 Paperbound **$2.00**

THE MERRY ADVENTURES OF ROBIN HOOD, Howard Pyle. The finest modern versions of the traditional ballads and tales about the great English outlaw. Howard Pyle's complete prose version, with every word, every illustration of the first edition. Do not confuse this facsimile of the original (1883) with modern editions that change text or illustrations. 23 plates plus many page decorations. xxii + 296pp.

22043-5 Paperbound $2.75

THE STORY OF KING ARTHUR AND HIS KNIGHTS, Howard Pyle. The finest children's version of the life of King Arthur; brilliantly retold by Pyle, with 48 of his most imaginative illustrations. xviii + 313pp. 6⅛ x 9¼.

21445-1 Paperbound $2.50

THE WONDERFUL WIZARD OF OZ, L. Frank Baum. America's finest children's book in facsimile of first edition with all Denslow illustrations in full color. The edition a child should have. Introduction by Martin Gardner. 23 color plates, scores of drawings. iv + 267pp.

20691-2 Paperbound $2.50

THE MARVELOUS LAND OF OZ, L. Frank Baum. The second Oz book, every bit as imaginative as the Wizard. The hero is a boy named Tip, but the Scarecrow and the Tin Woodman are back, as is the Oz magic. 16 color plates, 120 drawings by John R. Neill. 287pp.

20692-0 Paperbound $2.50

THE MAGICAL MONARCH OF MO, L. Frank Baum. Remarkable adventures in a land even stranger than Oz. The best of Baum's books not in the Oz series. 15 color plates and dozens of drawings by Frank Verbeck. xviii + 237pp.

21892-9 Paperbound $2.25

THE BAD CHILD'S BOOK OF BEASTS, MORE BEASTS FOR WORSE CHILDREN, A MORAL ALPHABET, Hilaire Belloc. Three complete humor classics in one volume. Be kind to the frog, and do not call him names . . . and 28 other whimsical animals. Familiar favorites and some not so well known. Illustrated by Basil Blackwell. 156pp.

(USO) 20749-8 Paperbound $1.50

EAST O' THE SUN AND WEST O' THE MOON, George W. Dasent. Considered the best of all translations of these Norwegian folk tales, this collection has been enjoyed by generations of children (and folklorists too). Includes True and Untrue, Why the Sea is Salt, East O' the Sun and West O' the Moon, Why the Bear is Stumpy-Tailed, Boots and the Troll, The Cock and the Hen, Rich Peter the Pedlar, and 52 more. The only edition with all 59 tales. 77 illustrations by Erik Werenskiold and Theodor Kittelsen. xv + 418pp. 22521-6 Paperbound $3.50

GOOPS AND HOW TO BE THEM, Gelett Burgess. Classic of tongue-in-cheek humor, masquerading as etiquette book. 87 verses, twice as many cartoons, show mischievous Goops as they demonstrate to children virtues of table manners, neatness, courtesy, etc. Favorite for generations. viii + 88pp. 6½ x 9¼. 22233-0 Paperbound $1.50

ALICE'S ADVENTURES UNDER GROUND, Lewis Carroll. The first version, quite different from the final Alice in Wonderland, printed out by Carroll himself with his own illustrations. Complete facsimile of the "million dollar" manuscript Carroll gave to Alice Liddell in 1864. Introduction by Martin Gardner. viii + 96pp. Title and dedication pages in color. 21482-6 Paperbound $1.25

THE BROWNIES, THEIR BOOK, Palmer Cox. Small as mice, cunning as foxes, exuberant and full of mischief, the Brownies go to the zoo, toy shop, seashore, circus, etc., in 24 verse adventures and 266 illustrations. Long a favorite, since their first appearance in St. Nicholas Magazine. xi + 144pp. 6⅝ x 9¼. 21265-3 Paperbound $1.75

SONGS OF CHILDHOOD, Walter De La Mare. Published (under the pseudonym Walter Ramal) when De La Mare was only 29, this charming collection has long been a favorite children's book. A facsimile of the first edition in paper, the 47 poems capture the simplicity of the nursery rhyme and the ballad, including such lyrics as I Met Eve, Tartary, The Silver Penny. vii + 106pp. (USO) 21972-0 Paperbound $2.00

THE COMPLETE NONSENSE OF EDWARD LEAR, Edward Lear. The finest 19th-century humorist-cartoonist in full: all nonsense limericks, zany alphabets, Owl and Pussycat, songs, nonsense botany, and more than 500 illustrations by Lear himself. Edited by Holbrook Jackson. xxix + 287pp. (USO) 20167-8 Paperbound $2.00

BILLY WHISKERS: THE AUTOBIOGRAPHY OF A GOAT, Frances Trego Montgomery. A favorite of children since the early 20th century, here are the escapades of that rambunctious, irresistible and mischievous goat—Billy Whiskers. Much in the spirit of Peck's Bad Boy, this is a book that children never tire of reading or hearing. All the original familiar illustrations by W. H. Fry are included: 6 color plates, 18 black and white drawings. 159pp. 22345-0 Paperbound $2.00

MOTHER GOOSE MELODIES. Faithful republication of the fabulously rare Munroe and Francis "copyright 1833" Boston edition—the most important Mother Goose collection, usually referred to as the "original." Familiar rhymes plus many rare ones, with wonderful old woodcut illustrations. Edited by E. F. Bleiler. 128pp. 4½ x 6⅜. 22577-1 Paperbound $1.00

TWO LITTLE SAVAGES; BEING THE ADVENTURES OF TWO BOYS WHO LIVED AS INDIANS AND WHAT THEY LEARNED, Ernest Thompson Seton. Great classic of nature and boyhood provides a vast range of woodlore in most palatable form, a genuinely entertaining story. Two farm boys build a teepee in woods and live in it for a month, working out Indian solutions to living problems, star lore, birds and animals, plants, etc. 293 illustrations. vii + 286pp.

20985-7 Paperbound $2.50

PETER PIPER'S PRACTICAL PRINCIPLES OF PLAIN & PERFECT PRONUNCIATION. Alliterative jingles and tongue-twisters of surprising charm, that made their first appearance in America about 1830. Republished in full with the spirited woodcut illustrations from this earliest American edition. 32pp. 4½ x 6⅜.

22560-7 Paperbound $1.00

SCIENCE EXPERIMENTS AND AMUSEMENTS FOR CHILDREN, Charles Vivian. 73 easy experiments, requiring only materials found at home or easily available, such as candles, coins, steel wool, etc.; illustrate basic phenomena like vacuum, simple chemical reaction, etc. All safe. Modern, well-planned. Formerly Science Games for Children. 102 photos, numerous drawings. 96pp. 6⅛ x 9¼.

21856-2 Paperbound $1.25

AN INTRODUCTION TO CHESS MOVES AND TACTICS SIMPLY EXPLAINED, Leonard Barden. Informal intermediate introduction, quite strong in explaining reasons for moves. Covers basic material, tactics, important openings, traps, positional play in middle game, end game. Attempts to isolate patterns and recurrent configurations. Formerly Chess. 58 figures. 102pp. (USO) 21210-6 Paperbound $1.25

LASKER'S MANUAL OF CHESS, Dr. Emanuel Lasker. Lasker was not only one of the five great World Champions, he was also one of the ablest expositors, theorists, and analysts. In many ways, his Manual, permeated with his philosophy of battle, filled with keen insights, is one of the greatest works ever written on chess. Filled with analyzed games by the great players. A single-volume library that will profit almost any chess player, beginner or master. 308 diagrams. xli x 349pp.

20640-8 Paperbound $2.75

THE MASTER BOOK OF MATHEMATICAL RECREATIONS, Fred Schuh. In opinion of many the finest work ever prepared on mathematical puzzles, stunts, recreations; exhaustively thorough explanations of mathematics involved, analysis of effects, citation of puzzles and games. Mathematics involved is elementary. Translated by F. Göbel. 194 figures. xxiv + 430pp. 22134-2 Paperbound $3.50

MATHEMATICS, MAGIC AND MYSTERY, Martin Gardner. Puzzle editor for Scientific American explains mathematics behind various mystifying tricks: card tricks, stage "mind reading," coin and match tricks, counting out games, geometric dissections, etc. Probability sets, theory of numbers clearly explained. Also provides more than 400 tricks, guaranteed to work, that you can do. 135 illustrations. xii + 176pp.

20335-2 Paperbound $1.75

MATHEMATICAL PUZZLES FOR BEGINNERS AND ENTHUSIASTS, Geoffrey Mott-Smith. 189 puzzles from easy to difficult—involving arithmetic, logic, algebra, properties of digits, probability, etc.—for enjoyment and mental stimulus. Explanation of mathematical principles behind the puzzles. 135 illustrations. viii + 248pp.
20198-8 Paperbound $1.75

PAPER FOLDING FOR BEGINNERS, William D. Murray and Francis J. Rigney. Easiest book on the market, clearest instructions on making interesting, beautiful origami. Sail boats, cups, roosters, frogs that move legs, bonbon boxes, standing birds, etc. 40 projects; more than 275 diagrams and photographs. 94pp.
20713-7 Paperbound $1.00

TRICKS AND GAMES ON THE POOL TABLE, Fred Herrmann. 79 tricks and games—some solitaires, some for two or more players, some competitive games—to entertain you between formal games. Mystifying shots and throws, unusual caroms, tricks involving such props as cork, coins, a hat, etc. Formerly *Fun on the Pool Table*. 77 figures. 95pp.
21814-7 Paperbound $1.25

HAND SHADOWS TO BE THROWN UPON THE WALL: A SERIES OF NOVEL AND AMUSING FIGURES FORMED BY THE HAND, Henry Bursill. Delightful picturebook from great-grandfather's day shows how to make 18 different hand shadows: a bird that flies, duck that quacks, dog that wags his tail, camel, goose, deer, boy, turtle, etc. Only book of its sort. vi + 33pp. 6½ x 9¼. 21779-5 Paperbound $1.00

WHITTLING AND WOODCARVING, E. J. Tangerman. 18th printing of best book on market. "If you can cut a potato you can carve" toys and puzzles, chains, chessmen, caricatures, masks, frames, woodcut blocks, surface patterns, much more. Information on tools, woods, techniques. Also goes into serious wood sculpture from Middle Ages to present, East and West. 464 photos, figures. x + 293pp.
20965-2 Paperbound $2.00

HISTORY OF PHILOSOPHY, Julián Marías. Possibly the clearest, most easily followed, best planned, most useful one-volume history of philosophy on the market; neither skimpy nor overfull. Full details on system of every major philosopher and dozens of less important thinkers from pre-Socratics up to Existentialism and later. Strong on many European figures usually omitted. Has gone through dozens of editions in Europe. 1966 edition, translated by Stanley Appelbaum and Clarence Strowbridge. xviii + 505pp. 21739-6 Paperbound $3.50

YOGA: A SCIENTIFIC EVALUATION, Kovoor T. Behanan. Scientific but non-technical study of physiological results of yoga exercises; done under auspices of Yale U. Relations to Indian thought, to psychoanalysis, etc. 16 photos. xxiii + 270pp.
20505-3 Paperbound $2.50

Prices subject to change without notice.
Available at your book dealer or write for free catalogue to Dept. GI, Dover Publications, Inc., 180 Varick St., N. Y., N. Y. 10014. Dover publishes more than 150 books each year on science, elementary and advanced mathematics, biology, music, art, literary history, social sciences and other areas.

athwartship
strop